STUDIES IN IRISH LITERATURE, CINEMA AND CULTURE

Series editor: Dr. Pilar Villar-Argáiz,
Senior Lecturer in British and Irish Literature,
Department of English Philology, University of Granada

1. Kathryn Laing and Sinéad Mooney (editors), *Irish Women Writers At the Turn of the 20th Century: Alternative Histories, New Narratives*.
2. Constanza del Río and José Carregal (editors), *Revolutionary Ireland, 1916–2016. Historical Facts & Social Transformations Re-Assessed*.
3. Adela Flamarike, *Women, Art And Nationalism in the Irish Revival. Presence And Absence*.
4. James Gallacher, *Bohemian Belfast and Dublin. Two Artistic and Literary Worlds in the Work of Gerard Keenan*.
5. E. A. J. Francisco, *Irish Dystopian Fiction*
6. Carlos M. Otero, *Ireland and the Irish in 20th Century British Cinema*.
7. Marjan Shokouhi, *Irishness in the Context of Current Environmental Discourse*.

We invite further submission for titles to be published in the series.

STUDIES IN IRISH LITERATURE, CINEMA AND CULTURE
No. 2
Series editor: Dr. Pilar Villar-Argáiz,

Revolutionary Ireland 1916–2016

Historical Facts & Social Transformations Re-assessed

Advance acclaim:

"Revolutionary Ireland covers a century of Irish history that is marked by major political, social and cultural change. Employing a variety of methodologies including historiography, post-colonialism, gender studies, discourse analysis, archival material, TV documentaries and literary criticism, the book provides a truly transdisciplinary analysis of the forces that shaped Ireland between the 1916 Rising and 2016, at which point the country seemed to be emerging from the ashes caused by the collapse of the Celtic Tiger. This book will appeal to a wide audience and will inform and entertain in equal measure." –
Professor Eamon Maher, Director, National Centre for Anglo-Irish Studies, Institute of Technology, Tallaght.

"The city of Zaragoza and its University hosted the XV International AEDEI Conference in 2016 on the centenary of the Easter Rising of 1916 and the revolutionary decade (1913–1923). This associated, interdisciplinary volume includes compelling contributions from historians and sociologists, and scholars analysing contemporary literary representations of the Irish revolution. The relationship between the past and present in key arenas - violence, gender, asylum, history, archives, politics, literature and culture - is illuminated by the exemplary scholarship and new original research provided in the text. Fundamentally, this collection represents a critical intervention in interdisciplinary Irish studies in a moment of contested commemoration and remembrance." – **Professor Linda Connolly,** Director, Maynooth University Social Sciences Institute.

Revolutionary Ireland 1916–2016

Historical Facts & Social Transformations Re-assessed

Edited by Constanza del Río and José Carregal

EER
EDWARD EVERETT ROOT PUBLISHERS, BRIGHTON 2020

EER

Edward Everett Root, Publishers, Co. Ltd.,
30 New Road, Brighton, Sussex, BN1 1BN, England.

Details of our overseas agents and how to buy our books are given on our website.

www.eerpublishing.com

edwardeverettroot@yahoo.co.uk

*Revolutionary Ireland 1916–2016
Historical Facts & Social Transformations Re-assessed*

Edited by Constanza del Río and José Carregal

Studies in Irish Literature, Cinema and Culture series, volume 1.

ISBN 9781911204800 Paperback
ISBN 9781911204817 Hardback
ISBN 9781911204848 eBook

First published in England 2020.

This edition © Edward Everett Root Publishers, 2020.

The editors and contributors have asserted their right under the Copyright, Designs and Patents Act 1998 to be identified as the authors of this work.

All rights reserved. No part of this publication may be reproduced, stored in a retrieval system or transmitted in any form or by any means, electronic, mechanical, photocopying, recording or otherwise, without the prior permission of the copyright owner.

Cover design by Pageset Limited, High Wycombe, Buckinghamshire.

Book production by Amanda Helm, St Leonards-on-Sea, East Sussex.

Printed by TJI Padstow, Cornwell.

Contents

Foreword: *Gerardine Meaney,* Professor of Cultural Theory in the School of English, Drama and Film, University College, Dublin ix

Acknowledgements xiii

Introduction: *Constanza del Río and José Carregal* 1

Part One: The Historical Facts

1. The Military Service (1916–1923) Pensions Collection: Evidence of a Revolution and New Perspectives
   Cécile Gordon and Robert McEvoy 21

2. Ireland's Revolutionary Years 1916–1923: An Oral History Record
   Maurice O'Keeffe 43

3. Violence against Women in Munster and Connacht in the Irish War of Independence, 1919–1921
   Thomas Earls FitzGerald 61

4. "We have not Committed any Sin": A Corpus-Based Critical Discourse Analysis of Brigid Lyons's Witness Statement of the Easter Rising
   Mariana Vignoli Figueroa 79

5. Resurrecting the Rebellion: A Postcolonial Reading of Two Historical Documentaries on the Easter Rising
   Paul O'Mahony 97

Part Two: Social Transformations

6. Politics, Sex and Land through the Lens of Exile in the Novels of Edna O'Brien
   Amor Barros-del Río 117

7. Evelyn Conlon's "What Happens at Night" (2014): Revolution, Art and Memory Practices
   Melania Terrazas 131

8. The Changing Status of Wounded Masculinity in Colm Tóibín's Ireland *José M. Yebra*	149
9. Direct Provision and Asylum Archive: Power and Surveillance *Vukasin Nedeljkovic*	167
10. Northern Irish Revolutionary Cinema: From Thriller to Comedy *Stephanie Schwerter*	183
11. Interview with Sarah Clancy: Poetry and Social Activism *Sara Martín-Ruiz*	201
New Poems by Sarah Clancy	209
Notes on Contributors	
Index	

List of Figures

1.1: Letter from Col. Vandeleur. MSPC. Con.Ran.23 (DP17)	28
1.2: Pension application form of Helena Molony. MSPC. MSP34REF11739	30
1.3: Letter from Margaret Skinnider. MSPC. MSP34REF19910	31
1.4: Letter from William O'Brien. MSPC. 1D178	36
7.1: Edwin Hayes, *An Emigrant Ship, Dublin Bay, Sunset*. © National Gallery of Ireland	132
7.2: Sarah Purser, *A Lady Holding a Doll's Rattle*.© National Gallery of Ireland	133
9.1: The Old Convent Direct Provision Centre, Ballyhaunis, 2008 (photo by Vukasin Nedeljkovic)	169
9.2: The Old Convent Direct Provision Centre, Ballyhaunis, 2008 (Nedeljkovic)	173
9.3: The Old Convent Direct Provision Centre, Ballyhaunis, 2008 (Nedeljkovic)	175
9.4: Object found in railway centre grounds, Kiltimagh, 2011 (Nedeljkovic)	176
9.5: The Old Convent Direct Provision Centre, Ballyhaunis, 2008 (Nedeljkovic)	177
9.6: Vaccine sheets found in Kilmacud centre, 2013 (Nedeljkovic)	177
9.7: The Old Convent Direct Provision Centre, Ballyhaunis, 2008 (Nedeljkovic)	179

Foreword

Gerardine Meaney,
Professor of Cultural Theory in the School of English,
Drama and Film, University College, Dublin

The focus on revolution in Ireland in this volume is an original and illuminating one, expanding out from the events of the 1916 Rising and the War of Independence to a century of social and cultural change. The editors' use of Hannah Arendt's definition of revolution as both a restoration of liberty and the beginning of a long process fits the case extremely well. The chapters in the volume chart both the limits of the liberty gained and the continuing struggle to extend it, to fulfil the promise of freedom, exceeding the history of political and social repression. The value of this volume lies in this open, reflexive approach to the meaning of revolution in Ireland, but also in the map it provides of the field of Irish Studies in the twenty-first century. It is indicative of the geographic range of Irish Studies, but at its heart is a dialogue between Ireland and Spain. Irish Studies in Spain has long been a dynamic contributor to the development of the field, with a particular strength in relation to issues of cultural memory and new approaches to texts, sources, and archives which is very much in evidence in this volume. Irish academics look forward to the AEDEI conferences for to get a sense of what new directions are emerging, for the informed and critical distance from which Spanish scholars look at Ireland opens up a particularly fertile ground for new ideas and approaches.

The volume situates itself very effectively between the revolutionary decade of 1913–23 and the Decade of Centenaries, a period of commemoration and critical reflection to which this book and the conference from which it derives make a significant contribution. The centenary of the Rising produced a kind of archive fever in Ireland, reflected in the projects to digitise and open up the records of the Bureau of Military History, initiating some oral history projects, bringing others into the multimedia age. Reflecting on the considerable enhancement of the archival record in relation to the 1916 Rising and its aftermath, this volume begins an important critical task, evaluating the evidence, asking how we can now work with this expanded treasure trove of sources. The application of appraisal theory here to Brigid Lyons's testimony of her involvement in the Rising is indicative of fascinating methodological challenges and opportunities offered by this expanded archive. Comparative documentary analysis and the analysis of art as memory practice in several chapters offer equally productive modes of engagement with the processes of cultural memory and commemoration stimulated by the Decade of Centenaries.

A particular strength of this volume is the attention to women as revolutionaries, whether military, social or cultural. The analysis of the difficulty women faced in gaining recognition as former military personnel with pension entitlements, even when they had been wounded in battle, as discussed in Chapter One, introduces the issues which women would address for the following century, in gaining rights and recognition. The description of the dangers women working in intelligence roles faced is enlightening, not least because such roles were of their nature low profile and easily sidelined in the historical account. The use of gender based violence, such as hair cutting, as a way of enforcing limits on women's sexual and political activities during the revolutionary period is linked in this volume with Edna O'Brien's searchlight on the scapegoating of women and the use of sexual violence as a political weapon in her late fiction. The overview of O'Brien's work as political fiction produces its own revolutionary history of Ireland, linking it to the broader currents of European history. O'Brien's work is set in productive context here by Evelyn Conlon's ekphrastic exploration of Irish women's cultural past, reaching back into the nineteenth century to create a counter-canonical history of the voiceless and overlooked. That history is counterpointed by the transitional masculinity celebrated in Colm Tóibín's work, challenging the poetics of sacrifice underpinning traditional ideals of Irish masculinity. The issues of cultural memory, commemoration and silencing recur across the volume. The processing of historical trauma and the trauma of processing history form a connective thread from the careful dispositions of the Bureau of Military History to the twenty-first-century novel.

The volume does not comfortably locate trauma in the past, the nightmare of history from which twenty-first century Ireland has awoken. It illuminates the ways in which pre- and post-ceasefire films set in Northern Ireland respectively use the conventions of the thriller and romantic comedy to explore the trauma of the recent past and the uneasy promise of a different future. The dislocation and isolation inflicted by what was once a nation of migrants onto the new century's immigrants is powerfully documented here. A new type of future facing a personal, dynamic, visual "asylum archive" stands in contrast to the monumental textual archives explored in Part One.

This is a highly interdisciplinary collection, spanning history, literature, film and media studies, and archival studies. It also succeeds in that most difficult endeavour, the creation of a productive interface between theory and practice, a dialogue between creativity, activism and scholarship. The inclusion of Vukasin Nedeljkovic's photographs and personal reflections, Sarah Martin-Ruiz's interview with poet Sarah Clancy, and Clancy's concluding poems make this something more complex than a collection of scholarly essays. Both Nedeljkovic and Clancy comment directly on the commemorative moment, and both challenge it, for the unrealised potential and stunted progress it marks. This volume concludes with Clancy's use of the language of the 1916 Declaration of Independence to satirise the state, in every sense, of the nation it heralded:

> you too will be cherished equally
> if you can afford it
> as soon as an operator
> becomes available
> which may well take
> another hundred years.

At the end of all the rigorous interrogation of the past, it is the future that is the shared space of artists, scholars, Ireland and Irish Studies in this volume. As the final section makes clear, that future is full of challenges. As the volume as a whole demonstrates, one of those challenges is a new appraisal of the legacies of the past. This volume is particularly welcome as the first major collection to critically reflect on a century of Irish culture and history through the lens of the national and international commemoration of the revolutionary decade of 1913–23. It does much more than that, in creating a meeting place for criticism, creativity, archives and history to consider where Ireland, and Irish Studies, go from here.

Acknowledgements

We would like to express our gratitude firstly to John Spiers, Managing Director of Edward Everett Root Publishers, and to Pilar Villar-Argáiz, General Editor of the EER Publisher's series 'Studies in Irish Literature, Cinema and Culture', and to Amanda Helm for her skills in production, for their inexhaustible patience, kindness and great efficiency in carrying out the publishing process. Apart from her extreme care and professionalism, Pilar deserves a lot of thanks (and hugs as well) for being such a loyal friend even in the most adverse circumstances. We also wish to thank all the contributors to this volume for making it attractive and interesting. We include here Linda, Gerardine and Eamon for their generosity in reading the book and writing about it, and also the colleagues that gracefully accepted the task of reviewing the different chapters.

This volume would not have been possible without the XV International AEDEI Conference celebrated in the University of Zaragoza, May 2016, so our gratefulness goes as well to AEDEI and all the participants in the Revolutionary Ireland Conference, too many to mention here, and now probably dispersed around the world.

In addition, we want to acknowledge the financial help of the Spanish Ministry of Economy and Competitiveness (METI) and the European Regional Development Fund (DGI/ERDF) (code FFI2015-65775-P), within the frame of the competitive research team "Contemporary Narrative in English" (H05), funded by the Government of Aragón and the European Development Fund (ERDF). This edited volume, which foregrounds previously silenced voices in Irish culture and history, is also part of a project funded by AEI/FEDER (code FFI2017-84619-P).

Because the edition of this book was completed in April 2020, we do not want to finish without making reference to the terrible and uncertain times we are all going through due to the Covid-19 health crisis. We sincerely hope that this devastating pandemic, which has claimed the lives of many and caused much suffering on a global scale, ends up providing a new social revolution for the sake of international cooperation and solidarity.

Introduction:

Constanza del Río and José Carregal

The present volume originated in an AEDEI (Spanish Association for Irish Studies) conference held in May 2016 at the University of Zaragoza, Spain.¹ In 2016 the centenary of the Easter Rising 1916 was comprehensively commemorated and celebrated in Ireland and, less ostensibly, in many other countries as well.² The sheer volume of events marking the centenary of the 1916 Rising in 2016 demonstrates that, together with the Great Famine of mid-nineteenth century, the Rising is among the most significant and iconic events in Irish history in that it transformed the face and future of the country. The conference held in Zaragoza was but a small piece in this commemorative collage, yet, rather than selecting the Rising as a single thematic core for this academic gathering, the organisers opted for the idea and the reality of revolution in Ireland in the twentieth and first decades of the twenty-first centuries, promoting the discussion of this topic from a multi- and inter-disciplinary perspective, and extending its scope to cover other possible "revolutionary" social transformations that may have taken place in Ireland from the 1960s onwards.

This volume also forms part of the wealth of literature devoted to the revolutionary decade (1913–1923), published in the years preceding and following 2016. Some of these books fill in previous gaps by uncovering the vital contribution to the revolutionary struggle made by particular individuals, many of them women, that were heretofore neglected; or revolve around the specificities of the revolution in different counties in Ireland (*The Irish Revolution [1912–1923]* series published by Four Courts Press); or deal more concretely with the Rising making use of new material, such as the files digitised and

---

1   This introduction is not aimed at providing an account of Irish history for the period 1916–2016. Rather the idea is to substantiate the volume's structure and contextualise its chapters.
2   For a more detailed account of celebratory and commemorative cultural events on the centenary of the Rising, see Christina Hunt-Mahony (215–217).

released by the Bureau of Military History (BMH) in 2003 (*The Rising. Ireland: Easter 1916* by Fearghal McGarry); or represent novel historical approaches to the revolutionary period (*Vivid Faces. The Revolutionary Generation in Ireland 1890–1923*, by R. F. Foster, a study that considers the Irish revolution from a generational perspective[3] and combines historical, biographical and cultural research). The massive *Atlas of the Irish Revolution* (Cork University Press, 2016) that covers the 1912 Home Rule crisis through to the end of the Civil War in 1923, has also represented a breakthrough in the scholarship on the Irish revolutionary period: it includes 120 multidisciplinary contributions from leading scholars, many of them based on newly released archival material – BMH together with files from the Military Pensions (1916–1923) Section Collection (MPSC), the latter being progressively made public from 2014 onwards – as well as a wealth of maps and visual materials, all these features making this vital period interesting and accessible to scholars, students and general readers.[4]

For all the historiography on and multiple representations – historical, literary, cultural, visual, musical, etc. – of the revolutionary period and, more particularly, of the Rising, these are historical events that still remain elusive and subject to divergent interpretations.[5] In McGarry's words. "Even now, there is a remarkable degree of uncertainty about fundamental aspects of the Rising" (8). Some of these "fundamental aspects" were already present in W. B. Yeats's famous poem "Easter 1916", such as: What were the motives of the republican revolutionaries behind the Rising? Why did it occur precisely at that time? Were the revolutionaries led by irrational and excessive impulses? Were the bloodshed and the violence necessary? Frequently, discrepancies in interpretation have been fostered by conflicting strands in Irish historiography, mainly nationalist, revisionist and postcolonialist, each one of these strands having its own political agenda, an issue that Chapter Five in this volume examines. Maybe, as poet Theo Dorgan has argued, the fundamental and ethical attitude when it comes to history is to avoid recruiting "the past to the service of a desired fiction – inevitably to excuse or promote an ideological position" (7).

---

3   McGarry's *The Rising* adopts a similar generational perspective and discusses the shared formative experiences – educational, cultural and political – of the revolutionary generation (40–43).

4   John Gibney provides a much more exhaustive account of and commentary on the rewritings of the Rising and the revolutionary decade issued on the occasion of the centenary (93–97).

5   Seamus Deane offered a critical close reading of F. S. L. Lyons's revisionist interpretation of the period 1919–1921 in Ireland (194–197). For a discussion of Roy Foster's and Joseph Lee's historical takes on the Rising, the Irish revolution and the Irish Free State, see Declan Kiberd (641–647). Fearghal McGarry also offers a commentary on conflicting historical interpretations of the Rising and of the early twentieth-century Irish Republican Movement (290–293).

Since Ferriter published his influential *The Transformation of Ireland 1900–2000* in 2004, and as stated above, new material (BMH and MPSC files, as well as other oral history collections, such as the *1916 Rising Oral History Collection*, from the Irish Life and Lore project led by Jane and Maurice O'Keeffe) has come to light in the form of oral recordings or written statements from participants in the Irish revolution and their descendants: that is, in the form of history as "lived experience" or "history from below," practiced and popularised by historian Raphael Samuel. Charles Townshend has commented on the value of such material:

> The release of the Witness Statements collected by the Bureau of Military History, intended to provide the basis for an official history of the war, but instead locked away for a generation, has had a dramatic effect on our knowledge of the personal experience of the revolutionary period. The release of the materials in the Military Service Pensions Collection (MSPC) will provide the final key to the inner life and activity of the revolutionary organisations. (111)

McGarry, who mainly based his book *The Rising* on the witness statements released by the BMH, also remarks on the value of these primary sources: "While the witness statements do not, for the most part, fundamentally alter our knowledge of what occurred, they enhance our understanding of the motivations, mentality, and experiences of the revolutionary generation, preserving something of the texture and complexity of the past rarely recorded by conventional sources" (5). Yet McGarry also cautions the reader against the subjective and potentially manipulated nature of the statements: "The Bureau's statements represent a heavily mediated form of oral history, recording those aspects of the past that interviewees were able or willing to recall, reflected through the lens of a state-sponsored historical project" (6). This is a drawback which, as Maurice O'Keeffe states in Chapter Two in this volume, the audio recordings from the Irish Life and Lore project do not show.

Apart from the questions mentioned above that still surround the Irish revolution,[6] there are other more general, and basic, issues that merit attention: Did a revolution actually take place in Ireland? And, when did it actually start? In this respect, Ferriter referred to Charles Townshend, who considered that "in its middle-class orientation and hostility to social revolution, it was perhaps more

---

6   In a special volume of *History Ireland* devoted to the 1916 Rising, Joe Culley compiled and edited a panel discussion on the justification, or lack thereof, of the Rising. The piece is subtitled "Heroic Sacrifice or Criminal Behaviour?" (87–92). The panel was chaired by editor Tommy Graham and the participants were Felix Larkin, Ronan Fanning, Padraig Yeates and John Borgonovo. They discussed issues such as the justification and morality of the Rising, its political legitimacy, the international context, the use of violence, partition, etc. The disparity of opinions among the speakers points towards the continuing existence of unresolved matters.

of a nineteenth- than a twentieth-century revolution" (*Transformation*, 187). For his part, Foster has acknowledged that although the War of Independence, Civil War and post-revolutionary consequences in Ireland resembled other bloody events in Europe after 1918, nevertheless, "the idea of the Irish revolution is still in the process of definition, and not just its duration. How far was it a 'revolution' in the generally accepted meaning of the word?" (xvii).[7] Well, first of all, it should be considered that, unlike the French or Russian revolutions, the historical process that came about in Ireland was fundamentally a de-colonising one, a struggle not so much against the British government as against the British empire, a struggle meant to restore sovereignty to the Irish people. In this pursuit, the Irish revolutionaries succeeded and a political revolution took place. Even if it was not fully a social class-driven process in the Marxist understanding of the term, other meanings of revolution may fit the Irish case, for example Hanna Arendt's. Arendt, one of the most famous twentieth-century philosophers and political thinkers, assimilated revolution with liberation, with the restoration of lost liberties and privileges marking a new beginning (34–40), and following this definition, we can say that indeed a political revolution took place in Ireland. This is the idea underlying the first part of this volume.

Arendt also comments on the difficulties of locating the beginning of revolutions, even if revolutions always signal the arrival of something new:

> It is in the very nature of the beginning to carry with itself a measure of complete arbitrariness. Not only is it not bound into a reliable chain of cause and effect, a chain in which each effect immediately turns into the cause of future developments, the beginning has, as it were, nothing whatsoever to hold on to; it is as though it came out of nowhere in either time or space. For a moment, the moment of beginning, it is as though the beginner has abolished the sequence of temporality itself, or as though the actors were thrown out of the temporal order and its continuity. (206)

In the Irish case, sometimes there are references to the revolutionary decade (1913–1923); the Dublin lockout and the establishment of Connolly's socialist Irish Citizen Army (ICA), the formation of the extra-parliamentary Ulster and Irish Volunteers and Redmond's support for the Great War being seen as the initial events in this process.[8] The reconstitution of the Sinn Féin as a fully republican party led by De Valera – a new Sinn Féin gathering very different

---

7   Marc Mulholland has recently written a nuanced examination of this matter ("Revolutionary").
8   Redmond was the leader of the constitutional Irish party (the United Irish League, inheritor of Parnell's Irish Parliamentary Party), opting for Home Rule and rejecting separatism. His support of the war effort alienated many Irish nationalists from the constitutional policies defended by Redmond's party.

separatist and republican mentalities and ideas[9] –, together with its electoral success in 1918 – a victory which amounted to the republican cause's winning the democratic mandate absent in the Rising –, the threat of conscription on the part of Britain (1918), plus the establishment of an underground Dáil, followed by the War of Independence (1919–1921) carried out through the Irish Republican Army (IRA), all these processes and events turn the years 1918 or 1919 into further possible candidates for the beginning of the Irish revolution. Yet, it is the unexpected and apparently arbitrary nature of the Easter Rising, the Rising's staging as a cultural and historical palimpsest, and particularly Pearse's reading of the Proclamation of the Republic among the neo-classical colonnade of the General Post Office, a moment suspended in time, that has transformed this event into a privileged catalyst or trigger for the revolution. Following this idea, the chapters in the first part of this volume generally take the Rising as the starting point of the revolutionary fight in Ireland.

Once warfare ended in 1923 after the Civil War, a key question remained: What do we want to make of Ireland? While reflecting on the sequel to decolonising processes, Franz Fanon said: "Independence has certainly brought the colonized peoples moral reparation and recognized their dignity. But they have not had time to elaborate a society or build and ascertain values. The glowing focal point where the citizen and individual develop and mature in a growing number of areas does not yet exist" (40). In this respect, there is an almost general consensus that the process of nation-building in Ireland fell terribly short of the promises of egalitarianism (in terms of religion, gender and class) expressed in the Proclamation, mainly gathered in the following paragraph:

> The Irish Republic is entitled to, and hereby claims, the allegiance of every Irishman and Irishwoman. The Republic guarantees religious and civil liberty, equal rights and equal opportunities to all its citizens, and declares its resolve to pursue the happiness and prosperity of the whole nation and of all its parts, cherishing all of the children of the nation equally, and oblivious of the differences carefully fostered by an alien Government, which have divided a minority from the majority in the past. ("Proclamation")

The conservative nature of the Irish revolution was explained by Terry Eagleton in the following words: "If the Irish revolution was to prove a conservative one, it was in part because 1916 was its coffin as well as its

---

9   The cohesive task achieved in political terms by the Sinn Féin at this stage had been preceded by the synergies within the Gaelic League (founded in 1893 by Douglas Hyde), a cultural movement that most nationalists from all fields supported. Undoubtedly, the convergence of cultural nationalism – with its emphasis on the significance of rural Gaelic Ireland for Irish identity – and political republicanism would be tremendously significant for the kind of state that emerged after the Civil War.

cradle, wiping out some of the most gifted and radical leaders" (291). Eagleton is possibly referring here to James Connolly, the socialist leader of the ICA executed by the British in May 1916, who tried to break the tension between socialism and nationalism and who believed in industrialisation and the future political role of the Irish working classes (Ferriter, *Transformation*, 168); or to the general oblivion and neglect into which revolutionary women, frequently more radical and progressive than their male counterparts, fell once the revolution ended.[10] Their names are many, although Constance Markievicz – feminist, socialist and republican activist – is the first one that most frequently comes to mind. But other female figures – suffragists, socialist activists and nationalists – should also be remembered: women such as Helena Molony, Kathleen Lynn, Eva Gore-Booth, Rosamond Jacob, Hannah Sheehy-Skeffington and many other less-known women who are mentioned in Chapters One, Two and Four in this volume. Their official mistreatment betrays the patriarchal orientation of the new state and the general idea that whenever women's politics and nationalist politics meet, the end result is that the former becomes absorbed by and subordinated to the latter (Radhakrishnan, 77–78). The eradication of feminism, secularism and socialism – probably the most progressive forces in the Irish revolution – from and by the new state certainly amounted to a great loss and contributed to its conservative nature, yet there were also other historical factors to take into account.

The Civil War (1922–23) had evinced the extent of the political discrepancies within the Irish Republican Movement, already latent in the Easter Rising in the frictions between the ICA and the Irish Volunteers in spite of Connolly's efforts to bridge the gap separating international socialism and (Catholic) Irish nationalism. The split in the Sinn Féin party explicitly revolved around the issues of partition and the oath of loyalty to the British crown. Additionally, Ferriter also referred to "the class bias of a revolutionary generation that had more in common with the administration they were attempting to overthrow than they cared to admit" (*Transformation*, 187) and wonders to what extent the divide between pro-Treaty and anti-Treaty republicans that led to the Civil War was not also a class divide, if only at the level of rank and file (256–257). The middle-class leaders of the pro-Treaty Sinn Féin party (later named Cumann na nGaedheal and then Fine Gael) won the Civil War. As members of a generation that had grown up absorbing Victorian and Edwardian values, they inevitably grafted those values onto the new state,[11] and the situation did not change once

---

10   It is not only that women's presence in future Irish governments was practically inexistent, but that they were also written out of the history of the revolution. As Connolly explains, in Ireland, the pioneers' of women's history – feminist and/or female historians – started their work in the 1980s by concentrating "on the role of prominent or 'worthy' women, particularly in Irish nationalist and suffrage movements" (18).
11   This paradoxical situation is superbly captured in Joyce's "The Dead," where a group of middle-class Catholic Irish gather to celebrate the Epiphany. The guests listen

the anti-Treaty Sinn Féin (named the Fianna Fáil party, led by De Valera) won the elections in 1932.

The conservatism of the Irish Free Sate can also be related to its leaders' capitalist mentality, values and practices, which had gradually infiltrated rural Ireland during the nineteenth century. In Scally's words:

> By the time of the famine, a large "middle" class of Roman Catholics farmers, graziers, tradesmen, and the beginnings of a native professional class had emerged in the vicinities of market towns. But probably most decisive and lasting of all, the inexorable intrusion of English capital into the Irish countryside through hundreds of such market towns … had already proceeded very far in the transformation of traditional Irish society. (20)

The process accelerated after the Great Famine, when the majority of those who died or emigrated were not land owners or tenants but landless labourers. The ensuing land clearance, combined with strict inheritance policies[12] and followed by the land reforms initiated by the Land League (founded in 1879 by Michael Davitt) – meant to shift land ownership from the Anglo-Irish Ascendancy to the tenants that farmed it (McGarry, 17) –, allowed for the emergence of a strong class of farmers whose progeny, nurtured in conservative and sexually repressive Catholic values, would later become the leaders of the revolution.

The role that the Irish Catholic Church would play in the new state,[13] a

---

to waltzes and dance quadrilles, a dance fashionable in the late eighteenth and nineteenth centuries and imported by English aristocrats in 1815 from elite Parisian ball rooms ("Quadrille"); a painting of the balcony scene in Romeo and Juliet and another of the two young sons of English King Edward IV adorn the walls; Robert Browning has been the poet chosen by Gabriel Conroy to quote in his speech; and all the guests follow strict norms of etiquette and propriety. Ironically, the only character that breaches manners, "assumes a very low Dublin accent" (183) and is drunk throughout the celebration is the Protestant Mr Browne.

12   These inheritance practices, known as "familism," were first studied by Conrad M. Arensberg and Solon T. Kimball (*Family and Community in Ireland* 1968). Basing themselves on Arensberg and Solon's work, Cairns and Richards defined "familism" in the following terms: "Familism consisted in a number of procedures to control access to marriage, including the imposition and perpetuation of strict codes of behaviour between men and women, general endorsement of celibacy outside marriage and postponement of marriage in farmers' families until the chosen heir [always male] was allowed by the father to take possession of the land" (42). One of the outcomes of these practices was that many of the sons from these farmer families, the ones not entitled to the land, would emigrate to Dublin and other Irish cities and towns in the 1890s and 1900s, carrying with them these conservative rural codes and forming the new middle-class that would later rule the country (60).

13   The historical role of the Catholic Church as badge of Irish identity and the frequent assimilation between Catholicism and Irishness should also be taken into account. When, for example, Spenser wrote the colonial tract *A View of the State of*

Catholic Church restructured and reinvigorated from the Great Famine onwards and imbued by a new Jansenist view of morality and emphasis on the dark side of human nature (Ferriter, "Irish Catholicism"), would be vital for the stringent moral and sexual principles governing the lives of Irish citizens in the first decades after independence. After the revolution, the Catholic Church, which had maintained at most a lukewarm and ambiguous attitude towards advanced nationalism, managed to consolidate its power by aligning itself with the pro-Treaty Sinn Féin (Foster, 142). The Catholic Hierarchy established a firm alliance with successive Irish governments – an allegiance enshrined in the 1937 Constitution – and took control over education and health in the whole country.[14] A combination of political conservatism, strong state centralism to the detriment of local democracy, economic autarchy, cultural censorship and sexual repression determined who the victims of the Irish revolution would be: not the British, not the losers in the Civil War (the anti-Treaty Sinn Féin, whose party renamed Fianna Fáil, and as previously mentioned, came to power in 1932) and not the Protestant community, a small minority in the new Ireland who, as Kiberd affirms, "posed no threat to the new order and, provided that they remained quiet and contented with their lot, were untroubled" (416). The victims were women, the working classes and deprived or orphaned children. The phrase "revolutionary Ireland" as applied to the country in the 1930s, 1940s, 1950s and early 1960s would certainly have been an oxymoron. This is the reason why this volume is structured in two different parts, with the second one, more cultural than historical in nature, dealing with social transformations occurring from the late 1960s onwards and emphasising, though not exclusively, questions related to gender and sexual identity, since this is perhaps the terrain where Ireland's conversion has become more drastic and has functioned as the most visible signpost of the country's modernisation and liberalisation. Even if these changes have taken place more gradually than the political revolution, considering the low liberal standards from which Ireland started and the country's profound transformation, they nevertheless merit to be termed "revolutionary" in the same sway as one now refers to a

---

Ireland (written in 1596; first published in 1633), characterising the Irish as a savage and barbaric people who could only be civilised if their culture were fully eradicated, who was there to raise a voice for Ireland and against these so negative stereotypes if not Catholic priests? Or, when the Penal Laws deprived the native Irish of many of their political and civil rights, which institution could in some way represent them other than the Catholic Church?

14 The privileged position of the Catholic Church in Ireland and its influence on state matters recalls the role of the Catholic Church in Spain after the Spanish Civil War (1936–1939) within Franco's regime (1939–1975). This close alliance between Church and State was called "national Catholicism" in Spain. There is an important caveat, though, and this is that Franco's regime was a cruel and bloody dictatorship while Ireland was, at least in theory, a democracy.

"technological revolution" or a "digital revolution."

Although from the late nineteenth century forwards women's movements coinciding with and influenced by the international first wave of feminism, such as the Irish Women's Suffrage Movement or Cumann na mBan, were active in Ireland fighting for social and legal equality, as well as in cultural and political nationalism, in post-independence Ireland women were marginalised and legally discriminated against in the 1937 Constitution. Yet, this is not to say that, from the 1930s until the late 1960s or early 1970s women's movements completely vanished from the scene. From 1930 to 1970 certain women's organisations (the National Council of Women, the National University Women's Graduate Association, The Joint Committee of Women's Societies and Social Workers, The Irish Women's Workers Union, the Irish Countrywomen's Association, the Irish Housewives Association) were set up which, even if not very visibly and practising some kind of "social feminism" (Ferriter, *Transformation*, 420), nevertheless opposed the gendered nature of the State. This is the reason why Linda Connolly considers that there has been a continuation between first wave and second wave feminism in Ireland through what she calls "a period of abeyance (1922–69)" (69–78).

In general terms, a wealth of domestic and foreign factors contributed to Ireland's flowering in the late 1960s. Beginning with the economy, the starting gun came with Séan Lemass's (Taoiseach from 1959 to 1966) determination to open up the economy, promote industrial growth and foreign investment, and develop the tourist industry. Lemass abandoned the autarchic economic policies of Éamon de Valera (Taoiseach from 1937 to 1948, from 1951 to 1954 and from 1957 to 1959; President of Ireland from 1959 to 1973) in an attempt to free the country from its endemic poverty, lack of industry and economic stagnation. Ireland's economic accomplishments took place in two phases: the first one starting in the mid-1960s, followed by a backlash in the 1980s which was the consequence of the international 1979 oil crisis. This backlash was social as well as economic and during the 1980s "the Irish women's movement increasingly felt the effects of an anti-feminist movement and a growing conservative backlash" (Connolly, 180). For some years, it seemed that Ireland had regressed to the fifties, with high levels of unemployment, emigration, crime and drug abuse. In terms of women's struggles, in this decade both the referendum for abortion and the attempt to legalise divorce were defeated. The country's economy finally left ground from the mid-1990s to 2007 (the period when Ireland became known as the Celtic Tiger), when an international crisis led to Ireland's bailout.

In social and cultural terms, the advent of TV (1961) and the traditional international connections of Irish citizens through the Irish diaspora – the latter exponentially increased through globalisation and the digital revolution[15] – put

---

15   According to the findings of the A.T. Kearney/Foreign Policy Magazine

Ireland in touch with other, more liberal, lifestyles, mores and manners, at the same time as a feeling of tiredness for the lack of social reforms in spite of a relative degree of economic affluence overtook a great part of the population. Industrialisation gave women access to jobs previously inexistent or denied to them, and made their presence more visible in the public arena (Ferriter, *Transformation,* 569). Politically speaking, international institutions, such as the United Nations, with its "declarations on the political rights of women and elimination of discrimination against women ... were also putting the Irish government under pressure" (Ferriter, *Transformation,* 574). In 1973 Ireland joined the EEC, a fact which helped Ireland open itself up to the world and cease seeing itself just in terms of the colonial relationship with Britain on one side and the USA on the other.

In terms of adherence to the Catholic faith and respect for the stern sexual and moral edicts of the Irish Catholic Hierarchy, hand in hand with modernisation gradually there came a desire for a greater degree of flexibility on the part of the Hierarchy, favoured by new currents pushing for change and coming from outside,

> ... from the top of the Church with Pope John XXIII. Pope John's pontificate began in 1958. The new Pope launched the process of *Aggiornamento,* that is to say a process which would enable the Church to adapt to the evolutions and meet the requirements of modern society and of the new economic and social order which emerged from World War Two. (Bevant, 43)

Nevertheless, it was the Catholic Church itself which finally became the agent of its own demise and loss of moral authority in Ireland when, from the 1990s onwards, a series of church related scandals – paedophilia and sexual abuses, brutality, enforced labour, kidnapping of children, etc. – were made public.

International second wave feminism and the "sexual revolution" that accompanied it had their impact as well, although, as Connolly argues, Irish women's activism during the abeyance period also favourably affected and characterised the emergence of second wave feminism in Ireland (89–90). In time, several amendments to the Constitution of Ireland were approved: namely, the Fifth Amendment in 1972, restraining the political intervention of the Church and favouring religious pluralism; the Thirteenth and Fourteenth Amendments in 1992, granting pregnant women the freedom to travel or obtain information

---

Globalisation Index, Ireland came out as the most globalised of 62 states for two consecutive years, 2001 and 2002 (78).This is an index that measures changes in categories such as engagement in international relations and policymaking, trade and financial flows, or the movement of people, ideas and information across borders. (The Index considers sixty-two countries representing 85 % of the world's population and more than 95 % of world economic output).

about abortion facilities abroad, the Fifteenth Amendment in 1995, allowing the dissolution of marriage under certain circumstances and, finally and most significantly, the removal of the Eighth Amendment in 2018, an amendment which guaranteed the "unborn" and the pregnant woman the same right to life and whose removal amounted to the right to abortion. As for LGBTQ+ rights, a similar, though belated process of liberalisation, has occurred, starting in 1993 with the decriminalisation of same-sex sexual relationships and, as for now, finishing with the legalisation of same-sex marriage in 2015. Chapters Six, Seven, Eight and Eleven in this book revolve around these questions.

In spite of all this progress, from 1969 to 1998 a dreadful shadow was cast upon the whole of Ireland in the form of the Northern Irish Troubles. Paramilitary violence and sectarian civilian street riots had occurred mainly in Belfast in the period 1920–1922, when the prospect of Home Rule and the signing of the Anglo-Irish Treaty in 1921 led to the confrontation between the Protestant and Catholic communities. From the moment of its establishment (1921), the Northern Irish Parliament was dominated by Protestants and the Prime Minister James Craig defined Northern Ireland as a Protestant state. Discrimination against Catholics was evident in terms of housing, employment and rights. Fuelled by the civil rights marches in the USA, the Northern Irish Civil Rights Association (NICRA) was founded in 1967. The NICRA's objectives were "to defend the rights of the individual and freedom of speech, highlight abuses of power and inform the public of their lawful rights" (Ferriter, *Transformation*, 615). Some of the protests and marches organised by the NICRA ended up with the intervention of the Northern Irish police force, the Royal Ulster Constabulary (RUC), or with loyalist attacks. In 1969 the British army occupied the streets of Northern Ireland with the initial purpose of being a pacifying force. Nevertheless, when during a civil rights march in Derry the British paratroopers killed 13 unarmed civilians in the infamous Bloody Sunday, the IRA decided to initiate reprisals and sectarian paramilitary violence escalated on both sides, lasting for three decades and leaving a toll of 3,600 deaths and thousands and thousands of injured and traumatised citizens. The peace process which started in the 1990s culminated in the 1998 Good Friday Agreement signed by all Northern Irish parties, the British government and the government of the Republic of Ireland. Chapter Ten in this volume deals precisely with the ways in which the 1998 Good Friday Agreement has radically altered the representation of Belfast in films produced in Northern Ireland.[16]

The last point in this introduction has to do with certain regressive social

---

16 We are aware that this summary of events in Northern Ireland is an oversimplification of a very complex situation which comprises historical, social-class, ethnic, political and religious factors. For more detailed and comprehensive explorations of this question, see for example David Miller's edited volume *Rethinking Northern Ireland: Culture, Ideology and Colonialism* (1998), and Marc Mulholland's *The Longest War: Northern Ireland's Troubled History* (2002).

processes that appeared in Ireland during the prosperous years of the Celtic Tiger. Despite the cultural and economic boom and the impression that Ireland had finally shaken off a history of deprivation, suffering and inferiority complexes, these were years when all that glittered was not gold. Sockets of poverty remained in the country and the digital breach evinced the increasingly widening gulf between the "haves and have-nots." In addition, it was precisely the new affluence that started reversing the traditional Irish migration patterns: that is, from a country that had historically provided labour force to other wealthier English-speaking countries (Britain, the USA, Canada, Australia), Ireland became the host country for migrants, refugees and asylum seekers from Eastern Europe, Africa, etc. The presence of these "new Irish" aroused racist and discriminatory attitudes which Vukasin Nedeljkovic, a former asylum seeker himself, reflects upon in Chapter Nine, where he offers a pointed critique of the Direct Provision system devised by the Irish government.

As previously suggested, Part One of this book, Historical Facts, concerns contemporary re-assessments of Irish history, more particularly, the turbulent years of the Irish revolution. Many of these new interpretations have emerged, as archivists Cécile Gordon and Robert McEvoy explain in Chapter One, entitled "The Military Service (1916–1923) Pensions Collection: Evidence of a Revolution and New Perspectives," thanks to the recent availability of The Military Service (1916–1923) Pensions Collection (MSPC), which contains records of the 1916 Easter Rising, War of Independence and Civil War. In their chapter, Gordon and McEvoy establish the provenance of the archives and highlight areas of special interest in the various sub-series that make up the collection – among them, files about Cumann na mBan, Ná Fianna Éireann and the Irish Citizen Army. Using evidence from the MSPC, Gordon and McEvoy then delineate vital themes to be further explored, like women's struggles for equality and participation in the independence movement, or the tensions and changes concerning social mores at a time of great political flux. As the work proceeds and more files become public, Gordon and McEvoy indicate, researchers will have the opportunity to expand on these themes and others, enhancing knowledge of the revolutionary period.

Moving from the MSPC archives to an appreciation of oral history as means to examine the past, Maurice O'Keeffe describes in Chapter Two, "Ireland's Revolutionary Years 1916–1923: An Oral History Record," the nature and scope of Irish Life and Lore, a project he began in 1990 with Jane O'Keeffe. Drawing on their vast archival material, more than 4,000 hours of recordings, O'Keeffe provides fresh insights into the Rising and the Irish Civil War through the life stories, perceptions and memories of participants and their close descendants. In this excavation of history, O'Keeffe points out, oral testimony works as the necessary complement to written resources, as the human voice reaches beyond the confines of official documents and forms – tightly structured and usually produced for administrative purposes –, which impose constraints on free expression. Omissions, contradictions, inaccuracies and imaginative projections may colour personal narratives, but these testimonies, as O'Keeffe tells us, facilitate a more nuanced understanding of the motivations, actions and reflections of those involved in historical events. Publicly praised by President Michael D. Higgins for its cultural value and breadth, Irish Life and Lore has greatly contributed to our renewed perceptions of the Irish revolutionary years, and will surely continue to do so.

Similarly, Chapter Three, by Thomas Earls FitzGerald, explores unknown stories of the revolutionary years. In "Violence against Women in Munster and Connacht in the Irish War of Independence, 1919–1921," FitzGerald concentrates on primary sources (contemporary journals and archival material) to tackle the issue of gendered violence against Irish women in the form of forced hair cutting, conducted by both revolutionary and counter-revolutionary actors in early 1920s Ireland. In comparison to other war scenarios, like occupied France in the First World War, forced hair cutting was not so common in Ireland, but, according to FitzGerald, this violence remained an intrinsic aspect to the 1919–1921 Anglo-Irish war. Making use of extensive archival material covering the areas of Munster and Connacht, FitzGerald relates that, while the British Crown forces were usually motivated by reprisal, revenge and demonstrations of power, the IRA had nationalist aspirations to homogenise the nation, and therefore punished any type of collaboration – no matter how politically insignificant – with the enemy. There were, of course, misogynistic implications behind forced hair cutting, and these attacks, FitzGerald maintains, responded to a traditional patriarchal obsession to control women's lives, imposing sexual stigma on those who were perceived to behave inappropriately. As FitzGerald foregrounds in Chapter Three, gendered violence has remained largely unexamined in the historiography of revolutionary Ireland and his chapter comes to fill this void, at least partly.

Chapter Four, Mariana Vignoli Figueroa's "'We Have not Committed any Sin': A Corpus-Based Critical Discourse Analysis of Brigid Lyons's Witness Statement of the Easter Rising," offers a linguistic analysis of Dr Bridget Lyons's witness statement. Lyons's testimony was registered in 1949 and now forms part of the Military Service (1916–1923) Pensions Collection. Dr. Lyons was involved in the Easter Rising as a member of Cumman na mBan. In her study, Vignoli Figueroa makes use of Appraisal theory not only to underline Lyons's cooperation and contribution to revolution, but also to analyse how she expressed her emotions. Vignoli Figueroa found that Lyons, when recalling her participation in the Rising, seldom used affect terms – those which centre on how one feels –, but relied mostly on appreciation and judgement expressions. Building on Monika Bednarek's concept of emotion talk, the author argues that Lyons's descriptions of events and situations, which largely replace expressions of personal feelings, vividly convey how she channelled her emotions through her sense of collective commitment towards revolution. Popular understandings of the Rising, which associate it with the sacrifice and martyrdom of male leaders, have traditionally obscured women's participation. Vignoli Figueroa's chapter ultimately calls for a wider recognition of women's involvement in the revolutionary struggle.

Part One closes with Chapter Five, Paul O'Mahony's "Resurrecting the Rebellion: A Postcolonial Reading of Two Historical Documentaries on the Easter Rising," where he develops a comparative analysis of two 2016 documentaries on the Rising: *1916: The Irish Rebellion*, an Irish–American production by Pat Collins and Ruan Magan, and the BBC documentary *Easter 1916: The Enemy Files*, by Andrew Gallimore. Informed by postcolonial theory, O'Mahony tackles the divergent representations of Irish rebels: as heroic martyrs in Collins and Magan's film, and as an unnecessarily violent crowd in Gallimore's. One key factor, O'Mahony argues, is the transnational perspective that each documentary projects in the depiction of the rebels' (il)legitimate use of violence. O'Mahony remarks how *The Irish Rebellion* romanticises the Rising by establishing parallels with the American and French revolutions, thus linking the rebellion to other culturally celebrated episodes of national liberation. On the contrary, *The Enemy Files* infantilises the rebels, perceiving no heroism in their actions, and then equates their religious zeal with Islamic extremism, invoking for the viewer the contemporary threat of global terrorism. Though these are recent documentaries, O'Mahony reminds us, they accurately reflect older tensions and contradictions between postcolonial, nationalist and revisionist interpretations of Irish history. The story of the Irish revolutionary past, O'Mahony concludes, continues to be a contested territory.

Shifting the focus from the revolutionary years to more recent manifestations of social change, Part Two, entitled Social Transformations, opens with Amor Barros-del Río's "Politics, Sex and Land through the Lens of Exile in the Novels of Edna O'Brien." Chapter Six examines the work of rebellious author Edna O'Brien, whose 1960 debut *The Country Girls* – banned and reviled in its time in Ireland – became (in)famous for its frank portrayal of Irish women's emotional and sexual lives. Whereas O'Brien's earlier novels, Barros-del Río remarks, contest the dominant cultural stereotypes for Irish women promoted by Irish law and the Church, her later work – from the mid-1990s onwards – extends the critical scope to engage with realities like transnationalism, sexual violence and contemporary socio-cultural restrictions on women's freedoms, both beyond and within Irish borders. In this way, O'Brien explores how recent global trends continue to affect women's lives. Central to O'Brien's approach, Barros-del Río argues, is a concern with place: home and locality, movement, travel, diaspora and exile, the latter offering the ultimate possibility of renewed self-perception. Through the trope of exile, Barros-del Río concludes, O'Brien exposes the silenced and subdued effects of legal, social and religious boundaries upon women's bodies and lives, portraying the protagonists' continuous negotiations with received ideas of womanhood, nation and identity.

Like O'Brien, another rebellious female voice is that of Evelyn Conlon, whose cultural contribution to Irish feminism – from her 1970s activism in Irishwomen United to her 2014 short story "What Happens at Night" – is analysed by Melania Terrazas in Chapter Seven, "Evelyn Conlon's 'What Happens at Night': Revolution, Art and Memory Practices." Drawing on scenarios like the Great Famine, the devotional revolution and first-wave feminism, Conlon's story imagines an encounter between two fictitious female figures represented in two different paintings – one by Sarah Purser (1848–1943) and the other by Edwin Hayes (1819–1904). This encounter, according to Terrazas, symbolises the need for women of different social strata to join together in dialogue and collaboration to achieve mutual empowerment. In her analysis, Terrazas makes use of Oona Frawley's interrelated concepts of "cultural memory" and "memory practices," just to highlight how Hayes' and Purser's paintings emerge as powerful transmitters of collective memory in Conlon's "What Happens at Night," a story infused as it is by the writer's contemporary gaze as a militant feminist. Terrazas points out that Conlon herself, as a representative of Ireland's second-wave feminism, uses the past to explain the present, paying tribute to women's mobilisation through art and memory.

Chapter Eight, by José M. Yebra, also tackles issues of gender and sexuality, but from the perspectives of masculinity and homosexuality in the work of Colm Tóibín. In this chapter, entitled "The Changing Status of Wounded Masculinity in Colm Tóibín's Ireland," Yebra observes that Tóibín – who, as a writer and journalist, has contributed to the latest sexual revolutions in Ireland, from pre-gay-decriminalisation to post-liberation times – carefully explores in his fiction traumata like AIDS and paedophilia cases among the Catholic clergy, aspects which connect with the contemporary "crisis" of Irish masculinity. The erosion of traditional hetero-patriarchal masculinity features as a key trope throughout Tóibín's canon, but, as Yebra argues, the writer does not focus on radical transformations, but on processes of transition and exposure of old wounds. Tóibín thus deconstructs the male body as a cultural artefact that bears witness to recent Irish sexual politics. In Tóibín's fiction, as Yebra notes, the AIDS-infected body serves to explore the constraints of being gay, whereas the sexualised body of the paedophile priest embodies the shortcomings of "Perfect Clerical Celibacy," which imposes a damaging model of asexual masculinity. As Yebra remarks, Tóibín effectively captures in his texts the tensions, paradoxes and evolving perceptions of masculinity in contemporary Ireland.

Chapter Nine, "Direct Provision and Asylum Archive: Power and Surveillance," by activist Vukasin Nedeljkovic, moves to the realm of politics and deals with the effects of the Direct Provision scheme, established in 1999 to house asylum seekers and refugees in isolated state-designed accommodation centres. From the viewpoint of civil rights and liberties, Nedeljkovic asserts, Direct Provision stands as a clear example of involution, as it condemns people to poverty, social exclusion and institutionalism. In recent years, victims of Direct Provision – among them, Nedeljkovic – have raised their voices in protest. One of their platforms is the Asylum Archive, founded by Nedeljkovic, which, as he explains, functions as a repository of personal experiences and creative work, in order to highlight the displacement, dispossession and trauma of asylum seekers and refugees in Ireland. To illustrate the nature of this project and the appalling conditions of Direct Provision centres, Nedeljkovic offers a fragment from his diary as originally written when he was seeking asylum and illustrates his chapter with several photographs which he took at the time. Mixing personal experience with critical reflection, Nedeljkovic reminds us that revolution today should not only be about centenary commemorations of the Rising, but also about the abolishment of systems of oppression like Direct Provision.

Chapter Ten, written by Stephanie Schwerter and entitled "Northern Irish Revolutionary Cinema: From Thriller to Comedy," directs our attention to Northern Ireland in the aftermath of the Troubles, an ethno-nationalist conflict characterised by long-standing sectarianism, violence and insecurity. A climate of optimism flourished after the 1994 IRA ceasefire and the 1998 Good Friday Agreement, and these revolutionary changes are examined by Schwerter in her filmic analyses of Thaddeus O'Sullivan's *Nothing Personal* (1995) and John Forte's *Mad About Mambo* (2000). Only five years separate the production of both films, but each projects radically different visions of Belfast, as Schwerter notes. If O'Sullivan's *Nothing Personal* draws on the tradition of the Northern Irish thriller, portraying Belfast as a gloomy place laden with crime and where no peaceful co-existence between Catholics and Protestants becomes possible, Forte's *Mad About Mambo*, which depicts a love story between a Catholic and a Protestant, uses comedy to demystify old rivalries and sectarian divisions, establishing social class as a major marker of difference in post-Troubles Northern Ireland. Notably, what also emerges from Schwerter's analysis is the recognition of popular filmic genres as powerful mediums to reflect and contribute to social change.

Finally, in Chapter Eleven, "Interview with Sarah Clancy: Poetry and Social Activism," Sara Martín-Ruiz interviews Sarah Clancy – who generously offered two of her unpublished poems – on her politically-engaged poetry and participation in social activism, ranging from women's, LGTBQ+ and migrant rights to ecological concerns. Asked by Martín-Ruiz about the cultural climate for poets in Ireland, Clancy argues that there is nowadays some prejudice against authors who use poetry as their vehicle for social protest. This situation, which stifles revolution and reinvention within the genre of poetry, somehow informs

Clancy's ambiguous relationship with Ireland. In her interview with Martín-Ruiz, far from adopting a complacent attitude towards present-day conditions, Clancy explains that Irish society has not really come to terms with its recent history of exclusion and cruelty inflicted upon numerous individuals, confined in state-run institutions like Direct Provision centres, Magdalene Laundries and Industrial Schools. Even though these realities, when made public, receive the condemnation of the majority, most people, Clancy maintains, still prefer not to stand against these and other injustices, unwilling as they are to confront the uncomfortable truths of today's society. Her two poems, "Things I Was Thinking when She Said She Wanted to Feed Me" and "Cherishing for Beginners," close the volume.

Drawing on various critical perspectives and recently available archival material, the contributors to this volume have re-examined contemporary interpretations of a number of drastic transformations that have shaped the political, social and cultural landscape of modern Ireland. The present decade, the 2020s, when the nation celebrates the centenary of its independence, becomes a most suitable moment to explore Ireland's past and present, its evolutions and involutions, as a step towards creating new paths for the future. Revolution, understood here as the need to effect positive change, remains an ongoing process.

Works Cited

Arendt, Hannah. *On Revolution*. Penguin, 1990 (1963).
A.T. Kearney/ Foreign Policy Magazine Globalization Index. "The Globalization Index." *Foreign Policy*, November and December 2006, pp. 74–81, www.ucg.ac.me/skladiste/blog_2212/objava_8666/fajlovi/Global%20Top%2020.pdf. Accessed 1 April 2020.
Bevant, Yann. "The *Aggiornamento* of the Irish Catholic Church in the 1960s and 1970s." *Études irlandaises*, vol. 39, no. 2, 2014, pp. 39–49.
Cairns, David and Shaun Richards. *Writing Ireland: Colonialism, Nationalism and Culture*. Manchester University Press, 1988.
Connolly, Linda. *The Irish Women's Movement: From Revolution to Devolution*. The Lilliput Press, 2003.
Culley, Joe, editor and compiler. "Moral Justification? Heroic Sacrifice or Criminal Behaviour?" *History Ireland. The Impact of the Irish Rising: 1916 Dream and Death*.Wordwell,2016, pp. 87–92.
Deane, Seamus. *Strange Country: Modernity and Nationhood in Irish Writing since 1790*. Oxford University Press, 1997.
Dorgan, Theo. "What's the Story?" *History Ireland. The Impact of the Irish Rising: 1916 Dream and Death*, edited by Joe Culley, Wordwell, 2016, pp. 6–7.
Eagleton, Terry. *Heathcliff and the Great Hunger: Studies in Irish Culture*. Verso, 1995.

Fanon, Franz. *The Wretched of the Earth*. Translated by Richard Philcox. Grove Press, 2004 (1961).

Ferriter, Diarmaid. *The Transformation of Ireland 1900–2000*. Profile Books, 2004.

———. "Irish Catholicism is rooted in class prejudice." *The Irish Times*, 25 August 2018, www.irishtimes.com/opinion/diarmaid-ferriter-irish-catholicism-is-rooted-in-class-prejudice-1.3606614. Accessed 4 April 2020.

Foster, R. F. *Vivid Faces: The Revolutionary Generation in Ireland 1890–1923*. Penguin, 2015.

Gibney, John. "Books: Rewriting the Rising." *History Ireland. The Impact of the Irish Rising: 1916 Dream and Death*, edited by Joe Culley, Wordwell,2016, pp. 93–97.

Hunt-Mahony, Christina. "Irish Studies around the World – 2016." *Estudios Irlandeses*, vol. 12, 2017, pp. 213–240.

Joyce, James. *Dubliners*, edited by Terence Brown, Penguin, 1992 (1914).

Kiberd, Declan. *Inventing Ireland: The Literature of the Modern Nation*. Vintage, 1996.

McGarry, Fearghal. *The Rising. Ireland: Easter 1916*. Oxford University Press, 2010.

Miller, David, editor.*Rethinking Northern Ireland: Culture, Ideology and Colonialism*. Longman, 1998.

Mulholland, Marc. *The Longest War: Northern Ireland's Troubled History*. Oxford University Press, 2002.

———. "How Revolutionary was the Irish Revolution?" *Academia*, 2019, www.academia.edu/41110690/How_Revolutionary_was_the_Irish_Revolution. Accessed 1 April 2020. Working paper.

"Proclamation of the Irish Republic," *CAIN Web Service – Conflict and Politics in Northern Ireland*,cain.ulster.ac.uk/issues/politics/docs/pir24416.htm. Accessed 23 April 2020.

"Quadrille." *Encyclopaedia Britannica*, www.britannica.com/art/quadrille-dance. Accessed 1 April 2020.

Radhakrishnan, R. "Nationalism, Gender, and the Narrative of Identity." *Nationalisms and Sexualities*, edited by Andrew Parker *et al.*, Routledge, 1992, pp. 77–95.

Scally, Robert James. *The End of Hidden Ireland: Rebellion, Famine, and Emigration*. Oxford University Press, 1995.

Spenser, Edmund. *A View of the State of Ireland*, edited by Andrew Hadfield and Willy Maley, Blackwell, 1997 (1633).

Townshend, Charles. "The Irish War of Independence: Context and Meaning." *Guide to the Military Service (1916–1923) Pensions Collection*, edited by Catriona Crowe, Óglaigh na hÉireann, 2012, pp. 110–123.

Part One
The Historical Facts

1

The Military Service (1916–1923) Pensions Collection: Evidence of a Revolution and New Perspectives

Cécile Gordon and Robert McEvoy

Introduction

The decision to afford public access to the Military Service (1916–1923) Pensions Collection (thereafter MSPC) was announced in 2006 by then Taoiseach, Mr Bertie Ahern, TD, in the context of the ninetieth anniversary of the 1916 Easter Rising. Following on from this decision, the Military Service Pensions Project was set up two years later: a Steering Committee, chaired by the Department of the Taoiseach and comprised of representatives from that Department, the Department of Defence, the Defence Forces and the National Archives of Ireland, was established to oversee the project. A team of four archivists was recruited by the Department of Defence. An Academic Advisory Board was also set up, composed of Professor Diarmaid Ferriter (UCD), Professor Eunan O'Halpin (TCD) and Professor Charles Townshend (Keele University). The Steering Committee decided that the material should be released in phases leading up to 2016, the first release to deal mainly with participants in the 1916 Rising, some leading figures in the Independence movement and selected files and material to place the collection in an overall context.

The first release was marked by an official launch that took place in the General Post Office (GPO) on 16 January 2014, a fitting space to present one of the flagship government projects for the centenary commemorations. On that day, 452,000 scanned images (files relating to more than 3,000 individuals) entered the public domain on time to enable journalists and researchers to become familiar with the new material, assess it and integrate it as a new source for the study of the revolutionary period. However, although the Project team's initial mission was to release and present the files of the participants involved in the Rising, it is important to note that many of the surviving men and women of the early revolutionary years did go on and served in the War of Independence and the Civil War. Therefore it should be understood that information concerning the years 1919–1923 has been released from the onset too.

To date, and only considering the files of individual applicants, the project has released the files of 8,007 individuals. On 11 December 2015, the Government announced through then Defence Minister Simon Coveney the decision to "extend work on the MSPC project with the retention of the current experienced staff who are employed" through to 2023 ("Minister"). In April 2016, more than 66,000 files were released relating to the award of the 1916 Medal and the Service (1917–1921) Medal.[1] Of course, the Government's commitment is good news for Irish history and historians, but it also demonstrates the conviction that projects of this kind do empower people to understand and appreciate their own history and that archival material is crucial in that process.

The purpose of this chapter is to outline the background of the material (provenance, nature and value as a primary source for the study of the revolutionary period in Ireland) while highlighting areas of special interest in the various sub-series that make up the collection. As the work is ongoing, many themes will continue to develop and others will come to the forefront as more files are processed by the Project team.

Background of the Collection

1. The Nature of the Collection

Charles Townshend observed that "the release of the materials in the Military Service Pensions will provide the final key to the inner life and activity of the revolutionary organisations" (111). The collection thus occupies a crucial and unique place in the Irish archival landscape. It is new, contains unheard voices and brings the historical narrative down to the personal, the rank-and-file Volunteer as well as the leadership. It illuminates the organisations, events and individuals in context and the collection is often referred to as "the last piece of the jigsaw" for the 1916–1923 period.

The popularity of the Bureau of Military History (1913–1921) Witness Statements (including among those who are not professional historians) is evidence of an interest in the public place for voices other than the big

---

1   The MD series (Medals Series) is available for access at Military Archives (research room). A database of those files and information on how to access them physically can be found on the MSPC website.

narratives, commonly featuring in some academic publications.[2] Due to an increasing popular engagement with history, sources such as the Bureau – only available since 2003 – are being "fed into" publications that are both scholarly and popular. However, people represented by the Bureau were identified and selected based on their Irish Volunteer/Irish Republican Army (IRA) credentials as well as their political involvement or their response to advertising to offer their testimony. This has proved a very worthy exercise although a little contrived due to exclusivity and the fact that the project commenced in 1947. In contrast, the MSPC not only contains the profiles of principal actors of Irish history but also the history of ordinary lives, those whose voices were never heard beyond the local narrative and who never spoke of their involvement beyond the family hearth or remained doggedly silent. The dead also have a voice, expressed as it is by the claims of dependants and the requirement to investigate and prove family circumstances. Because it contains tens of thousands of individual stories and narratives, the MSPC could prove to be the ultimate post-modern collection and certainly a contender-source for a "history from below."

2. The Files: Origins, Legislation and Provenance

The material contained in the MSPC[3] owes its origins to the decision of the Oireachtas of Saorstát Éireann in June 1923 to introduce the first Army Pensions Act. This decision recognised and compensated wounded members and the dependants of deceased members of Óglaigh na hÉireann, including the National Army, Irish Volunteers, Na Fianna Éireann, Irish Republican Army and Irish Citizen Army (ICA).[4] Subsequent acts made provision to include the members of Hibernian Rifles and of Cumann na mBan (1932), and certain members of the 1st Battalion Connaught Rangers, British Army (1936). The second strand of legislation addresses the adequate compensation of those members of the organisations whose livelihoods, careers or prospects had suffered due to their involvement in the struggle for independence. This brought about the enactment of the Military Service Pensions Act, 1924, under which applicants had to prove they had performed "active service" to be considered for a service pension. The 1924 Act was restrictive in that only members of the "National Forces" were considered. After the 1932 General Election, the new Fianna Fáil Government enacted the Military Service Pensions Act, 1934, opening applications to members of Cumann na mBan and the anti-Treaty Forces from the Civil War. The 1949 Act allowed for new cases to be considered and for the petition of unsuccessful cases under the earlier two acts.

---

2 The Bureau of Military History collection (Witness Statements and other material) is available online at www.bureauofmilitaryhistory.ie
3 All the MSPC material is available at: www.militaryarchives.ie/collections/online-collections/military-service-pensions-collection-1916-1923
4 The Army Pensions Acts and Military Service Pensions Acts are available at www.irishstatutebook.ie

The files generated by the Department of Defence under the Army Pensions Acts have remained under Departmental control from their creation. These files were originally located in the offices of the Ministry/Department at Griffith Barracks, South Circular Road, Dublin, later at Coláiste Caoimhín, Glasnevin, Dublin, and latterly at Finance Branch of the Department at Renmore, Galway. The non-current files relating to the collection were transferred to the Military Archives at Cathal Brugha Barracks, Dublin, in 1989 for storage and retrieval as required by the Department.

The majority of the files and material generated by the Board of Assessors[5] under the Military Service Pensions Act, 1924, were transferred from the Board's offices at Portobello Barracks to the Department of the President of the Executive Council (Department of the Taoiseach) on 30 March 1928. The Department of Defence retained files relating to 7,610 unsuccessful applicants ("Disposal," 13).

Following the passage of the Military Service Pensions Act, 1934, the Referee and Advisory Committee[6] sought various individual files generated by the Board of Assessors from the Department of the Taoiseach, and eventually all the files were transferred to the Office of the Referee. These files would remain under the control of the Referee, being added to significantly by the creation in that office of the Nominal Rolls and Activities file series as well as administration and applicants' files under the 1934 Act.

Finance Branch of the Department of Defence used the original applicants' files as "payment" files in the case of successful applications under the 1934 Act, and records, ledgers and index cards demonstrate the control and accountability of files within the Department and the Office of the Referee. All of the files generated by the Office of the Referee under the Acts of 1934 and 1949, including those files generated by the Board of Assessors (1924–1928), were passed to Finance Branch of the Department as the Referee and Advisory

---

5   The MSP Act, 1924, provided for the setting up of a Board of Assessors to investigate and report on all claims referred to them by the Minister. This Board was to consist of three members appointed by the Minister for Defence with the approval of the Executive Council. One of the members was to be a judge of the Supreme Court, High Court, Circuit Court or District Court of Saorstát Éireann or a practising barrister of no less than ten years standing. From 1924 to 1928, Mr Justice Cyril Beatty acted as chair of the Board of Assessors. Its other members were Mr Eamon Duggan –Parliamentary Secretary to Executive Council– and Mr. Fionan Lynch, Minister for Fisheries. Lt. Gen. Gearoid O Suilleavain was the secretary of this Board.

6   The MSP Act, 1934, provided for the investigation of applicants by a Referee and for the Referee to be assisted by an Advisory Committee. The Referee was to be a judge of the Supreme Court, High Court, Circuit Court or District Court of Saorstát Éireann or a practising barrister of no less than ten years standing. The Advisory Committee was to consist of four persons: two to be persons who held high rank in the forces before 11 July 1921, one person to be nominated by the Minister for Finance and one person to be nominated by the Minister for Defence.

Committee system was wound up in 1957.

The decentralisation of Finance Branch of the Department from Coláiste Caoimhín to Renmore, Galway, in 1989, saw a major examination of the files held at Coláiste Caoimhín. All non-current files generated under the Army Pensions and Military Service Pensions Acts relating to the period from 1916 to 1923 were transferred to the Military Archives for storage and retrieval as required for Departmental use. Those current applicants' files (relating to veterans and dependents still in receipt of payments) and the administration files created by the Office of the Referee and Advisory Committee, moved with Finance Branch to Galway. All files relevant to the MSPC and stored at the Military Archives were handed over to the Project Manager in March 2008. Following a detailed survey of files held at Finance Branch, Galway, identified files were also transferred to the Project office and reintegrated in the MSPC in July 2008.

Administration Files

1. Departmental Files

The Project team was acutely aware of the necessity to provide relevant contextual information to accompany the core of the MSPC since this material would also be released for public scrutiny to enable pertinent and quality research. An extensive survey was carried out in the Central Registry of the Department of Defence. Following a request to the Department, the relevant files identified were then made available to the Project through the standard process of examination and release by the relevant Certifying Officers. The files handed over in this manner proved to be of clear significance in understanding the nature of the collection.

To date fifty-five files have been released in this series, all of which are available online. These files are important in that they provide both context and supplementary information for the collection. Significant departmental files include "Casualties," which relates to those executed by the British military authorities during the War of Independence as well as to the burial location of the 1916 leaders. With respect to Civil War executions, departmental file "Executed irregulars" contains copy reports detailing name, date and place of execution, location of burial and name and address of next of kin for eighty-one executions recorded in the period from 17 November 1922 to 26 April 1923. There is also significant material relating to the awarding of the 1916 Medal and the Service (1917–1921) Medal, and detailed information on the construction of the vault and the ceremonial dealing with the re-interment of Sir Roger Casement in Glasnevin Cemetery on 1 March, 1965 ("Funeral").

2. Other Administration Files

Altogether (and counting the departmental files mentioned above) the administration series is comprised of six sub-series of files created while individual applications were being addressed, and together they offer an unprecedented background, bringing context to the inner workings of the pension machine, according to the legal strand they operate under (either Army Pensions Act or Military Service Pensions Acts). Some files deal with the routine administration of the Army Pensions Board and Army Pensions Department of the Department of Defence; others contain correspondence between the Army Pensions Branch and secretaries of various other departments or bodies such as the White Cross or Old IRA Associations. An interesting series is the Service Pensions General (SPG). This series offers a very informative contextual background to those applications lodged under the Military Service Pensions Act, 1924 – here, the key notion of "Active Service" is more fully developed ("Active"). Many other themes in this series include the dealing with applicants from Northern Ireland, the setting up of the Criminal Investigation Department (CID) and questions of affiliation to Cumann na mBan and Oglaigh na hÉireann.

Organisation and Membership

1. Brigade Activity Reports

The Brigade Activity reports are the most significant within the series of the MSPC. These files were compiled following a decision of the Referee and Committee to form Brigade Committees in order to assist in the verification of individual applications for pensions. The Brigade Committees were comprised of individuals who had previously held high ranking positions in the Divisions and Brigades of the IRA. The compiling work which started in April 1935 continued until 1946 and the resulting file series consists of 151 files and circa twenty-five thousand pages in total. A complete survey of the Brigade Activity files is ongoing and the files are currently undergoing conservation. To date, four files relating to counties Galway (two files), Louth and Wexford have been released online ("Easter Galway," "Louth" and "North Wexford"). These files relate directly to Easter Week activities in said counties. The remaining files in the series are waiting cataloguing and are expected to be released in the coming years.

The Brigade Activity Reports are submitted by each of the various Committees but differ in the level of detail they contain. However, mostly all include a brief description of operations planned or undertaken, locations, date of incident, number of enemy engaged and casualties on either side. The participants are broken down by Company/Battalion name and address and, on occasion, maps and sketches are filed with the reports. The importance of the Brigade Activity Reports lies with the fact that they will allow researchers to associate names (so far unknown) with a particular event.

2. Battalion and Company Nominal Roll

The Battalion and Company Nominal Roll (RO series) was the title assigned by the Referee and Advisory Committee to the series concerning membership. The series contains lists of membership for the ICA, IRA, Cumann na mBan and Na Fianna Éireann on two critical dates: 11 July 1921 (Truce period) and 1 July 1922 (outbreak of Civil War). The nominal roll series contains 817 files and a total of 49,982 individual documents, all of which are available via the military archives website. The majority of the files in the series were gathered from January 1935 onwards. The rolls prove interesting in that they allow comparison for both critical dates and allow researchers to track those individuals with continued membership during the Civil War and those who left the relevant organisations following the Truce, the latter possibly opting to remain neutral or enlist in the National Army.

While the bulk of these listings are particularly significant for the study of unit strength around the country for the periods covering the War of Independence and the Civil War, some do relate to Easter Rising 1916. As regards the IRA, this information is confined predominantly to the Dublin Brigade ("Easter Dublin"), but there is also a file that covers events in Tyrellspass ("Tyrellspass") and another focusing on the Kimmage garrison ("Kimmage"). A further unique file that deepens our understanding of lesser known aspects of the period is the only file (in this series) on the ICA ("Irish Citizen"). This file is particularly significant in the sense that, similarly to Cumann na mBan, the ICA was not fully known, the actions of its members not fully addressed, and its mission not always understood. The file contains a handwritten list giving names and ranks of ICA officers in 1916 and a twenty-five page handwritten listing giving names, addresses, periods of service and (recommended) pension grade of ICA officers and members from 1916 to the end of the Civil War (and in some cases their service location for 1916 and/or Civil War). Also on file is a statement (unsworn) dated 29 March 1935 from James O'Neill, erroneously named John O'Neill on the first page of the statement ("Irish Citizen," 17–22). The statement tackles important aspects, such as the ICA's hierarchy and structure, the appointment of officers, the status of female members, the question of the connection between the ICA, the Irish Volunteers and the IRA and operations where overlap occurred between the ICA and the IRA resulted in inefficiency.

Individual Applications

1. Connaught Rangers[7]

On 28 June 1920, five men from C Company, 1st Battalion, garrisoned at Wellington Barracks, Jullundur, Punjab, India, decided to protest against the effects of martial law in Ireland. The protest spread to a second company of the

---

[7] MSP Collection reference code is "Con.Ran" for online search.

battalion which was based at Solon. In a rush on the armoury at Wellington Barracks, Privates Patrick Smythe and Peter Sears were shot dead. In all, eighty-eight mutineers from both companies were tried by General Court Martial on 20 August 1920: nineteen men were sentenced to death – one Private James Daly was executed by firing squad (Figure 1.1) and the other eighteen had their sentences commuted to penal servitude for life ("Daly") –, fifty-nine were sentenced to periods ranging variously from life to twenty-one years', fifteen years' and three years' imprisonment – some of which cases were commuted to lesser sentences – and ten were acquitted.

In theory only those eighty-eight mutineers and the dependants of the three soldiers killed (Ptes Daly, Smythe and Sears) were entitled to apply under the Act, though, in fact, 258 individuals representing 280 files now in the collection did so. The 280 files are important because they contain many original British

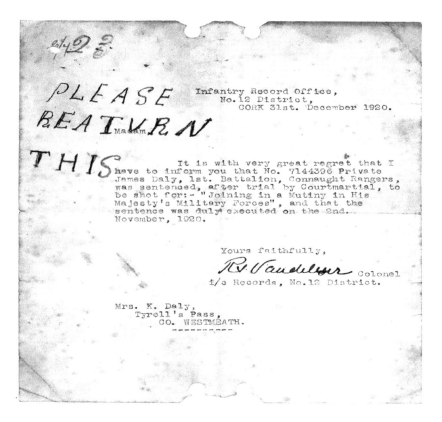

Figure 1.1: Letter from Col. Vandeleur (Infantry Record Office) addressed to K. Daly of Tyrrellspass, County Westmeath, informing her that James Daly was "duly executed on the 2nd November, 1920." Mr Daly submitted the letter to the Army Pensions Board as evidence ("Daly," 20).

1. THE MILITARY SERVICE (1916–1923) PENSIONS COLLECTION

Army records, an account of the Court of Enquiry into the Mutiny and into the deaths of Ptes Smythe and Sears and other related records that have not previously been in the public domain.

2. Women

The collection will also prove crucial in the reassessment of the role of women during the revolutionary years. Until now, sources have enabled researchers to unlock some private accounts and profiles of female participants, but the MSPC will prove to be a more solid base to analyse and study the female participation in a systematic manner and will also reveal unknown stories of ordinary women who got involved in the independence movement.

2.1. 1916 Women

The motivations that animated the 1916 women to join the insurrection are numerous and varied. Some women wrote eloquently about their awareness of the impact of their actions and, in relation to the award of pensions, many laid down their disappointment on paper and expressed their displeasure (Figure 1.2). Confronted with pensions jargon and the (strict) legal implications for her case, Helena Molony writes:

> It is difficult for the ordinary person to understand how such things are not classified as 'military service.' In any regular Army in any civilised country, I never heard of such 'no-combatants' as Army Service Corps, or Army Medical Corps, or Intelligence Dept. – being classified as 'non-military' and I respectfully suggest that to interpret such service in the IRA as 'non-military' is against the whole spirit of the act which was surely intended to give pensions to genuine soldiers of the Republican Army. I must be well known to members of your Board that I am not a person who is given as either bragging about their exploits or to making untruthful statements. (45–46)

The collection reveals that there are 225 women whose 1916 service was recognised (209 through the award of pension and medals, and sixteen with 1916 medals only). Cumann na mBan is revealed as the biggest organisation (for women) with 186 members recognised for 1916 service, while twenty-six women in the ICA get awarded a pension too. One woman, Linda MacWhinney (née Kearns), is recognised primarily through her work with the Volunteers. During Easter Week, she set up a first aid station in an empty house in North Great Georges Street but also transported ammunitions and guns from Hardwicke Street, North Great Georges Street to the GPO. Later she provided a link between Dublin and the west (mainly in the Sligo Brigade area), carrying despatches to and from the Supreme Council of the I.R.B. (Irish Republican Brotherhood) and to the Commanding Officers in Dublin and

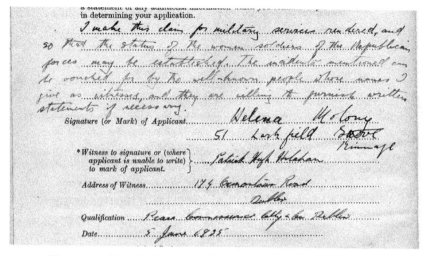

Figure 1.2: Detail of page 16 of the pension application form of Helena Molony.

the west. With regard to the Hibernian Rifles, seven of the sixteen members involved during Easter Week and who applied for a service pension were women. The rest, although the legislation insists on the fact that, to be eligible, the applicant must be a member of an organisation recognised under the acts, were not official members of any organisation but maintained strong links to key organisers able to offer strong enough references.

During the Rising, women were found at all main points of activity: sixty women (successful pension applicants) were located either in the GPO and/or more generally around the whole of O'Connell Street area. Some were positioned in the St Stephen's Green/Royal College of Surgeons area, Marrowbone Lane, Liberty Hall, City Hall, North King Street, Church Street, Jacob's Factory (Bishop Street) and Fairview. One of the great aspects of the collection is that although 1916 activities remain Dublin-centric, it shows other centres of activities: twenty-eight women were active in Enniscorthy, Co Wexford, twenty-two in Co. Galway; others carried despatches across county borders; others came from the north; and a handful, like Margaret Skinnider (Figure 1.3), came from outside Ireland.

Well before 1916, some women activists, trade unionists and feminists joined various socially and politically aware organisations such as Inghinidhe na hÉireann and later, the Irish Women Workers' Union. Others became involved due to their family members being involved: their brothers, husbands, fathers, uncles, sisters were active and therefore they became implicated too. Women involved in the independence movement thus come from different backgrounds: they are teachers, secretaries, shorthand typists, clerks, nurses and midwives but also dressmakers, shop assistants, housekeepers and factory

1. THE MILITARY SERVICE (1916–1923) PENSIONS COLLECTION

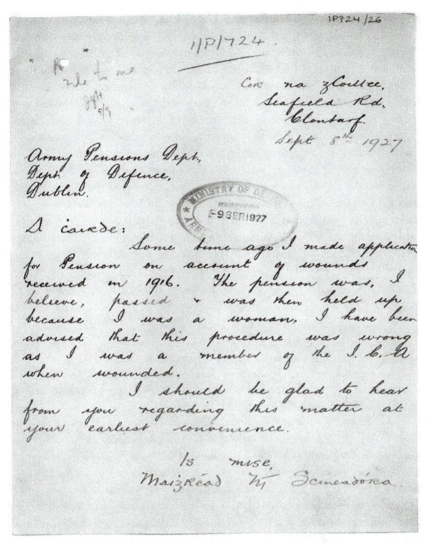

Figure 1.3: Letter from Margaret Skinnider to the Army Pensions Department.

workers. Post 1916, the files show that the background of female applicants changed for the periods covering the War of Independence and the Civil War. Many women were targeted and identified by the IRA as being valuable to employ due to their key location (if isolated, farm houses could be used for battalion or brigade meetings, with enough space to shelter men and store equipment), or key occupations in more urban areas where women had contact with the enemy through work: waitresses in public houses, restaurants or hotels, telephone operators, hotel employees, shopkeepers, secretaries.

31

2.2. Ignorance and Legal Discrimination

The files also show the unfamiliarity that the IRA leadership demonstrated towards women, the affiliation and structure of their organisation and their activities in general. In 1926, former Adjutant General Gearoid O'Sullivan writes to Senator Wyse-Power and Mrs Mulcahy to request some information regarding the affiliation of Cumann na mBan with particular reference to Easter Week ("Affiliation"). In her answer, Senator Wyse-Power insists that, during Easter Week, Cumann na mBan branches were attached to Volunteers units and that Cumann na mBan members were taking their orders from the Officers of the Volunteers. Margaret Skinnider's case is remarkable as it illustrates the discriminatory aspects of the legislation and the attitudes of the time regarding women. Originally from Glasgow, Skinnider fought in Easter Week as an ICA member and transferred to Cumann na mBan in 1918/1919. In February 1925 she lodged an unsuccessful wound pension claim under the Army Pensions Act, 1923, in respect of gunshot wounds (two gunshot wounds in her shoulder and one in her spine received in action while in charge of five men on Harcourt Street) on 27 April 1916. The Army Finance Officer, E. Fahy, wrote on 16 February 1925:

> The preamble to the Army Pensions Act, 1923, while mentioning allowances or gratuities to 'widows, children and dependants' presumably contemplates that the deceased members shall be of the male sex. It would be illogical, therefore, to include the female sex under the terms 'wounded members' and 'the definition of 'wound' in Section 16 only contemplates the masculine gender. ("Skinnider,", 18–19)

P. Coll, Treasury Solicitor, in a letter dated 18 March 1925, confirmed this view: "I am satisfied that the Army Pensions Act is only applicable to soldiers as generally understood in the masculine sense" ("Skinnider," 20).

Skinnider appealed the decision and applied again under the Army Pensions Act, 1932–1937. She indicated in the application form that she was now, in her profession as a teacher, unable to write on the blackboard in the school for any length of time or do any work involving her right arm. Medical examination indicated that her degree of disablement was 20%. Her wound pension was eventually awarded in 1938. She also succeeded in claiming for service between 1916 and 1923 and was granted eight years active service (Grade D) and awarded £80 per annum, under the 1934 Act.

The collection offers new perspectives on those revolutionary women and the strength of the collection lies also in the continuity that the files offer. Many women continued their activities beyond 1916. For them, post-Rising duties included election work and anti-conscription efforts, but the pension files convey evidence that women, influenced by the Rising, and within a wider context, possibly vitalised by the suffragette movement, truly found their voice through the events that followed.

2.3. Women in the War of Independence and Civil War

Individual files of women involved in the War of Independence and Civil War show new information about their organisation within Cumann na mBan and reveal an intensification of their activities. The files shed a light on Cumann na mBan as an organisation and its structure, and some do contain contemporary documentation and material directly relating to the Cumann na mBan structure. Many files relate to women who occupied prominent posts in their organisation (District Council or Executive) and who were awarded a grade D (rank of Captain or equivalent) for the calculation of their awards for pension purposes. Other files show the emerging profiles of women who did not join any organisation but who did special work, mostly directly for the IRA. Some of them also received Grade D for pension purposes.

During the War of Independence, Annie Kelly served as a Branch Secretary and a District Council President with Cumann na mBan for north Mayo. In her pension file, numerous documents (such as meetings notices, Cumann na mBan propaganda, members lists, attendance sheets or material relating to the Convention of October 1921) give evidence that Kelly was an important organiser pre- and post-Truce. The file also contains an original printed notice issued by Cumann na mBan Headquarters, Dublin, signed by Eilis Nic Eachnaidh and Sighle Nic Amhlaoibh, dated 24 February 1922, stating their position that the acceptance of "Dominion Home Rule is a denial of the Republic and hence treason to it" ("Kelly," 33), ordering members not to work for anyone supporting Dominion Home Rule during coming elections and stating that any members who supported a Free State candidate could not stay in the organisation.

The files also show the extremely significant work that women were undertaking on the ground, as much for the level of danger they were putting themselves in as for the utterly vital asset they represented for IRA Intelligence. Many were warned against joining an organisation like Cumann na mBan. Not being a member would allow them to move more freely as they were not tied down to a structure and could therefore be less visible and more useful. Intelligence work was carried out through the control over communications and the effective transmission of information.[8] Women, through their civilian occupations, or indeed their own businesses,[9] and through their connections,

---

8   Some of these women doing intelligence work include Nora Lonergan and Annie Barrett. Lonergan worked as a confidential typist for the 4th Battalion, Tipperary 3rd Brigade ("Lonergan"), while Barrett became responsible for furnishing vital information regarding the movement of British troops and police in the counties of Cork, Kerry, Limerick, Tipperary and Waterford. Barrett's collaboration led to the success of numerous important engagements ("Barrett").

9   Some of the women who created effective networks through their civilian occupations are the following ones: Celia Collins, a tobacconist based in 65 Parnell Street, Dublin ("Collins"); Margaret O'Callaghan, a waitress at Red Bank

were the key players in the field to create and maintain effective networks. Deciphering codes in post offices, transmitting information and providing reports to the IRA frequently and effectively without being identified, was a dangerous business. Madge Barnes (née Coughlan) and Lily Mernin carried out special intelligence work for the IRA and were instrumental in connection with major operations ("Barnes" and "Mernin").

These files show that, though some of these women relinquished a Cumann na mBan membership, they nonetheless retained strong connections with the IRA. Catherine Byrne, for instance, never served as a Cumann na mBan member and her primary duty was linked to the keeping and moving of arms. She had been involved in the Easter Rising, storing arms and ammunition for Paddy Daly. Later, she kept numerous arms, ammunition and explosives for members of the Dublin Brigade (Active Service Unit). During the War of Independence she was asked to bring her usual "shopping bag" to the locations of ambushes and attacks (Newcomen Bridge, Drumcondra) and was later linked to the storing and handing out of arms for Bloody Sunday ("Byrne"). Annie Maguire served as District Council President with Cumann na mBan and was heavily involved in organisational work in the south Down area. She was primarily involved in despatch carrying and intelligence work from 1919 onwards. In 1922, she took over the leadership of Cumann na mBan in the 4th Northern Division area, and in May 1922 she was officially appointed Divisional Director of Communications for the 4th Northern Division IRA ("Maguire").

More research is needed on the involvement of women in the Civil War. A number of women were arrested in 1922 and 1923, interned and participated in hunger strikes. Files present evidence of harsh treatment and health (physical and mental) breakdowns ("Brooks"). Further research may include social themes: for instance, some documents show the impact that the political context had on individuals. Nora Gavin of Castlebar, Co. Mayo, was working for the family business ("Gavin Brothers," contractors to British Garrison for foodstuff) and obtained information concerning the Crown Forces through her civilian work. She was very active during the whole period of the War of Independence, but in 1922 she explains that "when the Cosgrovian Government was formed my brothers became prominent supporters of his policy, a state of affairs which made my position both impossible and ridiculous" ("Gavin," 50). She continued for a time to help some "Irregulars" without telling her own brothers. However, they practically "outlawed" her from the family home because of her sympathies and eventually had to travel to England to stay with one of her sisters for a while. Many files show the impact of the events on families and family life (see, for instance, "O'Neill"). They illustrate that the choice that men enjoyed as to

---

Restaurant, on D'Olier Street, Dublin ("O'Callaghan"); Sheila McCarthy, who was the co-owner of a café at 6 Marlborough Street, Dublin ("McCarthy"); and also Nora and Sheila Wallace, who worked as shopkeepers.

whether to join or not was not as straightforward for women. They also show the daily violence that impacted on their lives throughout the period (frequent violent raids, burning of houses and furniture, or loss of business).

3. The Dependants

3.1. Legislation

Fatalities within the collection are recorded across four different sub-series and thousands of files. They are further supported through various accompanying series. The contents of a typical application in respect of a death may be summarised as follows: application form submitted by the dependant, plus reports from investigation officers assessing the degree and certificate of award if applicable. The Army Pensions Act 1923 outlined that a fatality had to fall within certain criteria. The death had to have occurred "in the course of [the deceased] duty while on active service, provided the death of the officer or soldier was not due to any serious negligence or misconduct" ("Army 1923"). Inquiries carried out by the investigating authorities would outline the circumstances surrounding the death and whether there was any negligence on the part of the deceased. An individual may have had up to ten files associated with their application.

Awards differed significantly with the legislation effectively producing a hierarchy of victimhood which left many with a certain degree of resentment. Under the Army Pensions Act, 1923, all veterans/members of the Irish Volunteers killed on active service in the 1916 Rising were awarded allowances at the rank of officer, qualifying their widows to be granted £90 per annum during widowhood. This award was doubled under the Army Pensions Act, 1927.

3.2. 1916 Signatories

In the case of James Connolly, following his execution in Kilmainham on 12 May 1916, eight files relate to claims for dependence lodged by Lily Connolly (widow), Moira Connolly-Beech (daughter: two files), Fiona Connolly-Edwards (daughter), Ina Connolly-Heron (daughter), Nora Connolly-O'Brien (daughter), Aideen Connolly-Ward (daughter) and Roderick James Connolly (son). Lily applies for a Dependence Allowance in December 1923. On 24 February 1924, William O'Brien (Irish Transport and General Workers' Union) writes to General Richard Mulcahy, Minister for Defence, stating that "she [Lily] has found it rather difficult to make ends meet during recent years and at the present moment is rather embarrassed for the want of ready money" ("Connolly," 13) (Figure 1.4). Two days later, General Mulcahy acknowledges O'Brien's letter and writes to the Army Finance Officer, firmly criticising the delay in processing the claim of Connolly's widow.

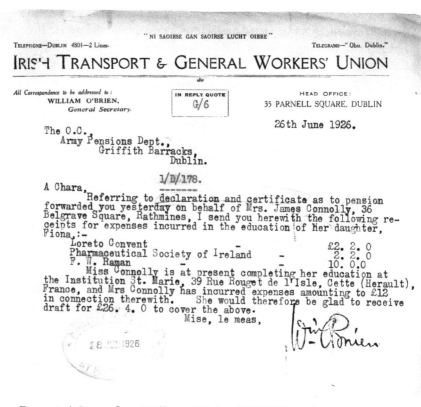

Figure 1.4: Letter from William O'Brien (ITGWU) to Army Pensions Department ("Connolly" 31).

The Army Pensions Act 1937 sets the families of the 1916 Proclamation signatories further apart in awarding additional allowance to their widows (£500 per annum for life), their children (£200 per annum until the age of twenty-five) and their sisters (£100 per annum for life). This is in stark contrast with the widows of soldiers. For example, the widow of a soldier in the National Army received seventeen shillings, six pence per week (approximately £42 per year). Allowances were also made for the children, parents and siblings of the deceased, again with degrees of disparity. Provision was also made for educational expenses. Receipted bills, not exceeding £35 per calendar year, could be submitted for each child between twelve and eighteen years of age.

3.3. War of Independence and Civil War Fatalities

With respect to the War of Independence the project has already released the files of 392 members of the IRA killed. Notable inclusions are IRA Commandant Charles Hurley, who led the IRA attack at the Upton train ambush on 15

1. THE MILITARY SERVICE (1916–1923) PENSIONS COLLECTION

February 1921 and was killed at Crossbarry ambush, Co. Cork on 19 March 1921 ("Hurley"). Another notable War of Independence fatality is Brigade Officer Commanding, Dublin Brigade, IRA Richard McKee. McKee had served in Jacob's Biscuit Factory, Dublin during the 1916 Easter Rising. He was captured by British forces in 1920 and shot dead along with Peadar Clancy and Conor Clune, while allegedly trying to escape from Dublin Castle on 22 November 1920 ("McKee" and "Clancy").

To date, the collection has revealed a total of 1,327 fatalities for the Civil War period. Of this there are altogether 914 National Army (pro-Treaty) fatalities and 413 Irish Republican Army (IRA anti-Treaty) fatalities. This figure will increase as the work on the collection progresses. What the figure does reveal is that the fatalities from this period in our history are greater than recognised to date. Figures have previously put the military fatalities at 1,100 (Ferriter, *Transformation*, 220). Those individuals who later died from wounds received are included in the casualties recognised by the Department of Defence. These deaths are recorded as taking place from 1924 until the late 1920s.

The full specifics of the Civil War are emerging as the collection is processed. What the files processed to date reveal of the Civil War dead is not statistically surprising in many ways. They were mostly young men with an average age of twenty-three, employed as labourers and farmers, the majority of whom were resident in Co. Dublin. What is perhaps more startling is that the National Army fatalities peaked in September 1922, when ninety-four deaths were recorded. Surprisingly, this peak came after initial heavy fighting in Dublin and the landing of National Army troops in Kerry (8 August 1922). The figure of fatalities on both sides continued in a downward trend until March 1923, when the most infamous incidents of the revolutionary period took place. Charles Townshend states, with particular reference to Co Kerry, that "a cycle of 'tit-for-tat' killings ... reached a gruesome climax in March 1923" (*Republic*, 443). This cycle began with an incident at Knocknagoshel in which five members of the National Army were killed during an IRA attack. What followed at Ballyseedy, Countess Bridge and Caherciveen were National Army retaliations which resulted in the deaths of seventeen members of the IRA and illustrate the "tit-for-tat" mentality Townshend refers too. The files of the fatalities and wounded of both the National Army and the IRA across those six March days make for difficult reading.

Retaliations were not only confined to Kerry. County Wexford also had its own particular incident at Adamstown on 24 March 1923, when three members of the National Army were executed and one wounded. This followed the execution of three IRA members in Wexford County Jail on 13 March 1923. In the Brigade Activity Report for the South Wexford Brigade this incident is referred to as "Operation 90" and indicates approval for the action at Brigade level.

The fatalities of the War of Independence and the Civil War contained within the MSPC offer more than merely a collection of names and circumstances of death. They also provide a wealth of information regarding their societal circumstances and the impact that their deaths had on their dependants. Thus, they very often reveal a great deal of the social mores of the time as well as the highly dependent nature of the families left behind.

This desperate need for support is acutely demonstrated in the letters of Margaret Mahony, the widow of National Army Sergeant Major Jeremiah Mahony, who was killed on 5 January 1923 at Millstreet, Co. Cork. Writing from Wales on 30 May 1924, some three weeks after her allowance from the Dependants' Section Army Pay Corps had ceased, she states: "I am actually starving I have had no food with a week I have every bit of clothes I had soled [sic] to get a bit of food for the children ... what in the name of God am I going to do" ("Mahony," 66). Mrs William O'Mahony was informed on 24 July 1924 that her application had been successful and she and her children were awarded the statutory amount (29). Her pleas demonstrate her ever increasing need and desperation. They serve to act as a reminder of the legacy of the revolutionary period.

4.1. Irish Life

The influential position of the Church in Irish life surfaces repeatedly in the MSPC. Religious were deferred to and were indeed used by the investigating authorities while gathering reports of an applicant's dependency on the deceased. One such case is that of National Army Private Martin Moloney, who died in September 1922. His mother, Bridget, made an unsuccessful application for an award as she was deemed not to be dependent on the deceased. The Army Pensions Board initially recommended a gratuity (lump sum) of £50 be awarded. However, following the intervention of Reverend J. Glynn, the award was withdrawn. Reverend J. Glynn wrote: "to give her any money, specially [sic] a lump sum would be altogether undoing her ... She is presently under a 'bail' and if I can, she'll be interned for a time next court. She was not depending on her son Martin" ("Moloney," 25). Indeed, tragedy seemed to follow the Moloney family. Bridget Moloney's husband, also Martin, was drowned in the sinking of the SS Laurentic during the First World War (a converted armed merchant cruiser which sank on 25 January 1917 with the loss of 354 lives) and another son, Michael, was killed as well in the First World War fighting for the British army at eighteen years of age (37).

A further example of the morality of 1920s "official Ireland" is revealed in the file of James Fox. Fox was a veteran of the Easter Rising, having served in Saint Stephen's Green and the Royal College of Surgeons, Dublin. He subsequently served with the National Forces between June and October 1922. However, in October 1927, he was refused a certificate of service, and consequently a pension, by the direction of the Minister for Defence, Desmond Fitzgerald T.D. Fox had been dismissed from the National Army in October 1922 on the instructions of the Director of Intelligence. This dismissal followed his arrest on 15 September 1922, while acting as Adjutant of Maryboro (Portlaoise) Military Prison, "due to suspicions regarding trafficking with prisoners" ("Fox," 64). However, in a letter of 29 August 1927 from the Director of Intelligence to the Department of Defence, the former refers to the use by Fox of "licentious" and "outrageous language" in letters written by Fox to his wife – these letters, which were seized during a search of Fox's home following his arrest, had "a very considerable influence in the decision to dismiss Fox from the Army," as "it was considered that Fox was not a proper person to hold such an important position in the Army" (62). Additionally, the Director of Intelligence considered the possibility that Fox may have been innocent of the formal charge against him. Under the Military Service Pensions Act 1924, Fox would have been eligible for a pension of just over five years' service of £25 per year. Instead his pension application was denied. The collection serves as a reminder "that military records can open a window on many strands of history, including class tensions and the social context" (Ferriter, "Archives").

4.2. Divisive Nature of the Civil War and Executions

Much has been made of the divisive nature of the Civil War and there are numerous accounts of the war separating families. One such is the case of the four Hales brothers – William, Thomas and Robert taking the anti-Treaty side while Seán was in favour of the treaty. One of the lesser known examples is to be found in the application of National Army Captain John Lynch. Lynch survived the Civil War but succumbed to pulmonary tuberculosis on 14 September 1925. His widow's, Nora Lynch, application was unsuccessful as she was deemed not to be dependent on her husband at the date of his death. Patrick Lynch, brother of the deceased, wrote on 18 April 1928: "she is the daughter of a big farmer and was to get a fortune of close on £1,000 but it was withheld [sic] when she married a Free State soldier" ("Lynch," 10). The marriage certificate notes John Lynch and Nora Blackburn were married on 11 July 1923 (87). A letter dated 13 June 1929 from An Gárda Síochána confirms that she married Lynch contrary to the wishes of her parents. Nora Lynch returned to her parents on "condition that she would not again live with her husband. She complied with the condition and was given her fortune of £400" (14). The file serves to illustrate the bitter and recriminatory nature that continued to exist in the immediate aftermath of the Civil War.

The policy of civil war executions marks one of the most contentious decisions by the Provisional Government. More concretely, the execution of Rory O'Connor, Liam Mellows, Richard Barrett and Joseph McKelvey in retaliation for the assassination of Seán Hales (T.D and Brigadier in the

National Army) proved particularly controversial ("O'Connor," "Mellows" and "Barrett"). To date, the majority of executions following the introduction of the Army Emergency Powers Resolution have been catalogued. These files are mostly contained within applications from dependants, with one notable exception: Erskine Childers, since the files relating to Childers are housed with the administrative series of the collection. These three files are concerned with the arrest, detention and administrative matters concerning his personal effects as well as protests on both the national and international stage following his execution ("Childers").

Conclusion

The collection is an excellent and, so far, largely untapped source of Irish history. It offers much more than a history of the revolutionary period 1916–1923. It endures as a history of twentieth century Ireland, and the fact that the collection is online will ensure that access to this history is open to all. President Michael D. Higgins, while speaking at the unveiling of a statue to Roger Casement, spoke of a "new and very positive readiness to engage with these sensitive aspects of our history." The MSPC will ensure that this willingness to engage can be fulfilled. The quantity of documents and the level of information released online is quite unprecedented and is serving those researching within Ireland and those who reside abroad. The collection will participate actively in the (continuous) shaping of the Irish collective memory.

There are no empiric truths to be found in archival material. However, the MSPC, because it contains a considerable amount of individual voices, represents a fantastic source as it refers to founding moments of the Irish State, with testimonies anchored in localities, which, when taken together, create a rich national story. The collection shows this "embeddedness" from the individual, familial, organisational and national movements and will provide alternative visions or redress selective narratives. It is in this that archives and their widespread availability can challenge official narratives in order to generate a sometimes painful but healthy interrogation of the past. And this has everything to do with the present and the future of a nation in search of its (historical) values.

Works Cited
Primary Sources

Irish Military Archives
Military Service (1916–1923) Pensions Collection:
"Affiliation of Cumann na mBán and Oglaigh na hEireann." SPG81.
"Barnes, Madge." MSP34REF60487.

1. THE MILITARY SERVICE (1916–1923) PENSIONS COLLECTION

"Barrett, Annie." MSP34REF5604.
"Barrett, Richard." 2RB734
"Brooks, Christina." MSP34REF8968.
"Byrne, Catherine." MSP34REF59728.
"Casualties IRA Exhumation of Remains of members by British 1916–1921." DOD/2/46751.
"Childers, Erskine." DOD/A15296-E4, DOD/2/15983 (A/7627) and DOD/P/387.
"Clancy, Peadar." 1D412.
"Collins, Celia." MSP34REF60813.
"Connolly, James." 1D178.
"Daly, James Joseph." Con.Ran.23 (DP17).
"Disposal of the Board's Files." SPG/117.
"Easter Week Dublin Brigade General." RO/10; RO/11; RO/12; RO/13; RO/14; RO/15 and RO (10/16).
"Easter Week County Galway." A21_4_A. and A/21/4/B.
"Executed Irregulars." DOD/2012/2.
"Fox, James." 24SP10468.
"Funeral/burial Roger Casement and others." DOD/3/47020.
"Gavin, Nora." MSP34REF55990.
"Hurley, Charles." 1D189.
"Irish Citizen Army G.H.Q." RO/10A.
"Kelly, Annie." MSP34REF34790.
"Kimmage Garrison 1916." RO/607.
"Lonergan, Nora." MSP34REF5604.
"Louth Area Easter Week 1916 Activities 1st Brigade, 4th Northern Division." A51_3.
"Lynch, John." 24SP4518.
"McCarthy, Sheila." MSP34REF48950.
"McKee, Richard." DP23324.
"MacWhinney, Linda." MSP34REF1307.
"Maguire, Annie." MSP34REF56373.
"Mahony, Jeremiah." 3D245.
"Mellows, Liam." DP10200.
"Mernin, Lily." MSP34REF4945.
"Moloney, Martin." 2D451
"Molony, Helena." MSP34REF11739.
"North Wexford Brigade. Easter Week 1916 – Enniscorthy North Wexford Brigade." A66_2.
"O'Callaghan, Margaret." MSP34REF20537.
"O'Connor, Rory." DP6664.
"O'Neill, May/Mary." MSP34REF59221.
"Operation 90." IE/MA/MSPC/ A65.
"Skinnider, Margaret." MSP34REF19910.
"Tyrellspass 1916."RO/503B.
"Wallace, Nora." 34D2124

41

"Wallace, Sheila." 34D1846.

Secondary Sources:

"Active Service." *Irish Military Archives: Military Service Pensions Collection (1916–1923),* www.militaryarchives.ie/en/collections/online-collections/military-service-pensions-collection-1916-1923/about-the-collection/definition-of-active-service. Accessed 20 Feb. 2020.

"Army Pensions Act, 1923." *Irish Statute Book,* www.irishstatutebook.ie/eli/1923/act/26/enacted/en/print.html. Accessed 17 Feb. 2020.

Ferriter, Diarmaid. *The Transformation of Ireland 1900–2000.* Profile Books, 2005

———. "Military Archives Open Window on the Revolutionary Experience." *The Irish Times,* 30 April 2016, www.irishtimes.com/opinion/diarmaid-ferriter-military-archives-open-window-on-the-revolutionary-experience-1.2629664. Accessed 28 Oct. 2016

Higgins, Michael D. "Speech at the Unveiling of a Statue of Roger Casement, Ardfert, Co. Kerry." *President of Ireland Media Library,* 21 April 2016, www.president.ie/en/media-library/speeches/speech-at-the-unveiling-of-a-statue-of-roger-casement. Accessed 26 Oct. 2016.

"Minister Coveney Announces Third Release of Material from the Military Service (1916–1923) Pensions Collection and Extension of the Project." *Merrion Street: Irish Government News Service,* 11 December 2015, merrionstreet.ie/en/News-Room/Releases/Minister_Coveney_announces_Third_Release_of_material_from_the_Military_Service_1916-1923_Pensions_Collection_and_extension_of_the_Project.html. Accessed 19 Feb. 2020.

Townshend, Charles. "The Irish War of Independence: Context and Meaning." *Guide to the Military Service (1916–23) Pensions Collections,* edited by Catriona Crowe, Óglaigh na hÉireann, 2012, pp. 110–124.

———. *The Republic: The Fight for Irish Independence, 1918–1923.* Allen Lane, 2013.

2

Ireland's Revolutionary Years 1916–1923: An Oral History Record

Maurice O'Keeffe

Introduction

The rich heritage of Ireland is an unrivalled treasure. Without the human connection, however, this heritage is diminished. All the components of "heritage" – landscape, geology, wildlife, archaeology, and architecture – are of value because they speak to us of the life experiences and activities of the people who went before us. But that which speaks most strongly and persuasively of these experiences and activities is the human voice. Learning what the voice has to tell us is, of course, of great importance, but hearing the voice proclaim, in all its richness of timbre and accent, is as joyous and stimulating as it is valuable. Our unique personal and familial histories, together with the places in which they were created, provide the deep foundations for the people we ultimately become.

Ireland is changing fast, and the people who remember the country as it was before motor and telecommunications began the process of homogenisation are now dying or have already gone. Very soon, the eye-witnesses to the 1916 Rising, the War of Independence, the Civil War and the first laborious decades of the Irish Free State will no longer be here to narrate their experiences. Indeed, Fr. Joseph Mallin, S.J., who was interviewed at his home in Hong Kong in 2013, died on 1 April 2018 at the age of 104. Fr. Mallin was the last surviving direct descendant of an executed signatory of the 1916 Proclamation.

There are substantial oral history archives in this country, for example, that maintained by RTÉ (the national broadcaster) and that of the Irish Folklore Commission, which, between 1935 and 1970, assembled one of the world's largest folklore collections. The Commission was the initiative of Éamon de Valera's government and the collection is housed in University College Dublin. However, there are information deficits in terms of eyewitness accounts of the

Irish revolutionary period, particularly of the Irish Civil War, 1921–1922, and neither organisation is currently making the collection of oral history recordings a priority. In addition, material is not readily accessible from the Commission. The Bureau of Military History, which is maintained in Cathal Brugha Barracks in Rathmines, Dublin, was established by the Fianna Fáil government in 1947, and is a further source of oral history material. The Bureau was a State sponsored body, the function of which was to collect and examine written and oral history of the 1919–1921 period. The Bureau interviews were tightly structured, posing mostly closed questions and the format was designed to discourage participants from inference or opinion. Also, because the interviewee was seeking to qualify for an IRA pension, the content may sometimes have been not entirely accurate.

In some measure, these deficits have been addressed by Irish Life and Lore, founded by independent oral historians, Maurice and Jane O'Keeffe, in 1990. For thirty years, we have been recording, archiving and publishing Irish oral history. Our archive of over 4,000 hours of recordings covers a broad sweep of social, military, political and cultural history. On 21 January of 2016, I made a presentation of the Irish Life and Lore *The 1916 Rising Oral History Collection* to the National Library of Ireland. On that occasion, our guest speaker President Michael D. Higgins acknowledged the value and breadth of the collection in his address:

> The Irish Life and Lore 1916 Oral History Collection leads us deeply into the story of 1916, into its back streets and covert corners and into the quiet heroism of those whose names, despite not being widely known perhaps to later generations, are as permanently stitched into the fabric of the Irish Republic as the names of James Connolly, Padraig Pearse, Cathal Brugha or Michael Collins ... Two hundred and thirty individuals have taken part in the recording of this audio material. That is a greatly significant addition to the material already available to us on the 1916 Rising and will allow for a deeper and wider understanding of the events and perspectives of that time.

The Historical Context of this Paper: 1916–1923

On Easter Monday 24 April 1916, an armed insurrection took place in Ireland. The Rising was launched by Irish Republicans in a bid to end British rule and establish an independent Irish Republic, at a time when the Great War was consuming Britain's attention in Europe. The rebellion was led by poet, educator and Irish language activist Patrick Pearse, and was joined by James Connolly's Irish Citizen Army and 200 women of Cumann na mBan (McGarry). The rebels seized a number of key locations in Dublin and proclaimed an Irish Republic from the General Post Office on Sackville Street. Although initially taken by surprise, the British authorities quickly brought in reinforcements from Britain as well as artillery and a gunboat. There was fierce street fighting on the routes into the city centre from Kingstown harbour, where military reinforcements from Britain were put ashore, and the rebels offered stiff resistance, slowing the British advance and inflicting heavy casualties. However, over the coming days, the rebel positions were surrounded and isolated; having much greater numbers and heavier weapons, the British Army suppressed the Rising. On Saturday 29 April, Pearse gave the order to surrender. During May, after courts martial, fifteen rebels were executed by firing squad at Kilmainham Gaol, including all seven signatories of the Proclamation.

The following years were turbulent in Ireland. Although support for the insurgents had been limited, there was now a profound shift in public opinion as a result of the brutal British response: the execution of fifteen rebels by firing squad, the imprisonment or internment of hundreds more, and the imposition of martial law in Ireland. In addition, the unprecedented threat of Irishmen being conscripted into the British Army in 1918 for service on the Western Front accelerated this change. The change of heart among the population favoured the Republican Movement: in the December 1918 elections, Sinn Féin, the party of the rebels, won three quarters of all seats in Ireland. Twenty-seven of these elected Members of Parliament assembled in Dublin on 21 January 1919 to form a thirty-two-county Irish Republic parliament, and the first Dáil (parliament) declared sovereignty over the entire island. Unwilling to negotiate any understanding with Britain short of complete independence, the army of the newly declared Irish Republic waged a guerilla war, the Irish War of Independence, from 1919 to 1921. In December 1920, the "Better Government for Ireland Act" implemented Home Rule, while separating the island into what was termed Northern Ireland and Southern Ireland. In July 1921, the Irish and British governments agreed to a truce, and in December of that year, representatives of both governments signed the Anglo-Irish Treaty, creating the Irish Free State. Under the terms of the Treaty, the six northern-east counties, from then onwards to be known as Northern Ireland, could opt out of the Free State and stay within the United Kingdom, which the majority protestant population chose to do.

The great part of those who opposed the Treaty in the Dáil withdrew from the assembly and, having formed an opposition "republican government" under Éamon de Valera, began a political campaign denouncing the Treaty from March 1922 onwards. At the same time the powerful IRA Army Executive divided, and its anti-Treaty members refused to be bound by the Dáil vote which had ratified it. This led to the outbreak of Civil War in June 1922. Following the General Election on 16 June 1922, held just before the outbreak of the Civil War, the Irish Provisional Government took power, and went on to wage guerrilla warfare against the Anti-Treaty side. Families and siblings divided on either side in a most bitter and brutal campaign that continued for another year. The tragic legacy of this endures to the present day.

The oral testimony explored in this paper will allow the reader to capture some sense of the lived experience of ordinary individuals in extraordinary times, who observed and participated in seismic events in Ireland a century ago. In the pages that follow, I will focus on the 1916 Rising and include excerpts of interviews from *The 1916 Rising Oral History Collection*, released in 2015, comprising 230 recordings carried out by Irish Life and Lore with people central to events during that momentous time in Ireland's history. Jane O'Keeffe is editor of the volume which accompanies the audio material for the 1916 Rising Oral History Collection. Work on this project quickly became a race against time and, sadly, several of the people recorded for the project since it began in 2012 have now passed away.

This task of recording an oral history of 1916 was an independent enterprise, and unlike the Bureau of Military History some sixty years earlier, the interviewer was, in the words of Helene O'Keefe, "unhindered by any particular remit other than a personal commitment to collect as many interesting stories connected to the Rising as possible, from as many different perspectives as possible before they vanish from living memory" (7). In the second part of this chapter, the interview excerpts are taken from an Irish Life and Lore project on the Civil War in Kerry 1922–1923. Carried out over fifteen years ago, the collected testimony is from those involved on both sides of the divide. There also followed, in 2006, a book written by Jane O'Keeffe, *Recollections of 1916 and its Aftermath: Echoes from History*, for which the author used the documentary evidence collected during the recording process.

Research Methodology

Recorded and preserved oral testimony derived from interviews is what we define as oral history. In this regard, qualitative research methods are favoured, because the primary concern of the researcher is the lived experience of the participant, and the crucial importance of context is more effectively revealed in this way. The interview is undertaken by the researcher and participant, with both parties having the conscious aim of creating an authentic and permanent record of a topic or an event. This assists us in our understanding of the complexities of the past and presents a diversity of viewpoints, rather than the accepted "truth" regarding that event. Over recent years, the recording of oral testimony has emerged as a powerful instrument in attaining details of personal memory, which are often in imminent danger of being lost. The narrative approach is a technique yielding rich and complex data, leaving the participants in control of the interview.

The methodology employed in the compilation of oral history recordings must comply with existing guidelines in qualitative research. In utilising oral history, it is necessary to adopt a critical approach to the content of oral testimony and its interpretations. In *To Speak of Easter Week* (2015), Helene O'Keeffe asserts that an oral history interview is the product of interaction between interviewer and interviewee and, by its nature, such a process determines what is going to be recalled and how it is recalled. It is a subjective process, a record of perception rather than a recreation of an historical event. However, O'Keeffe goes on to state that this is precisely its value rather than its limitation; it is an expression of the personality of the interviewees and of the influences that shaped their point of view. Memory, therefore, is both the source and the subject of study.

If we accept memory as a guide to assist us in shedding light on events in the past, we must ask the same questions about its origins as we would of a more traditional source; the same steps of conventional scientific inquiry apply to those who compile oral history collections. Although oral history is a form of naturalistic inquiry, we cannot reject the concept of rigour, and must provide evidence of credibility and validity as would be required in any research study. Also, as Helene O'Keeffe observes, we should not confuse memory with history and, in this regard, she quotes Richard White, who asserts that:

> History is the enemy of memory. The two stalk each other across the fields of the past, claiming the same terrain. History forges weapons from what memory has forgotten or suppressed … But there are regions of the past that only memory knows. If historians wish to go into this dense and tangled terrain, they must accept memory as a guide. (6)

A further consideration is that of reflexivity, a vital quality for the researcher. Linda Finlay describes this quality as "thoughtful, conscious self-awareness" (532), with contextualisation being its key dimension. Reflexivity allows us to step outside our own individual frame of reference, in order to see how others might perceive reality. In the context of the oral history interview, reflexivity allows the interviewer to be present and attentive while not derailing the interviewee's narrative with argument or confrontation.

1. Ethical Considerations

The first step in the process towards the final recording is for the researcher to telephone or meet a potential interviewee, explain the reason for meeting and the process and purpose of recording oral history. If the individual agrees to be interviewed and allows the interview to be recorded, the researcher arranges a suitable time, informing the interviewee that, if they wish, they may invite a person of their choice to be present. The matter to be discussed at interview is reviewed with the interviewee in advance. The interviewee then signs informed consent and the interview is recorded. The interviewer's reflexivity is important during this process.

The authenticity and validity of the research is evidenced through the commitment to provide a written synopsis of the interview to the interviewee for approval. Interviewees may also request a copy of the recorded interview. This procedure gives participants the opportunity to say whether their intended meaning is represented faithfully in the recording. Until approval is secured, no further work on the interview is undertaken.

The written agreement between participant and interviewer is an important component in the archiving of oral history. The document should clearly state that copyright and related rights are assigned to the interviewer, in order to allow the material to be available to the interviewer's successors and to those to whom the interviewer may wish to assign the benefit.

The researcher is responsible for safeguarding the data protection rights of the participant, ensuring that the material is safely stored and is used only for the purposes on which they are agreed.

2. Selection Procedures

In the compilation of oral history, the interviewer or his sponsors select potential candidates for interview who are deemed to be knowledgeable on the subject under consideration, articulate, reflective and willing to discuss the matter. Those selected are identified through local research on the subject matter and consequent identification of key individuals for interview. Initial contact is then made with these individuals, who may be known to either the researcher or his sponsors. Discussion is undertaken with these individuals regarding further sources known to them, in respect of this subject.

3. Data Collection

Recording techniques involve initial research into the subject to be discussed. Once an individual agrees to be interviewed, the interviewer arranges a suitable date, time and place for the compilation of the interview. The interviewer prepares for the interview by investigating the subject matter and formulating a number of relevant interview questions. The narrative technique does not impose strict discourse guidelines on participants but encourages them to be the ones who decide what to recount. It is always preferable to record participants in their own homes, where the surroundings are familiar and where they may have access to old records or memorabilia. At the initial stage, it is necessary to spend time in relaxed conversation, perhaps over a cup of tea, while participant and interviewer get to know each other sufficiently to become comfortable in one another's company. Good eye contact with the interviewee and a focus on the subject or subjects under discussion should be maintained. When an interviewee begins to stray from the subject or subjects being examined, a gentle prompt may be required to steer the discussion back to its original track. Ample time for answers to questions posed should be allowed at all times. An enquiring approach, rather than an interrogatory one, is always to be recommended.

Access to photographs, illustrations and documentation as an *aide-memoire* can be most useful on occasion. Acceptance of the reaction of the interviewee to a particular line of questioning, in terms of a positive or negative emotional response, is paramount. All material offered should be recorded and the interviewer should refrain from correcting any part of an answer given to a posed question. Additionally, testimony should be recorded in a chronological manner where possible. Repetition of a question posed earlier in a recorded interview, to which an opaque answer was given, may sometimes result in a more detailed and valuable response at a later stage in the process. Most interviews take one to two hours to complete. Before leaving, it is important to request copies of family memorabilia pertinent to the interview, such as photographs, letters or family papers. Participants also have their photograph taken for the cataloguing process.

4. Data Analysis

The interviewer listens carefully to the recording in its entirety as soon as possible after the event, noting responses to key questions and also any matters that may be sensitive. It is important that the recording is not changed in any way that might alter its meaning – editing is limited to the removal of extraneous noise and any comments that are not pertinent to the topic under discussion.

Once the participant has approved the written account of their interview, the material is indexed with all other relevant information, including the interviewee's photograph, date of birth, and date and location of recording. This material is then compiled into the catalogue page, which, with other relevant work, goes to form an oral history collection.

5. Findings

The edited recording of the interview is catalogued and deposited with educational institutions and other interested bodies and also onto the Irish Life and Lore designated website page.[1] Making the recorded interviews available to researchers and the communities to which they are relevant is a means of returning the information to its source and expands the boundaries of our definition of community.

This study now moves to its central focus – to explore excerpts from recorded interviews with people who were involved in the revolutionary years in Ireland, from 1916 to 1923, and their families.

---

1 All material is available at www.irishlifeandlore.com

Interviews: 1916 Rising

The paper now moves to explore the events of 1916 in Ireland as described and narrated through the perceptions and memories of participants and their descendants, the latter carrying the historical legacy into the present day. These interviews are taken from *The 1916 Rising Oral History Collection*, which comprises 230 interviews, offering diverse and detailed accounts of the events surrounding Easter Week 1916 and its aftermath. Many of those interviewed recount stories which were told to them by survivors of the insurrection. Also included are some original recordings made with those directly involved, where some of them reflect on the idea of sacrifice and how in Ireland this is a notion inextricably linked to myth, culture and history; and on how the sacrificial action has been a powerful carrier of Ireland's separatist legacy.

Here, I will examine excerpts taken from the recordings compiled with five individuals for the 1916 Oral History Collection, in the following order:

1. **Fr. Joseph Mallin**, S.J., son of Michael Mallin. Fr. Joseph, who passed away recently, was the last surviving son of a 1916 executed leader. He was interviewed in Hong Kong in December 2012.
2. **Alf MacLochlainn**, grandson of Emily Pearse, half-sister of the Pearse brothers Patrick and Willie. Both men were executed after the Rising. He was recorded in March 2013.
3. **Lucille Redmond**, daughter of Barbara Redmond and granddaughter of Thomas McDonagh, an executed leader. She was recorded in February 2013.
4. **Sean Holahan**, son of Paddy Holahan who, during the week of the Rising, took command of men fighting at North Brunswick Street and the Four Courts. Sean Holahan was recorded in August 2015.
5. **Alex Findlater**, grandson of Captain Henry de Courcy-Wheeler, Staff Officer to General W.H.M. Lowe, Officer Commanding the British Forces in Dublin at Easter 1916. He was recorded in October 2015.

1. Fr. Joseph Mallin

The difficulties and hardships endured by the widows of those who were executed in the aftermath of the Rising are clearly recalled by Fr. Jospeh Mallin, who says:

> In the beginning, we lived on the White Cross, [aid organisation] that kept us going, but my mother was a very good manager, and we learned to live poorly, with not much, but it was hard on her I know. When my mother had to go to hospital she broke down. Dr. Kathleen Lynn [member of Cumann na mBan and senior officer in the Irish Citizen Army] was looking after us. I remember the day she was walking up to the house; I

didn't know what was going on at the time; that would be 1924, and she wrote this letter to my mother. She brought myself and my sister Maura down to St. Enda's. I stayed there then to do the rest of my studies. (Part 1, 00:14:00)

As Mallin's words reveal, his widowed mother, Agnes, was made to suffer physically, financially and emotionally in the years following her husband's execution

2. Alf MacLochlainn

Very little provision was made for the wellbeing of the bereaved women whose husbands had faced a firing squad in the Stonebreaker's Yard of Kilmainham Gaol in the weeks after Easter 1916. Alf MacLochlainn, the grandnephew of Patrick and Willie Pearse, recalls his grandmother's, Emily Pearse, personality and determination. He articulates the necessity to access funds for those bereaved:

> There was a White Cross fund for those involved in 1916 and that would have helped her a small bit. In fact, there is a famous portrait of Patrick and Willie Pearse sitting on the side of a gateway. This is in all of the books. My father, [Alfred MacLochlainn], who was a keen photographer, apparently took that photograph, and my mother [Marcella Dowling, whose three brothers were involved in the revolutionary period from 1916–1923] gave the copyright to the White Cross and it was sold widely as a keepsake. (00:02:00)

In 1966, when Ireland commemorated the fiftieth anniversary of the Easter Rising, Alf MacLochlainn was employed in the National Library of Ireland as Assistant Keeper of Manuscripts. The owners of No. 16 Moore Street (now a National Monument), the building which the Volunteers occupied after evacuating the GPO, paid him a visit. No. 16 Moore Street was the location of the last meeting of the rebel leaders to confer, after which Pearse ordered the unconditional surrender on Saturday 29 April 1916. MacLochlainn describes this event as follows:

> In 1966, there came to the National Library people who had re-entered a house in Moore Street, and when they reoccupied their house they found a rectangle of cardboard which was taken out of the back of a picture frame and it was a document in the hand of Patrick Pearse, which I knew, being a Manuscript Librarian; and it was the draft of the surrender in 1916, and this was different from the usually received version of the surrender document – decided by a majority to surrender. So that means there was a vote. (00:19:00)

The document indicates that there was reluctance on the part of some of the leaders to surrender; the words of Eamonn Ceannt, one of the executed leaders of the Rising, resonate here. In the recording, MacLochlainn states the words of Eamonn Ceannt on the eve of his execution: "I see nothing gained, but grave disaster caused by the surrender which has marked the end of the Irish Insurrection of 1916 – so far, at least, as Dublin is concerned" (cit. in Henry, 179).

The handwritten draft of the surrender is now in the archives of the National Library. To be so closely related to the Commander-in-Chief of the Irish Volunteers and to have the privilege of witnessing first-hand a draft of the surrender in his granduncle's own hand was indeed a moving reminder for Alf MacLochlainn of the last moments of the failed insurrection.

3. Lucille Redmond

In the aftermath of the Rising, the National Aid Association made an effort to assist widows and orphans. Lucille Redmond's grandmother, Muriel, was a sister of Grace Gifford, who had married Joseph Plunkett in Kilmainham Gaol the night before his execution. Muriel and her two children, Barbara and Donagh, went on holiday with Grace Plunkett (née Gifford) to the seaside resort of Skerries. The holiday was organised by the Aid Association and it ended in tragedy, the two children without either father or mother. As Lucille Redmond explains,

> In July 1917, my mother and grandmother [Muriel McDonagh] were collecting pretty seashells just before she [Muriel] went swimming and drowned. Died of a heart attack, yes. She was a well-known swimmer, a superb swimmer, but the weather had turned terribly cold and the sea was icy. She wasn't in the best of health. The sisters had the children [Barbara and Donagh], mainly Katie, her eldest sister; then the children were kidnapped by the McDonagh side of the family, and after that all was chaos. (00:21:00)

In order to contextualise the truly desperate conditions endured by revolutionaries and their leaders as Easter Week progressed, up to the point when they received the handwritten surrender note from Commandant Patrick Pearse, Commander-in-Chief, the next extract from the 1916 Rising Oral History Collection has been selected.

4. Sean Holahan

Sean Holahan is the son of Paddy Holahan, who in Easter Week fought with the Four Courts Garrison under the command of Edward Daly. He took command when Captain Laffan was shot and surrendered with great reluctance following receipt of a note from Patrick Pearse. Paddy Holahan and his men were arrested and detained for some time at Frongach prison camp in North Wales. According to Sean Holahan:

> My father negotiated the surrender. He insisted on getting the signed note from Pearse, which Fr. Augustine or Fr. Aloysius (I'm not sure) brought to him, and it was then that he surrendered. He said it was the hardest task he had to do, to actually surrender, and then he marched them off to Richmond Barracks. (00:15:00)

5. Alex Findlater

Alex Findlater is the grandson of Captain Henry De Courcy-Wheeler, Staff Officer to General W.H.M. Lowe, Officer Commanding the British Forces in Dublin at the time of the Rising. In April 1916, he was ordered to Dublin from his base at the Curragh to report to Brigadier General Lowe. He was to serve as Staff Captain to General Lowe during Easter Week. Captain De Courcy-Wheeler took the surrender of James Connolly, Thomas McDonagh, Michael Mallin and Countess Markieviecz, and was present when Patrick Pearse, accompanied by Nurse Elizabeth O'Farrell, surrendered to General Lowe at 2.30pm on 29 April 1916.In the following extract, Alex Findlater contextualises the surrender of Patrick Holahan and his men at the Four Courts:

> There was a small detachment around the Four Courts, and his actual name was Patrick Houlihan [Holahan], and he was a young man, and he was cut off in North Brunswick Street. He refused to surrender, and General Lowe was concerned about this. He said to Pearse: would you write another surrender note? There was this particular one that was firing away, and so Pearse wrote another note out in hand, which was on the 30th, and then the two monks went to young Patrick Houlihan [Holahan], and said: Look, Pearse says surrender. The monks were permitted to pass through the embattlement lines to see him, and when this document was presented, the young desperate rebel reluctantly laid down his hands. (00:56:00)

Immediately after the Rising, Captain De Courcy-Wheeler wrote up his impressions in an army issue field notebook and his grandson surmises that it was his idea to keep the surrender notes in his possession after the events of 1916, partly for the purposes of clarity and for production at the courts martial. The notes were subsequently kept within the family and were not published. In 2015, having recorded Alex Findlater, Irish Life and Lore encouraged him to publish the findings on his grandfather's original notes. *1916 Surrenders: Captain H.E. De Courcy-Wheeler's Eyewitness Account*, with research by Alex Findlater and foreword by Jane O'Keeffe of Irish Life and Lore, was published in February 2016.

These interview excerpts detail individual perspectives on the same historic days in our troubled past. The contrasting voices offer a useful demonstration of how oral history can be an important instrument in painting a broader and more nuanced picture of events as they occurred. As Donald A. Ritchie writes in *Doing Oral History* (2003):

> Public history is an organised effort to bring accurate, meaningful history to a public audience, and oral history is a natural tool for reaching that goal. The oral history and public history movements share a natural affinity, both having attracted practitioners and audiences different from those for more traditional history writing. (41)

The pages that follow move on to discuss events which occurred after the War of Independence, when the Civil War began.

Interviews: The Irish Civil War

In order to demonstrate the unique capacity of oral testimony to illustrate divergent points of view, while still remaining true to fact, the paper will now address an incident in Kerry which occurred during Ireland's Civil War in 1922. In the following excerpts, we will hear a number of accounts of this incident from witnesses; these witnesses provide multiple perspectives on the same event. While the Civil War was heart-breaking for those who were actively involved, it is also interesting to note the neutral eyewitness account. As Ritchie writes in his *Doing Oral History*, "researchers will want to hear the first-person observations of events great and small, and to learn what sense people made in their own lives of these events"(45).

The oral history researcher's job, as will be seen in the following examples, is to pull together the strands of evidence from a number of sources, such as documents, objects, and a crossover of testimony from different interviewees who describe the same event. The interview excerpts explored here are taken from an oral history project on the Civil War in Kerry carried out by Irish Life and Lore over fifteen years ago. Testimony was recorded from those involved on both sides of the conflict.

Simon Brouder, a staff journalist with *The Kerryman* newspaper, puts into context the episode of the Civil War which we are about to examine, writing in *Rebel Kerry* in 2017,

> On 2 August, the National Army's Dublin Guard landed at Fenit [in Co. Kerry].They were commanded by Brigadier Paddy O'Daly, the former leader of Collins's elite Assassination Unit, "the Squad," who had led the National Army forces that retook Dublin. Anti-Treaty forces, aware of the danger of a potential invasion from the seas, had intended to blow up the

pier at Fenit should an attack be launched, but the charges were rendered inoperable by persons unknown – though most likely to have been a disillusioned anti-Treaty fighter – in an attempt to minimise damage to the port. With the charges decommissioned, *The Lady Wicklow* had no difficulty mooring at Fenit and 450 Free State troops were rapidly landed and quickly made their way into Tralee. The main engagement of the day occurred at Boherbee, where a large group of anti-Treaty supporters fought the Free State troops in a fierce one-hour long firefight. This ferocious battle provided cover for most of Tralee's anti-Treaty forces to retreat from the town and into the countryside, from where they intended to launch a sustained guerrilla campaign. The Free State troops had landed in Fenit at 10.30 am and, by 6pm, Tralee was in Free State hands. Further landings took place at Tarbert and Kenmare. (175)

In the summer of 2002, in the company of Lt. Col. Sean Clancy (b.1901), I enquired him about his memory of that historic day in 1922, when the Dublin Guard arrived by boat to Tralee Bay:

> I remember the Dublin Guards went down by boat to take Kerry. Sailing into Fenit pier, they misjudged the tide and were stuck in the harbour for several hours, and some of them tried to wade across to dry land. They were fired on anyway from the mainland and at least six of them were killed. The bodies were brought back to Dublin and I saw their remains laid out in the gymnasium in Portobello Barracks. So, it wasn't all one-sided. (Part 3, 00:15:00)

Col. Sean Clancy was dealing with records and troop payments during the Civil War and was stationed at Portobello Barracks when the bodies were brought back to Dublin. He had a clear recall of events during the Civil War in Kerry. In 1924, he was sent to the county to assist with demobilisation and was to experience several narrow escapes on the roads where snipers were very active. Having experienced the fighting in Kerry and having knowledge of the atrocities carried out by Free State soldiers, he was quick to point out that "it wasn't all one-sided." Not recorded in *The Kerryman* article at that time was the shooting by anti-Treaty individuals of the soldiers who were wading to shore.

Next to be explored is an account from a member of the Dublin Guard who was landed at Fenit on that day. In October 2015, I interviewed Fred O'Connor, the son of John Joe O'Connor (b.1902) whose involvement in Kerry's fighting story began when he was put ashore at Fenit as a member of the Dublin Guard in August 1922. Fred O'Connor describes events at that time:

> It was after Collins was killed that they went down to Fenit on *The Lady Wicklow*. They came ashore and took Fenit and then they started moving but they were fired on every so often. He said that when the others were retreating into a village or a town, they would burn the Big Houses that

they were occupying. The army couldn't understand that; they did more damage than the army did going in after them. (00:30:00)

John Joe O'Connor was stationed in Kerry during the worst of the atrocities carried out by both sides. His eyewitness account of events as they unfolded was clearly articulated to his son and might have been altogether forgotten had the stories not been passed on. From Fred O'Connor's recall of his father's account of the landing, it is evident that the anti-Treaty side were causing major destruction to buildings as they retreated from Fenit to Tralee.

Following this, the next excerpt deals with the awareness of a young eyewitness of rumours concerning the landing at Fenit and his memory of the battle that followed. Archdeacon Rowland Blennerhassett (b. 1909) was recorded in 2002. In 1922, he was living on the outskirts of Tralee when Free State soldiers passed his house on their way into the town:

> I particularly remember the landing at Fenit; there were all sorts of rumours going around, rumours that there was a landing and that there was an invasion. Nobody knew anything; there was no communication. However, this morning I was going to the dentist for a dental appointment, and as I passed the police barracks, which at that time was held by the Republican forces, I saw a very decrepit looking armed car pulled into the gateway, and they were filling it with petrol, and there were all sorts of activities which weren't in the normal course of events, and I got home as fast as I could. I remember lying on the floor under the table, and shots fired in all directions. (00:01:00)

Archdeacon Blennerhassett further recalls:

> The pier in Fenit was mined, but the charges were withdrawn before the landing, so of course the mine never went off, and they had more or less a free rein, because there were only a few Republicans in the Coastguard House up there. They retreated. The Free State soldiers came along anyway. They had an 18 pounder, and on the way, they took somebody's mare, and she pulled it from Fenit to Tralee, approximately 7 miles. There was fairly stiff opposition when they reached the town; you could hear the firing going on. (00:03:00)

Between the lines of the anecdote, a more nuanced picture emerges, which helps the reader to draw conclusions relating to events as they unfolded on that historic day in Kerry. Blennerhassett recalls that there was much confusion in the town as to whether it was a German invasion or that Free State forces had landed at nearby Fenit. Also, the lack of communication caught the anti-Treaty side off-guard, as did the removal of the mine from Fenit pier before *The Lady Wicklow* docked.

Chief of General Staff Richard Mulcahy gave an address in Kerry in 1923,

2. IRELAND'S REVOLUTIONARY YEARS 1916–1923

in which he recalled the landings in Fenit from the perspective of the Free State command. This address was published in Volume I No.15 of *An tÓglach* on 6 October 1923, but is now out of circulation and the only copy is in private hands. Mulcahy eulogises the bravery and loyalty of the Dublin Guard, who he says fought a bitter battle all the way to Tralee, leaving comrades dead by the roadside.

Next, we meet a revolutionary figure who takes a diametrically opposing view to that expressed above. In 2002, I recorded Dan Keating (b. 1902). After the signing of the Treaty and the outbreak of Civil War in 1922, Keating supported the anti-Treaty side, joining the IRA Boherbee 13 Company in Tralee:

> After the fight for freedom, the Civil War was on. It was very bitter, you know; it must be said the Free Staters were like the Black and Tans, you had quite a lot of atrocities. It was 70% Republican in Kerry at the time of the landing at Fenit and the taking of Tralee by the Staters. We retreated to Listowel, taking it easily; then we went into west Limerick, cleaned up Newcastle west, all the areas the Free State soldiers were. The Staters then retreated to Limerick city; Limerick was there for the taking. (00:05:00)

By listening to the hours of recordings compiled with Dan Keating during the period 2002–2005, it is possible to understand his unrepentant stance as a member of the IRA; until the 1950s he held a high-ranking position in the organisation. It is revealing of Keating's mind-set that much more detail was provided on the years of the fight for freedom from British rule than of the Civil War period, about which he spoke only in relation to republican successes. His memory of the successes of the anti-Treaty forces against the Old Dublin Guard, as he put it (the Free State forces) was clear and detailed. Even though he had fought side by side with these men in the years following the 1916 Rising, during the War of Independence he referred to them as being worse than the Black and Tans, who were British soldiers sent to Ireland in 1920 to quell the struggle for independence. Notorious for brutality, the Black and Tans caused havoc and mayhem throughout the country during an extended period.

The next excerpt contrasts with Keating's and presents the view of a man who supported the Treaty. Tom Slattery was recorded in 2001 and again in 2015. His father, Thomas, was a native of Tralee, and his family home was on Rock Street, where much of the fighting took place. Thomas Slattery joined the Free State army after the signing of the Treaty, and in July and August 1922 was on board the ship which landed at Tarbert in north Kerry, a stronghold of the anti-Treaty side. This was one of several landings by the army along the south and west coast which marked the end of the conventional phase of the Civil War. Tom Slattery relates:

> When they advanced up Tralee town and the army took the town, there

was a machine gun put in our house in Rock Street by the Free State troops, to have control of Pembroke Street and Rock Street. There was also a Free State ship that landed in Tarbert to secure the north Kerry section of the county, and my father was on that ship. There was a major gun battle at the corner of Rock Street and Pembroke Street in Tralee. The circumstances that gave rise to this were that the Free State army had landed at Fenit and fought their way into Tralee, and there was also a machine gun mounted on top of the Shamrock Mills and to the best of my knowledge there was six Free State soldiers shot in Rock Street. The soldiers were laid out beside O'Keeffe's Mills before their removal to be buried in Dublin. (00:30:00)

Tom Slattery's excerpt, from a long interview detailing the landing at Fenit and the battle that ensued in Tralee, was related from his memory of stories told to him by his father Thomas, who had been stationed there for the duration of the Troubles – from August 1922 to October 1923. Interestingly, the full weight of the legacy of the Civil War was more evident in the interviews with the second generation than with the eyewitnesses to the events. The memories of Tom Slattery and Fred O'Connor recall the post-traumatic stress endured by their fathers.

Conclusion

As outlined above, oral historians adopt a different approach to that of the traditional historian. They explore the lives and experiences of historical figures in a more rounded, nuanced and human way. Oral history offers a greater understanding of the motivations, actions, experiences and reflections of those involved in historical events. As social historian Jane O'Hea O'Keeffe has noted in *Recollections of 1916 and its Aftermath*, oral tradition can sometimes convey vital information which may be incidental to the story being told but delivers valuable insight and wider context to an event from the past which helps its clearer emergence from the mists of time. Although a not entirely reliable historical source, the spoken word transmits an indelible echo of another time and illustrates the social and historical circumstances in which events are rooted.

Over many years of recording oral history for Irish Life and Lore in Ireland, particularly that of the early years of the 20th century, involving historical events such as the Lockout of 1913, the 1916 Rising, the War of Independence and the Civil War, the contested legacy of these crucial events became ever clearer. In this context it is right and proper to acknowledge the complex tapestry of nuanced human experience in times of conflict, and to engage sensitively with inherited memory.

The study of inherited memory conducted for the Irish Life and Lore oral history collections, and specifically the 1916 Rising Oral History Collection, reinforces the point made by Helene O'Keeffe in *To Speak of Easter Week*, regarding the rich understanding of the complex legacy of history which we may gain when we study oral recordings, combining these with more traditional historical sources.

Works Cited

Primary Sources

Irish Life and Lore: Oral History Archive
Blennerhassett, Rowland. 2002.
Clancy, Lt. Col. S. 2012.
Keating, Dan. 2002.
MacSwiney Brugha, Máire. 2009.
O'Connor, Fred. 2015.
Slattery, Tom. 2001; 2015

The 1916 Rising Oral History Collection, 2015
Findlater, Alex.
Holahan, Sean.
Mallin, Joseph Fr.
McLochlainn, Alf.
Redmond, Lucille.

Secondary Sources

Brouder, Simon, editor. *Rebel Kerry: From the Pages of* The Kerryman. Mercier Press, 2017.
Findlater, Alex. *1916 Surrenders: Captain H.E. de Courcy-Wheeler's Eyewitness Account.* A. & A. Farmar, 2016.
Finlay, Linda. "Outing the Researcher: the Provenance, Process and Practice of Reflexivity." *Qualitative Health Research*, vol. 12, no. 4, 2002, pp. 531–45.
McGarry, Fearghal. *The Rising. Ireland: Easter 1916.* Oxford University Press, 2010.
Mulcahy, Richard. "The Spirit of Loyalty and Comradeship." *An tÓglach*, vol. 1, no. 15, 1923.
Henry, William, *Éamonn Ceannt: Supreme Sacrifice.* Mercier Press, 2012
Higgins, Michael D. "Speech at the Presentation of the 1916 Rising Oral History Collection to the National Library." *President of Ireland,* 21 January 2016, president.ie/en/diary/details/president-gives-an-address-at-the-presentation-of-the-1916-rising-oral-hist/speeches. Accessed 20 Feb. 2020.
O'Hea O'Keeffe, Jane. *Recollections of 1916 and its Aftermath: Echoes from History.* Irish Life and Lore, 2005.
O'Keeffe, Helene. *To Speak of Easter Week: Family Memories of the Irish Revolution.* Mercier Press, 2015.
O'Keeffe, Maurice and Jane O'Keeffe. *The 1916 Rising, Oral History Collection.* Irish Life and Lore, 2015.

———. *The Old Kerry Journal. Vol 4.* Irish Life and Lore, 2017.
Quinn Patton, M. Q. *Qualitative Research and Evaluation Methods.* 3rd ed., Sage Publications Ltd., 2002.
Ritchie, Donald A. *Doing Oral History.* 2nd ed., Oxford University Press, 2003.

3

Violence against Women in Munster and Connacht in the Irish War of Independence, 1919–1921

Thomas Earls FitzGerald

Introduction

The role of women in the Irish revolution is becoming an increasingly discussed and researched topic. However, a tendency does exist to focus primarily on the role of Cumann na mBan, the female auxiliary branch in the Republican movement, and on individual Republican women. These studies focus on the role of Republican women in the bohemian and radical circles that existed before the 1916 Rising, leaving post-1916 Republican women's groups under researched.[1] The activities, motivations and role of Cumann na mBan between 1919 and 1923 are clearly worthy of further academic analysis, though Cumann na mBan volunteers were not the only women who experienced the Irish revolution. During the revolutionary period, civilian women also became victims of the combatants. This chapter explores the nature of the intimidation and violence that specifically targeted women in these years. Initially, it deals with how the issue of violence against women has been considered in the historiography, then examines the various examples and forms of violence against women in the south and west of Ireland, followed by an exploration of the motivations behind the attacks together with how these attacks compared to violence against women in continental Europe.

The issue of violence against women in the revolutionary period has received a certain degree of attention in the historiography. In 2000, Louise Ryan explored violence against women in her essay "'Drunken Tans': Representations

---

1   See for instance Senia Paseta's *Irish Nationalist Women, 1900–1918* (2013), R.F. Foster's *Vivid Faces: The Revolutionary Generation in Ireland, 1890–1923* (2014) and Sinead McCoole's *Easter Widows: Seven Women who Lived in the Shadow of the 1916 Rising* (2014).

of Sex and Violence in the Anglo-Irish War," where she examined a number of cases of violence against women conducted by the Crown forces and the IRA between 1919 and 1921, but the piece is mainly concerned with perceptions of masculinity, femininity and violence. Gemma Clark, recently, in *Everyday Violence in the Irish Civil War* (2014), has shown the prevalence of Republican/ agrarian incidents of violence against women and some cases of sexual violence in the Civil War. However, Clark does not explore the precedents set for these forms of intimidation and violence in 1919–1921 by both the Crown forces and the IRA. Clark writes:

> Social norms and expectations certainly are challenged during conflict. Civil War enables the invasion by males of the usually female denominated domestic arena. House burning, for example, a viciously destructive yet common tactic, employed throughout 1919–1923, affected directly these groups who would have otherwise avoided serious violence. (190)

Arson, along with the actual killing of civilians, was certainly one of the most extreme forms of violence against civilians in this period, but, importantly, the "female dominated domestic arena" was consistently intruded upon between 1919 and 1923 in the form of raids on private houses and assaults. Clark identifies a small number of cases but concludes that sexual violence against women was not widespread and in fact "sexual assault has never been made a wartime tactic in Ireland" (193). T. K Wilson has identified eight cases of sexual assault by loyalists in 1921–1922 in County Londonderry, south Armagh and Kilkeel (76). Recently, Marie Coleman in her essay "Violence against Women in the Irish War of Independence 1919–1921" concludes:

> Violence against women was certainly a feature of the war of independence yet the evidence available indicates that it was limited in nature and scope, especially by contemporary European standards. The targeted killing of females was very rare. Most of the violence carried out against women by both the Crown Forces and the IRA can be categorised as physical, gendered and psychological. Sexual violence took place but was very rare. Rape was not employed by either side as a weapon of war. (154)

My own research indicates that women were consistently targeted through 1919–1921, primarily in the form of forced hair cutting. Coleman recognises the existence of this form of violence against women highlighting an example in Galway city in September 1920, when five members of Cumann na mBan had their hair cut off by Black and Tans after the IRA had cut the hair off a young woman who gave evidence against the IRA in court. Coleman writes that this was a form of non-sexual gendered violence "displayed as a method of disciplining women" (141), and she recognises that both Republicans and the security forces used this tactic, but does not give any other examples, preferring instead to deal with the absence of widespread sexual violence and the reasons for this absence.

Though few women were ever killed in the Irish revolution, consistent patterns and forms of gendered intimidation and violence emerged. Women, while not the victims of "serious" violence, were threatened, humiliated, boycotted, had goods or property stolen, were beaten and had their hair cut by combatants. Like other forms of violence and intimidation directed against civilians in this period, violence against women was largely inspired by association with the enemy. The violence that emerged was gender specific in that women were attacked for fulfilling typical gender roles – namely young women who had relationships with members of the Crown forces. The violence of the Crown forces tended not to be quite as gender specific in that they would usually target whole families and communities at a time. Nevertheless, they also adopted gender specific violence by cutting off the hair of young women whom they believed were connected to the IRA.

Hair Cutting

The extreme form of intimidation or violence against women was hair cutting and it was also the most obviously gendered. On the night of 11 September 1919 Norah Williams of Lisdoonvarna, Co. Clare, "was pulled out of bed and had her hair cut off because she kept company with soldiers" (Inspector General of the Royal Irish Constabulary,[2] September 1919). Norah Williams was the first such case of hair cutting in the south and west of Ireland and set a pattern that would be followed in nearly every subsequent case of hair cutting by Republicans. Forty-four women had their hair cut off by Republicans in Connacht and Munster in the period 1919–1921. The following cases are a select few examples. The sources for this piece are drawn from Royal Irish Constabulary (R.I.C.) reports, British army records, contemporary newspapers[3] and contemporary Republican documents and memoirs produced later.

At 2 a.m. on 17 March 1920, Mary Brandon, from Ballybunion in north Kerry, was attacked for the second time in two months. The police reported that "twelve masked men cut off Mary Brandon's hair at Ballybunion because she was intimate with a policeman. On 24.2.20 portion of her hair was cut off and tar thrown on her clothes" (R.I.C., 29 March–11 April 1920). On 9 May a notice was posted outside Killavullen chapel, outside of Mallow, County Cork, declaring "any girls seen speaking to the police from this day forward are liable to the penalty of hair cut" (R.I.C., 9–16 May 1920). In May 1920 in Ballinasloe, east Galway, a notice was found declaring that any girl found in the

---

2   Henceforth I.G.
3   The newspaper articles referenced in this study are available at www.irishnewsarchive.com (*Irish Newspaper Archive*).

company of the Crown forces would have their "hair cut and ears amputated" (R.I.C., 9–16 May 1920). These were by no means empty threats.

The Cork Examiner reported on 5 May that, just outside Tuam in County Galway, seven men singing "we're out for Ireland free" cut the hair off an unnamed young woman in her night dress leaving "her unconscious from shock and exposure." The men also threatened to blow up the house where she lived. In late May the woman was named as Bridget Keagan of Cloondarona, near Tuam. While cutting her hair, the attackers reportedly said: "That's what you get for going out with Tommies." Mr Golding, Crown solicitor for Tuam, who sentenced three brothers – William, Jack and Frank Jordan – with six months' imprisonment for the offence, said "God help Ireland if these are the acts of Irishmen and God help Ireland if these are the men to free her."

In Tralee, County Kerry, in May 1920, the IRA put up posters that, according to the R.I.C., "warned girls against keeping company, or walking with soldiers. The girls are reminded that in 1916 England's soldiers shot down their brothers. Soldiers are warned that if they are found with girls, they will be shot" (R.I.C., 16–23 May 1920). In Kerry, the IRA were not slow to act if these warnings went unheeded. On 27 June "three masked men entered a house in Cahirciveen District, in the south-west of the County, and beat and cut the hair off two young girls named Julia and Margaret McCarthy. The girls are friendly with the police" (R.I.C., 27 June–4 July 1920). On 1 July in Annagh, outside Tralee, Norah Walsh was taken from her family home by armed and masked men "out to the road, where they cut off her hair and tarred her head. The injury was inflicted because she did not induce her brothers to resign from the R.I.C. One brother is serving in Clare, and the other is a recruit training at the Depot" (R.I.C., 27 June–4 July 1920). According to the British Army's Record of the Rebellion, produced following their departure from what became the Irish Free State, the operation was conducted by fifteen men and Norah was then seventeen years old (Kautt, 77).

On Monday, 5 July, in Youghal, east Cork, a young unnamed woman, "daughter of a prominent public official," while cycling was waylaid and had her hair cut off. Interestingly, those responsible were, reportedly, men and women, and women did the actual cutting (*Cork Examiner*, 6 July 1920). Possibly, the most insensitive or cruel case occurred in Mallow, in north Cork, on 7 July. The police reported:

> ... about 10.30. p.m. ... about 50 armed men called at the house of Mrs Deedy, publican and widow of the ex-head constable, Mallow district, and asked for her daughter Mary Ellen, who was to be married to [R.I.C.] constable M. McNieve next morning. She was at her cousin's house and on being so informed the raider took her to her mother's place. In reply to a raider she said she was going to marry a policeman. A raider then went to cut off her hair. She asked that her mother be allowed to cut it. The mother cut some but the raiders cut what remained. (R.I.C., 4–11 July 1920)

3. VIOLENCE AGAINST WOMEN IN MUNSTER AND CONNAGHT 1919–1923

On 10 August in Roscommon District (presumably near the town of Roscommon), twelve armed and disguised men entered the home of Kathleen Loughnane, a dressmaker, at 1 a.m.,

> ... and having asked her if she was keeping company with a policeman, received the reply that she was. She was then informed that they were going to cut her hair. She told them "cut away" that would not alter her mind. They forced her onto a chair, one man held her arms, while another cut off her hair. When the hair was partly cut she told them to do it up nicely. So that it would not be noticed unless closely observed. The constable has made the necessary application to his authorities to marry the girl. (R.I.C., 4–11 July 1920)

On 12 August in Abbeydorney, north of Tralee, while Catherine Fitzgerald was walking home, "she was accosted by a masked man who caught her by the arm and took her into a laneway, where four other masked men were. They blindfolded her, cut off her hair, and tarred her blouse and skirt. The girl was friendly with the police, and often went on errands for them, hence the motive" (R.I.C., 15–22 August 1920).

Family connections to the police, as well as what appear to have been romantic attachments, could also sometimes result in the IRA deciding to cut a girl's hair. The police reported that on 24 October

> a number of armed and disguised men visited the house of Jeremiah Sullivan, farmer, Listowel district. They beat his two sons Patrick and Daniel, cut the hair of his daughter's head, and burned a rick of corn. Miss Sullivan is friendly to the police, and her brother Daniel was examined for the police about two years ago, and it was thought he would again present himself. (R.I.C., 24–31 October 1920)

On 1 December Margaret Nash, a domestic servant to Dr Garny in Kildysart, in west Clare, while on her way home was "held up by three men who threw her down on the road and cut off her hair. The motive is evidently intimidation, as this girl was on friendly terms with Constable Flynn of Kildysart" (R.I.C., 12–19 December 1920).

In late 1920 and early 1921, as the Crown forces vigorously pursued their policy of shootings and reprisals, IRA activity against civilians connected to the Crown forces became more murderous and a notable decrease in hair cuttings is evident from police reports. *The Manchester Guardian* did, however, state that on 23 April, an unnamed, woman's hair was cut off in Kilgarvan, Co. Kerry, by the IRA (30 April 1920).

The following is a breakdown of a complete list of the attacks that occurred based on *The Cork Examiner*, *The Manchester Guardian*, *The Kerryman*, and the reports of the R.I.C. Inspector General and of the R.I.C. County Inspectors, together with the Weekly Summaries of outrages from 1920–1921:

Name	Date	Location
Norah Williams	11 September 1919	Lisdoonvarna, Clare[4]
Ciss Brandon	2 March 1920	Ballylongford, Kerry[5]
Unnamed	16 March 1920	Hollycross, Tipperary[6]
Mary Brandon	17 March 1920, also 24 March	Ballybunion, Kerry[7]
Bridget Keagan	5 May 1920	Tuam, Galway[8]
Annie Devine	17 May 1920	Tuam, Galway[9]
Unnamed	June 1920	Sligo[10]
Unnamed	June 1920	Sligo[11]
Kathleen Meade	17 June 1920	Clonakilty, Cork[12]
Kate Sullivan	18 June 1920	Kilrush, Clare[13]
Unnamed	18 June 1920	Castletownroche, Cork[14]
Unnamed	18 June 1920	Castletownroche, Cork[15]
Julia McCarthy	27 June 1920	Cahirciveen, Kerry[16]
Margaret McCarthy	27 June 1920	Cahirciveen, Kerry[17]
Unnamed	Late June 1920	Clonakilty, Cork[18]
Norah Walsh	1 July 1920	Tralee, Kerry[19]
Unnamed	4 July 1920	Cahirciveen, Kerry[20]
Unnamed	4 July 1920	Cahirciveen, Kerry[21]
Unnamed	5 July 1920	Youghal, Cork[22]

---

4 I.G., September 1919.
5 *The Kerryman*, 6 March 1920.
6 *Cork Examiner*, 16 March 1920.
7 R.I.C., 29 March–11 April 1920.
8 *Cork Examiner*, 11 May 1920.
9 R.I.C., 16 May–23 May 1920.
10 *I.G.* June 1921.
11 *Ibid.*
12 R.I.C., 20–27 June 1920. See also Kautt 77.
13 R.I.C., 20–27 June 1920.
14 *Cork Examiner*, 18 June 1920.
15 *Ibid.*
16 R.I.C., 27 June–4 July 1920 and *The Kerryman*, 3 July 1920.
17 *Ibid.*
18 *Cork Examiner*, 22 June 1920.
19 R.I.C., 27 June – 4 July 1920.
20 *Cork Examiner*, 6 July 1920.
21 *Ibid.*
22 *Ibid.*

Mary Ellen Deedy	7 July 1920	Mallow, Cork[23]
Nellie Fitzgerald	23 July 1920	Newpallas, Limerick[24]
Annie Fitzgerald	23 July 1920	Newpallas, Limerick[25]
Unnamed	23 July 1920	Nenagh, Tipperary[26]
Unnamed	23 July 1920	Nenagh, Tipperary[27]
Unnamed	26 July 1920	Newport, Tipperary[28]
Unnamed	Early August	Kenmare, Kerry[29]
Kathleen Loughnane	10 August 1920	Roscommon town, Roscommon[30]
Catherine Fitzgerald	12 August 1920	Abbeydorney, Kerry[31]
Unnamed	Late August 1920	Tubbercurry, Sligo[32]
Unnamed	Late August 1920	Tubbercurry, Sligo[33]
Unnamed	September 1920	Cahirciveen, Kerry[34]
Ms Greany	September 1920	Limerick city, Limerick[35]
Ms Baker	8 September 1920	Galway city, Galway[36]
Ms Sullivan	24 October 1920	Listowel, Kerry[37]
Mary Connolly	14 November 1920	Limerick city, Limerick[38]
Unnamed	Late November 1920	Quilty, Clare[39]
Unnamed	Late November 1920	Quilty, Clare[40]
Unnamed	Late November 1920	Quilty, Clare[41]
Unnamed	Late November 1920	Quilty, Clare[42]

23 R.I.C., 4–11 July 1920.
24 *Ibid.*
25 *Ibid.*
26 *Cork Examiner*, 26 July 1920.
27 *Ibid.*
28 *Cork Examiner*, 27 July 1920.
29 *The Kerryman*, 7 August 1920.
30 R.I.C., 29 August–5 September 1920.
31 R.I.C., 15–22 August 1920.
32 *Cork Examiner*, 26 August 1920.
33 Farry, 196.
34 *The Kerryman*, 18 September 1920.
35 *Cork Examiner*, 25 September 1920.
36 Leeson, 45.
37 R.I.C., 24–31 October 1920.
38 R.I.C., 14–21 November 1920.
39 *Cork Examiner*, 22 November 1920.
40 *Ibid.*
41 *Ibid.*
42 *Ibid.*

Margaret Nash	1 December 1920	Kildysart, Clare[43]
Minnie Keane	Mid December 1920	Kilrush, Clare[44]
Annie O'Shea	Mid December 1920	Kilrush, Clare[45]
Nina Wright	12 December 1920	Lismore, Waterford[46]
Unnamed	23 April 1921	Kilgarvan, Kerry[47]
	Total	**44**

Like a number of aspects of the IRA's campaign in the period from 1919 to 1921, hair cutting was a spontaneous reaction by local units to local conditions. Unlike say IRA policing, that also developed in reaction to local conditions but was regularised by G.H.Q. ("IRA Police"), hair cutting was never regularised. In fact, I have never come across a contemporary document at Battalion, Brigade, Divisional or Headquarters level that even references the practice. Why this was the case cannot be ascertained. Perhaps some IRA commanders may have been uncomfortable with the practice; others maybe wanted to ignore it and others might have been content for it to happen without any interference from higher ups. But such assaults on women were by no means one sided.

The Crown Forces and Forced Hair Cutting.

In the late summer and autumn of 1920, the Crown forces began a vigorous campaign against IRA violence. Often fuelled by drink, Black and Tans, Auxiliaries and regular army troops would indulge in indiscriminate reprisals against provincial towns such as Fermoy, Tuam, Balbriggan, Cork city, Ballylongford and Tralee. In these reprisals, arson, looting and beatings were common. D.M. Leeson has, however, recently shown in his 2011 study *The Black and Tans: British Police and Auxiliaries in the Irish War of Independence* that on the whole violence conducted against civilians by the Crown forces was largely discriminate rather than indiscriminate. They knew who they wanted to punish. Leeson writes that "in many cases the police chose their victims with care, even in the midst of a riot," and adds that "the police attacked well known Republicans and left other people alone" (273).

The tactics of both sides in many respects came to mirror each other. As 1920 progressed and the IRA continued to punish women associated with the Crown forces, the Crown forces retaliated by punishing women associated with the IRA. The following are a select number of examples of forced hair cutting by the Crown forces.

---

43 R.I.C., 12–19 December 1920.
44 *Ibid.*
45 *Ibid.*
46 *Ibid.*
47 The *Manchester Guardian*, 30 April 1921.

3. VIOLENCE AGAINST WOMEN IN MUNSTER AND CONNAGHT 1919–1923

In mid-October 1920, the Crown forces around north Kerry began attacking civilians to break the power and influence of the IRA. On 18 October, Black and Tans from Listowel came to the home of the O'Sullivan's two miles outside the town, beat two brothers living there and cut the hair off two girls living there (*The Manchester Guardian*, 30 October 1920). It is not clear whether the Sullivans were connected to the IRA, but it seems more than likely. The party of Black and Tans then drove to Lixnaw village and the home of IRA member Steve O'Grady. Steve escaped in his nightshirt across the fields but his sister Bridget was caught and had her hair cut off. Hugh Martin, an English journalist reporting on the situation in Ireland, later interviewed Bridget, who said that "one of the men said 'we are doing this because your brother had something to do with cutting the girl's hair in the village,' and they also threatened to murder Steve" (Martin, 124). The Black and Tans then proceeded to burn the Lixnaw creamery (*The Kerryman*, 5 February 1921). They then visited the home of John Lovatt, whose son Maurice was in the IRA. Maurice was beaten with rifles and kicked while on the ground. His sister Mary was then taken outside in her night clothes and had her hair cut off. Mary was told: "This is on account of our lady friend whose hair was bobbed for being friendly with us" (Martin, 124–25).

The raiders then visited the McElligott household. John and Tom McElligott, both volunteers, were accused of shooting policemen and cutting off a girl's hair. The two brothers were made to stand against a wall in the pouring rain wearing only their shirts and were then beaten up. Their sisters, aged fifteen and eighteen, were then made to come outside: the elder got away but the younger had her hair cut off. The raiders again maintained it was on account of a girl who had her hair cut off for being friendly with the Crown forces (*The Manchester Guardian*, 30 October 1920).

Later in the month of October 1920, Babe Hogan of Cumann na mBan in Milltown Mallbay, County Clare, was attacked by masked men who came to the house of her father at 1 a.m. Babe tried to escape but was caught and brought back inside where the raiders managed to cut off some of her hair. Babe, however, managed to escape her attackers before much damaged was done and reached an adjacent yard where she spent the rest of the night (*The Kerryman*, 30 October 1920).

In Galway city, in the autumn of 1920 and in reaction to the death of Black and Tan Constable Krumm, Black and Tans attacked the house of Sean Broderick who was the O/C of the 4th Galway Battalion ("Broderick"). Sean's sister, Peg Broderick of Cumann na mBan, had her hair cut off. Peg's statement to the Bureau of Military History[48] is the only first-hand account of what the experience was like. Peg recalled:

---

48 Files belonging to the Bureau of Military History collection are available at www.bureauofmilitaryhistory.ie

Sometime afterwards another raid took place when they asked if I was in. I called down from the top of the stairs and said: 'Surely I am allowed to dress myself.'" They replied: 'No, come down as you are ...' I went down and snatched a coat from the hall-stand. My mother shouted after me: 'Be brave, Peg': I thought at first they were going to shoot me, but they took me out and closed the door, then grabbed my hair, saying 'What wonderful curls you've got' and then proceeded to cut off all my hair to the scalp with a very blunt scissors. I might say they did not handle me too roughly, which is strange to say. There was no further comment until they finished, when they pushed me towards the door and said, 'Goodnight ...' All spoke with English accents. I had to have my head shaved by a barber next day in order to have the hair grow properly. ("Broderick-Nicholson")

The cutting of a girl's hair by the Crown forces could also be one incident in a series of attacks against a Republican family. Thomas Mannion, of Dunmore in north Co. Galway, recalled that his house was attacked on several occasions by the Crown forces: "One night, they had a big scissors with them. A Black and Tan grabbed my sister Nora by the hands. She said: 'what are you going to do?' One of them, a Black and Tan also, said: 'We're going to cut your locks, lass.' They cut her hair right to the scalp."

Unfortunately, it is not possible to produce a solid figure for the number of women who had their hair forcibly cut by the Crown forces for a number of reasons: the Crown forces kept extensive records on the activities of the IRA, but not on their own actions, resulting in the reprisals and other activities of the Crown being not as well documented as the activities of the IRA. The main sources for the activities of the Crown forces remain contemporaneous newspapers which, unfortunately, were often hazy on specifics. Also, due to shame many women would not report the issue. From the available documentation, it does appear that the Crown Forces did not practice forced hair cutting as frequently as the IRA.

Motivations and Context

Members of the Crown forces rarely left written testimonies on their experiences in Ireland. Other than the claim by Black and Tans in Lixnaw that they were taking revenge, their own views and motives for cutting a woman's hair are hard to discern. John M. Regan, the County Inspector for Limerick, described encountering the experience as very upsetting:

> We had not a real hatred for those who fought us fairly as circumstances allowed. At the other end of the scale from them, however, were the savages who attacked women. I loathed them. A very attractive looking girl was shown into my office one day and at once she burst into tears. She removed a covering from her head, and I nearly wept in sympathy. She had

been keeping company with one of my men, when a coward had charged with it and cut her hair right to the scalp, leaving long strands here and there. She was a pitiable sight, and wanted to know from me what on earth she was to do. She was a waitress in a restaurant and could not possibly carry on with her work. I did not know what to say to the poor girl, and could do nothing for her. (Augusteijn, 162)

Douglas Duff, who was serving with the Black and Tans in Galway city, recalled the issue of hair cutting in a rather unsettling way in his memoir *Sword for Hire* (1934). Duff believed it was so common an occurrence in County Galway, as conducted by both sides, that "it seemed likely that half the Galway girls would be bald" (Duff,76). Strangely, Duff did not consider hair cutting to be a serious assault: he saw it like the acts of "mischievous children" rather than the work of professional soldiers (76). Duff also believed that there had never been a single case, on either side, of what he described as "violence or insult to womenfolk" or at least not in Connacht (76). Regan seems to have been more compassionate in his reading of how such attacks affected women.

Occasionally, an IRA veteran would discuss the issue in later years. Dan Keating, a lifelong physical force Republican from Castlemaine in Kerry, felt the cutting of girls' hair in Tralee was successful in that it scared other girls into not fraternising with the Crown forces: "Their hair was cut and they were warned off" (Keating and Fleming, 39). James Moloney, from Bruff county Limerick, recalled

Some young girls created a problem. The British uniform was an attraction for them, as indeed would any uniform. They could be a real danger to the movement and gave a bad example by consorting with the enemy. They were warned repeatedly and stronger measures had to be resorted to. No Volunteer liked the job, but on occasions these girls' hair had to be cut. Years later Dame Fashion was to dictate bobbed hair but at this period of revolution it was deemed shameful.

Leo Buckley, from the Cork No.1 Brigade, recalled: "I remember at the time, young girls from Cork going out to Ballincollig to meet the British soldiers. We curbed this by bobbing the hair of persistent offenders. Short hair was completely out of fashion at the period, and the appearance of a girl with 'bobbed' hair clearly denoted her way of life." Michael Higgins, from Tuam, who was involved in the cutting of a girl's hair, recalled that "she was a very beautiful girl before her hair was sheared and I pitied her although I knew I should not in the circumstances." Geraldine Dillon, the sister of the executed 1916 leader Joseph Plunkett, who was in Galway during this period, simply recalled that the cutting of a girl's hair was "more of tragedy than it would be now."

Some of these last comments tell us perhaps more than anything else. It was not until the mid-1920s that in some circles short hair on women was considered fashionable but still, for most people, highly unusual. In rural Ireland, long hair would have been a defining feature for most women. Having it forcibly removed would have, as Leo Buckley observed, "denoted" some type of transgression for the world to see. By cutting off a woman's hair, combatants were taking away a woman's sense of normality, right to pride in her appearance, exposing her to ridicule and mistrust. More than this, these women were displayed as traitors to Ireland. Standards had been set and these women had failed to uphold them and were publicly shamed as a consequence. Like many other examples of IRA violence and intimidation, these attacks were far from random, IRA volunteers must have watched young women who they felt they could not trust, gathering proof of misconduct before deciding to make the attack.

On the other hand the hair-cutting by the Crown forces seems more spontaneous. Usually acting out of anger and frustration, and often drunk, the Crown forces attacked swiftly, striking at any known Sinn Fein supporter. The Black and Tans, like their opponents, cut hair as a means of sending a message or statement that this was punishment for IRA violence. However, though female victims of the Crown forces were publicly shamed, it does not appear they were attacked on account of their supposed lack of morality. It was a case of rough spontaneous vengeance against the "Shinner's" women rather than the response to activities the women had engaged in.

The IRA, however, attacked these women for what were considered to have been their morally reprehensible decisions. Interestingly, the blanket term used in police and press reports is that these women were "friendly" or sometimes "intimate" with the police or military. This could, of course, mean almost anything. However, the clear implication is that these women developed romantic relationships with members of the Crown forces or perhaps even simply went on a few dates together. This was what constituted the morally reprehensible action. These women were attacked, seemingly, for lacking a moral code and what would have been seen as sexual misconduct. Tom Barry, an IRA leader from west Cork, characterised the type of women who would have gone out with a member of the Crown forces as "unfortunates," presumably referring to prostitutes (Barry, 209). From the opposite perspective the British 6th Division's report on the conflict, similarly characterised female Sinn Féin members or sympathisers as "disaffected old maids, whom no decent person would be seen near" ("Irish rebellion"), which would also suggest the same connotation as that made by Barry.

The clear international comparison to make is the liberation of France from German dominion during World War I, when French women believed to have been collaborators with the Germans had their hair forcibly removed. In those years, France presented as many differences from and similarities with the Irish situation in the revolutionary period. Not least in terms of scale, across

3. VIOLENCE AGAINST WOMEN IN MUNSTER AND CONNAGHT 1919–1923

France, it has been estimated that between ten- and thirty-thousand women experienced forced hair cutting. In Ireland, the number appears to be well under one hundred. Also in France the hair cuttings occurred in public, the women in question were dragged through the streets and large numbers of spectators came to watch. The shavings were seen as having an almost medieval, carnival-like feeling. In Ireland, the attacks happened within the home of the victim and often at night. But the similarities included the fact that the attacks in France tended to be carried out by the Resistance, like the IRA, an idealistic guerrilla force that faced far superior opponents. Historian Julian Jackson has described the process as being motivated by the idea that "before 'resurrection' and 'renewal' could occur, France had to 'cleanse' herself cutting out those 'gangrenous' elements" (582). According to the attackers these women would have been regarded as defiled. In terms of the language used and ideology behind these attacks, the French Resistance behaved similarly to the IRA, drawing on concepts such as national honour and betrayal for justification.

It does, however, need to be asked, in cases by both the Black and Tans and the IRA, if there is some sexual aspect to their actions. Images of women being dragged into alleys, tied up, beaten and thrown to the ground give some sense of how traumatic and brutal the experience must have been. James Moloney believed that "no volunteer liked the job." However, such conduct is also suggestive of deliberate cruelty, misogyny and possible sexual violence on the part of the IRA volunteers and the Crown forces involved. T.K. Wilson, for instance, addresses this subject in the following terms: "The issue of haircutting might be seen as a sexualised punishment in that it deliberately targeted the femininity of (usually Catholic) women who were held to have betrayed their national responsibilities" (120). However, I would argue that for the IRA these attacks were motivated by desire to punish sexual misconduct rather than overt sexual gratification. In fact, members of Cumann na mBan sometimes seem to have been involved in haircutting, such as for example Kathleen O'Connor, from Milltown County Kerry, who in her pension application[49] claimed to have been involved in the cutting of a girl's hair.

However, it is more than possible that some elements of these incidents were deliberately not written down. Charles Townshend has written that members of the Crown forces probably did rape women but they would have been "hushed up" by the families of the victims (171). This is, of course, a common problem. In 1914, as the German army advanced into France and Belgium, rape became a widespread occurrence, but French and Belgian women were unwilling to discuss what had happened to them. One woman raped by a German soldier in Audun-le-Roman later told a police commissioner that she had never gone

---

49 These applications can be found in the Military Service (1916–1923) Pensions Collection: www.militaryarchives.ie/collections/online-collections/military-service-pensions-collection-1916-1923.

to report it to the German authorities "due to fear and shame" (Horne and Kramer, 196). Perhaps the German invasion of France and Belgium can be considered further in relation to violence against women as perpetrated by the British Crown forces in Ireland. John Horne and Alan Kramer write in *German Atrocities, 1914: A History of Denial* (2001) that "rape demonstrated in the starkest possible way that the relationship between the invader and invaded was also one of gender. If male civilians were more likely to be shot, only girls and women (as far as we know) were raped, so that the invader's absolute power to violate the body was expressed in different gendered ways" (199).

Surely, this can extend to hair cutting in Ireland. The Crown forces, acting out of anger at IRA violence, wanted to give out an aggressive message that they were in charge and any challenge to this authority would result in severe punishments. Hair cutting is the clearest example of gendered punishment. Horne and Kramer also write that "the readiness of German soldiers to think of their antagonist as a dehumanised *franc-tireur* (French/Belgian civilians attacking the Germans behind their lines) lowered their inhibitions against committing inhuman acts" (197). German actions, as well as those of the Black and Tans and Auxiliaries, need to be understood within the context of soldiers in fear of civilians. The most usual complaint expressed by members of the Crown forces in Ireland was that they could not see their enemy, since they did not wear uniforms and were thus indistinguishable from regular civilians, and they would only use guerrilla tactics rather than the open style of warfare they were familiar with (Leeson, 211). The future Field Marshall Montgomery, who served with the British Army in Ireland in the period 1919–1921, would famously write that he regarded all civilians as "Shinners" (Ó Ruairc, 45). Hair cutting by the Crown forces should be seen not only as a product of this belief in all civilians being possible opponents, but also as part of a desire to appear to be in control of a difficult situation and having a right to control, revealing the invader's power.

These women were punished for their actions and for who they were associated with, rather than for the sexual gratification of the aggressors. Reported instances of rape between 1919 and 1923 were rare. This is not uncommon in particularly localised conflicts. The conflict between pro and anti-union militias in Kansas and Missouri in the American Civil War has been described as being a form of brutal conflict "exceeding anything else in the war," and mainly affecting civilians (McPherson, 784). However, as in Ireland in the years 1919–1921, instances of rape rarely occurred in the Kansas –Missouri conflict, despite being of both a greater scale and displaying much fiercer brutality than the Irish conflict (McPherson, 784). But, on the flip side, British officers and troops were accused of raping Russian women in the Crimean war (Figes, 345). Presumably, the British soldiers felt that so far from home they would not be held responsible, while the guerrillas in Missouri may have been subject to communal retribution. This latter may have been the case in Ireland, as the British born members of the Crown forces were still technically operating within the United Kingdom and with English speaking people. On the other hand, the rape, notably, of black South African women during the second Anglo-Boer war by British soldiers was reported (Tabitha Jackon, 168). This would suggest that the further the troops were from home or in more "foreign" surroundings, the likelier they were to engage in serious transgressions.

The issue of hair cutting has not been analysed in the ever increasing historiography of this period. Charles Townshend, T.K. Wilson, John O'Callaghan, D.M. Leeson and Peter Hart have referred to the existence of the practice, as conducted by all sides, but cite it in passing as an example of tactics used, and do not take the issue further. John O'Callaghan's 2010 work *Revolutionary Limerick: The Campaign for Independence in Limerick, 1913–1921* addresses the issue but presents it as being connected to the IRA's campaign against civilian spies and informers. O'Callaghan claims that women "were more likely to have their hair cut off than to be executed" (173). But, as my own research shows, these women were never described as spies or informers. All the women targeted were described as being "friendly" or for having associated with the Crown forces rather than for giving information to the Crown forces. Interestingly, in 1998 Peter Hart also wrongly confused the two issues describing the victims of forced hair cutting as "suspected female informers" (310).

Although the practice of hair cutting in the revolutionary period has not been researched and written about extensively, it has entered the popular perception and understanding of the revolution. For example, in Ken Loach's 2006 film *The Wind that Shakes the Barley* Orla Fitzgerald's character, Sinead Sullivan, a Cumann na mBan volunteer, having previously watched her brother being tortured and killed by the Black and Tans for refusing to say his name in English, has her hair cut off by Black and Tans in a reprisal after a successful IRA ambush. The Tans are shown as vicious thugs who beat and taunt Sinead whilst tearing her hair out and burning her home. Later on Sinead's lover Damien is executed by Free State troops for refusing to give up information about his fellow IRA men. Sinead goes through tremendous physical and emotional suffering throughout the film for her loyalty and her friends and family's loyalty to the Republic. Despite this suffering Sinead does not give up on her principles and remains a proud Irish Republican. Sinead and the people around her can be seen as almost the living embodiment of the Republic and representative of the suffering of all those who defended it.

On the other hand, in 1972, in David Lean's film *Ryan's Daughter*, set in the west coast of Ireland during the Irish War of Independence, Sarah Miles' character Rosy Ryan also has her hair cut off. Rosy, a publican's daughter, is a beautiful, adventurous yet innocent young woman eager to escape the narrow minded and rustic environment in which she lives. Disappointed with her intellectual yet rather aloof husband Charles Shaughnessy, played by Robert Mitchum, Rosy begins a passionate affair with a handsome young British officer. The cruel and vicious townspeople find out and round on Rosy tearing off her clothes and cutting off her hair. Rosie's vanity and cruelty towards some people around her make her hard to like as character. Yet her decision to have an affair is presented as the product of boredom and the desire of any person for romance and intimacy rather than a politically driven rejection or treason to Ireland. The townspeople do not see it that way and come off as cruel and narrow minded.

In my view, both Loach and Lean present equally valid interpretations of the forced hair cutting which occurred at this time. The attacks against women highlighted in this chapter should not be looked at in isolation but rather as part of a broader pattern of violence and intimidation in the Irish revolution. In the years 1919 and 1920, the IRA put up notices, across Ireland, warning people of the consequences of dealing with the R.I.C. or the British army. The IRA would also put up notices naming business people who did not heed their warnings. In late 1920 and 1921 the IRA began to label their civilian victims with placards proclaiming "Spies and informers beware." These tactics were designed to ensure civilians would not inform, and were presented as the cost of betraying the nation. Likewise, the Crown forces, by burning and stealing the property of Republicans and their families, and often simply members of the broad nationalist population, were giving a clear message to Republicans and their supporters of the consequences of their actions. Women with bruised faces and a few remaining tufts of hair were likewise intended as a message to other women of either the very real dangers of associating with the R.I.C. and, on the other side, of the very real dangers of being in any way connected to the IRA. It is necessary to recognise the shame and humiliation that must have been felt by the victims of these attacks. However, it is just as necessary to recognise the fear and horror these attacks must have created in the minds of dozens, if not hundreds, of other women across Ireland.

Works Cited
Primary Sources

Imperial War Museum, London
Sir General Peter Strickland Papers:
"Irish rebellion in the 6th divisional area after the 1916 Rebellion to December 1921 compiled by the General Staff of the Division." Box P.363.

Irish Military Archives
Bureau of Military History (1913–1921):
"Broderick, Sean." WS1677.
"Broderick-Nicholson, Margaret." WS1682.

"Buckley, Leo." WS1714.
"Dillon, Geraldine." WS0424.
"Higgins, Michael." WS1247.
"Mannion, Thomas." WS1408.
"Moloney, James." WS1310.

Military Service Pensions Collection (1916–1923):
"O'Connor, Kathleen."MSP34REF14007.

Irish Newspapers Archives
The Cork Examiner.
The Kerryman Examiner.
The Manchester Guardian.

National Library of Ireland, Dublin
Piaras Béaslaí Papers:
"IRA Police." Instructions for the organisation of IRA police units. MS 33,913(1).

Trinity College Dublin, Berkeley Library
Royal Irish Constabulary Collection:
Inspector General of the Royal Irish Constabulary. Monthly Report. September 1919. MS 904/110.
——. Monthly Report. June 1921. MS 904/115.
Royal Irish Constabulary. Weekly Summaries of Outrages. 29 March–11 July 1920. MS 904/148.
——. Weekly Summaries of Outrages. 15 August–19 December 1920. MS 904/149.

Secondary Sources

Augusteijn, Joost, editor. *The Memoirs of John M. Regan. A Catholic Officer in the R.I.C. and R.U.C., 1909–1948.* Four Courts Press, 2007.
Barry, Tom. *Guerrilla Days in Ireland.* Anvil Press, 1949.
Clark, Gemma. *Everyday Violence in the Irish Civil War.* Cambridge University Press, 2014.
Coleman, Marie. "Violence against Women in the Irish War of Independence." *Years of Turbulence. The Irish Revolution and its Aftermath. In Honour of Michael Laffan,* edited by Diarmaid Ferriter and Susannah Riordan, UCD Press, 2015.
Duff, Douglas. *Sword for Hire – The Saga of a Modern Free Companion.* John Murray, 1934.
Farry, Michael. *Sligo 1914–1921: A Chronicle of Conflict.* Irish Books and Media, 1992.
Figes, Orlando. *Crimea: The Last Crusade.* Oxford University Press, 2010.
Foster, R.F. *Vivid Faces: The Revolutionary Generation in Ireland, 1890–1923.* Penguin, 2014.

Hart, Peter. *The IRA and its Enemies. Violence and Community in Cork, 1916–1923.* Oxford University Press, 1998.
Horne, John and Alan Kramer. *German Atrocities, 1914: A History of Denial.* Yale University Press, 2001.
Jackson, Julian. *France: The Dark Years, 1940–1944.* Oxford University Press, 2001.
Jackson, Tabitha. *The Boer War.* Channel 4 Books, 1999.
Kautt, William H., editor. *Ground Truths: British Army Operations in the Irish War of Independence.* Irish Academic Press, 2014.
Keating, Dan and Diarmaid Fleming. "Interview: Last Man Standing: Dan Keating." *History Ireland,* vol. 16, no. 3, 2008, pp. 38–41.
Leeson, D.M. *The Black and Tans: British Police and Auxiliaries in the Irish War of Independence.* Oxford University Press, 2011.
McCoole, Sinead. *Easter Widows: Seven Women who Lived in the Shadow of the 1916 Rising.* Doubleday, 2014.
McPherson, James. *The Battle Cry of Freedom: The Civil War Era.* Oxford University Press, 1988.
Martin, Hugh. *Ireland in Insurrection. An Englishman's Record of Fact by Hugh Martin with a Preface by Sir Philip Gibbs, K.B.E.* Daniel O'Connor, 1921.
O'Callaghan, John. *Revolutionary Limerick. The Campaign for Independence in Limerick, 1913–1921.* Irish Academic Press, 2010.
Ó Ruairc, Páidraig Óg. *Truce: Murder, Myth and the Last Days of the Irish War of Independence.* Mercier Press, 2016.
Paseta, Senia. *Irish Nationalist Women, 1900–1918.* Cambridge University Press, 2013.
Ryan, Louise. "'Drunken Tans': Representations of Sex and Violence in the Anglo-Irish War (1919–1921)." *Feminist Review,* no. 66, 2000, pp. 73–94.
Townshend, Charles. *The Republic: The Fight for Irish Independence, 1918–1923.* Allen Lane, 2013.
Wilson, T.K. *Frontiers of Violence: Conflict and Identity in Ulster and Upper Silesia, 1918–1922.* Oxford University Press, 2010.

4

"We have not Committed any Sin": A Corpus-Based Critical Discourse Analysis of Brigid Lyons's Witness Statement of the Easter Rising

Mariana Vignoli Figueroa

Introduction

This chapter analyses the particular usage of emotion and judgement in the witness statement of an Irish woman, Dr Brigid Lyons, who was involved in the 1916 Easter Rising.[1] The traditional approach to emotional talk is to measure the frequency and nature of explicit emotive terms, like "love" and "hate" (language about emotion). This study, however, endorses Monika Bednarek's concept of "emotion talk" (language as emotion), which covers "all sorts of human behaviour that signal emotion without the recourse to linguistic expressions that explicitly denote emotion" (11). This means that emotion talk also accounts for features like pronoun use, intensifiers, vagueness, markedness, intonation and so on, which "conventionally signal the speaker's emotions" (Bednarek, 12). By looking at emotion talk, we may also analyse the ideology underlying the speaker's usage of emotion and judgement terms, since "ideologies may influence the ways social attitudes are expressed in discourse" (Van Dijk, 1).

My study, as already observed, centres on the witness statement given by Dr Brigid Lyons, who was a member of Cumann na mBan,[2] a republican women's paramilitary organisation that helped the Irish Volunteers during the Rising.

---

1   Lyons's witness statement is part of the Military Service (1916–1923) Pensions Collection. All files belonging to this collection are available at www.militaryarchives.ie/collections/online-collections/military-service-pensions-collection-1916-1923.
2   Cumann na mBan translates as "The Irishwomen's Council" and also as "The League of Women."

The research questions that trigger this study are:

1. How did Brigid Lyons portray her emotions in relation to the 1916 Easter Rising events?
2. How did Brigid Lyons judge the events that took place in the 1916 Easter Rising?

Taking into account the above, the main objectives that guide this study are the following:

(a) To identify her beliefs and ideas as reflected in her witness statement.
(b) To describe her participation in the Rising and the violence she faced.
(c) To understand her view on imprisonment and death.

In order to assess the emotions and judgments prevalent in Lyons's statement, I shall make use of Appraisal Theory (Martin and White, 2005), a methodology which will be briefly explained in what follows. I have also attached, in an appendix to this chapter, some of Lyons's most relevant appreciations of her experiences in the Rising.

An Overview of Appraisal Theory

Emotions are powerful and have thus remained a constant object of analysis and appreciation throughout history. Greek philosophers, among them Plato and Aristotle, used a vast array of emotional expressions in order to emphasise their intellectual discoveries, and it has been further remarked that "ancient Greek literature exhibits a wealth of emotions, whether in the behavior of characters in narratives or in the response elicited in the audience or readers" (Konstan). In modern times, emotions have been predominantly studied from the perspectives of psychology (Griffith) and sociology (Gordon). It was not until late in the twentieth century that linguists stepped into this area of analysis, a task which has proved to be complex. As Johnny J. R. Fontaine argues, this complexity lies in the fact that people are constantly expressing emotions consciously and unconsciously, and speakers modulate their emotion talk according to the particular situations in which they are immersed (7). Linguists have developed various methodologies to study language and emotion. One of these is Systemic Functional Linguistics (Halliday, 1985), whereby "the organizing principle adopted is that of system: the grammar is seen as a network of interrelated meaningful choices" (Halliday and Matthiessen, 49), which reflect the "subjective presence of writers/speakers" in language production (Martin and White, 1).

Following Halliday (1985), we perceive language as having three basic metafunctions: (i) ideational, (ii) interpersonal, and (iii) textual. The ideational metafunction concerns the speakers' construction of human experience, as they draw on the "resources of the lexicogrammar of [their] language" (Halliday and Matthiessen, 30). The second metafunction is the interpersonal one, where language is perceived as "enacting our personal and social relationships with the people around us" (30). The textual metafunction, on its part, can be regarded as an "enabling or facilitating function," because it "organiz[es] the discursive flow and creat[es] cohesion and continuity" (31).

My study of Dr. Brigid Lyons's statement focuses on its interpersonal metafunction and, in particular, on one of its systems: appraisal, which addresses the ways in which "evaluation is established, amplified, targeted and sourced," an evaluation that is often constructed via emotion talk (Martin and White, 9). Emotion talk, as previously observed, relates to "all those constituents (verbal, non-verbal, linguistic, non-linguistic) that conventionally express or signal affect/emotion" (Bednarek, 11).

Appraisal Theory, which contends that "emotions are elicited by evaluations (appraisals) of events and situations" (Roseman and Smith, 3), emerges as an appropriate framework for my analysis of Lyons's emotional, ethic and aesthetic evaluation of her Easter Rising experience. When it comes to describing an emotional evaluation, we can distinguish three important aspects of emotional experience: (i) the emoter, (ii) the emotion and (iii) the trigger. Following Bednarek, the emoter refers to "who is said to 'feel' an emotion," while the trigger defines "what causes the emotional response" (Bednarek, 70). Similarly, the category of "appraiser" centres on the individuals who evaluate, judge or express an opinion about other people or events, the "appraised" entities.

Appraisal Theory is divided into three systems: (i) attitude, (ii) engagement, and (iii) graduation. The attitude system, the one that informs my assessment of Lyons's statement, encompasses "emotional reaction, judgements of behaviour and evaluation of things" (Martin and White, 35). The attitude system is at the same time divided into three categories: (i) affect, (ii) judgement and (iii) appreciation:

Appraisal Theory	{	Engagement Attitude Graduation	{	Affect Judgement Appreciation

Table 1. Attitude and its categories within Appraisal Theory.

The category of affect describes "positive and negative emotions, both of the speaker (authorial affect: *I love*) and third parties (non-authorial affect: *s/he loves, you love, they love*)" (Bednarek 14). Affect can be classified into different subcategories: (i) un/happiness, (ii) dis/satisfaction, (iii) in/security, (iv) dis/inclination, and (v) unclear affect. The subcategory of un/happiness revolves around "affairs of the heart-sadness, hate, happiness and love," whilst the dis/satisfaction subcategory "covers emotions concerned with telos (the pursuit of goals)-ennui, displeasure, curiosity, respect" (Martin and White, 49). The in/security subcategory is "concerned with ecosocial well-being anxiety, fear, confidence and trust," while the fourth, dis/inclination, relates to the desirability attached to any entity (49). The fifth one, the subcategory of unclear affect, serves to mark instances in which the affect being described does not fit any of the previous subcategories.

A second category within the attitude system is that of judgement, which deals with the "resources for morally evaluating human actions, behaviour or character, by reference to a set of ethic norms" (Bednarek, 15). This category comprises six subcategories, which may express judgements of social esteem or social sanction. Judgements of social esteem, whose function is to construct social values and build up social networks, are regulated "in the oral culture, through chat, gossip, jokes and stories of various kinds" (Martin and White, 52). The subcategories of normality, capacity and tenacity belong to the arena of social esteem. Normality is concerned with how usual an event or entity is, while capacity refers to how capable the entities are to perform specific tasks; as for tenacity, it refers to how resolute the evaluated entities are. Judgements of social sanction, on their part, concern notions of propriety and veracity, and are not regulated by oral culture, but "codified in writing, as edicts, decrees, rules, regulations and laws about how to behave as surveilled by church and state" (52). People who do not abide by the laws and decrees of their communities can face penalties and punishments; these judgements, as suggested, depend on evaluations of propriety and veracity. Propriety considers how ethical or moral an entity is, while veracity assesses the truthfulness of an idea or event.

The last category within the attitude system is appreciation, which provides the necessary resources to "evaluate the (aesthetic) quality of processes, things and products (and human beings when they are seen as entities)" (Bednarek, 15). There are three subcategories within the appreciation category: (i) reaction, (ii) composition and (iii) valuation. Reaction "concerns the impact of the text/process on our attention (impact: *captivating–dull*) and its attitudinal impact (quality: *beautiful–ugly*)" (15). It is important to highlight that there "are strong links between the appreciation variable reaction and affect" (Martin and White, 57), since reaction makes reference to values of affect which have been detached from human experiencers. Speakers, instead of saying that they are frustrated, can say that something is frustrating, therefore voicing the "social significance of the appreciated entity" (57), which is what the subcategory valuation refers to. Such significance is, of course, culturally contingent. For this reason, I have included in this chapter the historical background to Lyons's statement, as it will help recognise instances of social-valuation. On its part, composition refers to "perceptions of proportionality/balance (balance: *harmonious–discordant*) and detail (complexity: *intricate–simplistic*)" (57). As shall be explained later, the perceived importance of Easter Rising has an effect on the ways in which Brigid Lyons recalls her emotions and participation in the event.

As regards Appraisal Theory, a final consideration to make is that, though affect, judgement and appreciation are presented as independent categories, there are no rigid boundaries separating them, since speakers often "combine affect with judgement or appreciation" (Martin and White, 61). When analysing Lyons's emotion talk, I shall attempt to find meaningful connections between the three categories of affect, judgement and appreciation.

Corpus: Dr Brigid Lyons's Witness Statement

The corpus used for this study, Dr Brigid Lyons's witness statement, was part of her application in order to receive a military-service pension. She gave her statement to the Irish army on 4 June 1949, that is, thirty-three years after the Easter Rising took place. Lyons's statement is part of the archives of the Military Service (1916–1923) Pensions Collection. In his *Modern Ireland and Revolution* (2016), Cormac O'Malley summarises the importance of these archives for a more nuanced re-interpretation of Ireland's revolutionary years:

> In all, over 2,000 former combatants gave a first person account … concerning some aspect of their involvement in Ireland's independence struggle from 1913 to 1923. The often scant descriptions of IRA actions in newspapers, British records and IRA brigade and battalion reports can now be fleshed out with hundreds of accounts of ambushes, engagements, arms raids, assassinations, intelligence gathering, prison life, hunger strikes, the separatist movement's wider organization and supporting networks during the Easter Rising, War of Independence and Civil War.

Lyons's witness statement, as well as many other testimonies like hers, was made public online in 2013.

As suggested earlier, for a better understanding of Lyons's emotion talk, we need to account for the exceptional historical circumstances informing her witness statement as a participant of the Easter Rising, an event regarded by many as the starting point for Irish independence.[3] Two years before the Rising, in 1914, members of the IRB (Irish Republic Brotherhood), former Fenian members and Volunteers from the Citizen Army, came together to discuss "what

---

3   Generally understood as a vital episode of recent Irish history, the Easter Rising is still today a much debated issue. A number of historians, like Diarmaid Ferriter, while unsupportive of the revisionists' focus on "native failings rather than externally created problems" (750), maintain that the rebels did not have a popular mandate and that a general revolutionary situation did not exist in Dublin at that time – it was only after the Rising that a revolutionary climate clearly emerged (136–147).

they should do during the war" (Kee, 156). Around the same time, in April 1914, a republican women's organisation, Cumann na mBan, was founded. Aside from being an "auxiliary to the Irish volunteers" they also attempted "to advance the cause of Irish liberty," women's equality included ("Cumann"). At the time of the Rising, Cumann na mBan was led by Countess Markievicz, also a member of the Irish Citizen Army (ICA), and Helena Molony was one of its most notorious members. According to Molony, they tried to facilitate "political engagement by women, who were denied the vote and excluded from most political and cultural organisations" (McGarry, "Molony"). Members of the organisation believed that, after national independence, women would have the opportunity finally to achieve social equality. Their feminist aspirations arose some hostility among Irish Republicans, but Cumann na mBan continued to help the Irish Volunteers and to promote the idea of women's rights (Sebestyen).

As part of their activities, the members of Cumann na mBan had to learn First Aid, carry out intelligence work, take care of the wounded, collect supplies, help with propaganda and publicity, raise funds and assist "in the escape of prisoners" ("Cumann"). By the time the Easter Rising started, there were nearly forty-three active branches of Cumann na mBan, and all its members were performing various activities to help the Irish Volunteers. These women did not take "direct part in the fighting, but performed assigned tasks as nurses, cooks and dispatch-carriers (probably the most dangerous activity in Easter Week)" (Kiberd, 399). Even though Cumann na mBan members were not expected to fight during the Rising, they were trained and taught "how to parade and drill. In Belfast and Dublin, but apparently not elsewhere, women were even taught how to handle guns" (McGarry, *Rising* 65).

Among these women was Brigid Lyons, sometimes referred to as Bridget, a medicine student who joined Cumann na mBan in Galway. Lyons was "born into a prominent Roscommon nationalist family in 1896" in Northyard, Scramouge, and, ever since she was a child, she became acquainted with Irish nationalism (Sayers). Her father, being a farmer, had been imprisoned for having been an active member of the Land League during the Land War in the 1870s. As Lyons declared with a tinge of admiration, her father went on to join the Volunteers "although he was 65 years of age." In her witness statement, Lyons claimed that her family was reduced to poverty, so at the age of eight she was sent to live with her aunt and uncle, Frank McGuinness, in County Longford. Both Frank and his brother, Joe, became members of Sinn Féin and the Irish Volunteers, which encouraged Lyons to uphold Irish separatism.

In Lyons's family, women were also involved in nationalist organisations: her aunt, for example, was a member of Cumann na mBan, and worked as a courier before and during the Rising. Following her aunt's steps, Brigid Lyons carried out activities to raise money for the Volunteers and even attempted to found a nationalist organisation, a "Liberty Club on the receipt of a request from

Count Plunkett" ("Lyons"). From a young age, Lyons remained determined to collaborate on the cause of independence, even at the risk of her own safety. Life stories like Lyons's give the lie to the long-held assumption that women were not actively involved in the revolutionary struggle.

At the outbreak of the Rising, Lyons decided to accompany her uncle, Frank, in order to support the separatist movement. Access to Dublin was not easy, since, as she remarked, "drivers and owners would not undertake the risk [to enter the city]," a description that underscores Lyons's and her uncle's bravery and resolution. Once in Dublin, Lyons and her uncle managed to reach the Four Courts and the General Post Office (GPO), which became the main areas of insurgent activity. Being a medicine student,[4] Lyons was allowed to stay in the Four Courts and work as a nurse; her first patient got "a bullet near the liver" within a few hours from her arrival ("Lyons"). She was therefore one of the women who experienced the violence of war personally: "The fighting was terrifying, the activities were unceasing" ("Lyons"). Although scared of being in the battlefield, Lyons remained in the Four Courts assisting the Volunteers. After defeat, she was arrested together with other women who, like her, had aided the revolutionaries.

As Lyons explains in her statement, she and other women were sent to Richmond Barracks, even though they had been promised by a British officer that they would not be arrested or sent to prison. Once there, they met their superior, Countess Markievicz, and other fellow comrades. After their stay in Richmond Barracks, they were sent to Kilmainham. During their time in Kilmainham Gaol, they witnessed the executions of the Easter Rising leaders – "we were there for all the executions. We used to hear the shots in the morning" –, and suffered much pain and diseases provoked by the "dreariness, squalor and sordidness of Kilmainham" ("Lyons"). After having spent a couple of weeks in prison and being interrogated daily, Lyons was eventually released from Kilmainham jail, but was made to promise that she would not engage in any subversive activities again. Far from becoming submissive to British power, Lyons continued to be involved in the struggle for Irish independence in the years that followed.

Analysis: Reading between the Lines

To analyse Lyons's emotion talk in her witness statement, I have used a software programme, the UAM Corpus Tool (UAM).[5] This is a free-downloadable software that allows annotation of linguistic corpora and that facilitates the

---

4   Despite the poverty she suffered, with the economic support of her relatives Lyons was able to complete secondary school in Sligo. She then moved to Galway to study Medicine at University College Galway thanks to a scholarship she had won (Crowe).
5   UAM Corpus Tool can be downloaded from the official website: http://corpustool.com/download.html

design of a scheme appropriate to the researcher's needs.[6] This software allows for annotation of multiple texts as well as annotation of each text at different levels. Once the annotation is done, this software facilitates statistical analyses of the annotated words/phrases.

A UAM-Corpus-Tool-built-in scheme for Appraisal Theory was the starting point to develop the tagset[7] that would eventually be used in this research. The built-in scheme had only the three categories that make up the attitude system: affect, judgement and appreciation. Each one of the categories also had its own subcategories, as proposed by Bednarek in *Emotion Talk*. The tagset had to be modified in order to fit the purposes of this study, so new features were added to the original scheme. Subcategories to indicate polarity, attitude, explicitness, appraiser, appraised, valence, realisation, voice, emoter, and trigger were included in the final tagset, as this was the most accurate scheme for the purposes of analysis.

A total of 839 items were annotated and included for analysis. Table 2 gives a first impression of how Brigid Lyons perceived the world around her. As can be observed, there is a sharp contrast between the frequency of affect terms and of those of judgement and appreciation:

ATTITUDE SYSTEM	%
Affect	12.61
Judgement	45.25
Appreciation	42.14

Table 2. Attitude categories in percentages.

The percentage of affect terms –the explicit expression of emotions as experienced by the speaker– is surprisingly low (12.61%), which may give the false impression that Lyons was emotionless when recalling the events of the Rising, a crucial moment in her life. Instead of using affect terms to articulate her emotions, she did so by making use of appreciation and judgement terms mostly. This means that, instead of putting herself as the experiencing subject, she customarily opted for a more "detached" approach, as in the following example: "The fighting was terrifying." Emotion is here described by means

---

6 I downloaded a copy of Lyons's witness statement, which had been digitised and converted into PDF format. Later, I copied and pasted her statement to txt format, as this is the necessary format for the software to work.

7 A tagset may be defined as "a list of part-of-speech tags (POS tags for short), i.e. labels used to indicate the part of speech and sometimes also other grammatical categories (case, tense, etc.) of each token in a text corpus" ("Tagset").

of negative appreciation. Notably, she generally expressed her evaluations and judgements by appreciating the quality of the events, the social value of the actions or people, the behaviour of the people involved in the Rising and so on. This focus on a spirit of collectivity, far from making her statement emotionless, highlights the importance of the event.

Despite the low preponderance of affect terms, the findings within this category are revealing. In Table 3, the results for the subcategories of affect are shown:

AFFECT CATEGORY	%
Un/happiness	63.53
Dis/satisfaction	9.41
In/security	16.47
Dis/inclination	5.88
Unclear	4.71

Table 3. Affect categories in percentages.

As observed, the subcategory un/happiness presents, by far, the highest rate of usage. What is relevant here is that the instances denoting happiness or unhappiness mainly refer to other people's emotions, not her own (1). Fewer are the moments when Lyons relates her own emotions (2), although in some cases, she denotes affect by using a language of proximity towards her relatives and friends (3).

1. My uncle Joe was delighted to see us.
2. I was thrilled with him.
3. My uncle Joe often spoke about ...

Moving on to the subcategory of in/security, we find an overwhelming prevalence of terms denoting states of disquiet:

IN/SECURITY SUBCATEGORY	%
Disquiet	92.86
Quiet	7.14
Trust	0
Distrust	0

Table 4. Insecurity categories in percentages.

87

The fact that Lyons expressed much disquiet seems reasonable enough, as they all were in the middle of a war. The uncertainty as to what was going to happen next would have caused Lyons to feel extremely insecure. In (4) and (5), Brigid portrayed those feelings of disquiet when talking about herself and others:

4. We were challenged at every corner, the city being under martial Law.
5. My aunt was in a great state of distress.

As stated earlier, Lyons seldom portrayed herself as the experiencer of emotions, not even in those cases where she used affect terms. Yet, as examples (4) and (5) show, there is no doubt that she was emotionally affected by the violence surrounding her. Since Lyons was actively involved in the Republican Movement, this probably gave her a sense of a collective commitment though which she channelled her emotions.

Unlike the affect category, the judgment category presents a high prevalence within Lyons's discourse. And, within the judgement category, the subcategories of propriety, tenacity and capacity feature as the most salient ones:

JUDGEMENT CATEGORY	%
Normality	13.77
Capacity	24.59
Tenacity	24.59
Propriety	34.43
Veracity	2.62
Unclear	0

Table 5. Judgement categories in percentages.

It is interesting to note that Lyons frequently expressed judgements of propriety. Propriety reflects the judgments people make about others' actions, which are then evaluated in terms of morality or ethics. Her statement reflects how "Irish nationalism became a genuine mass phenomenon" (O'Connor, 599) – in the revolutionary years, Irish nationalists greatly appreciated mutual solidarity and loyalty in their armed struggle against the British, probably more than ever before. It is therefore no surprise that Lyons often refers to other people's sense of propriety, as in the following example:

6. One of the Church St. priests, Fr. Columbus, stayed in the room with us till morning by way of protection.

Lyons emphasises here the priest's benevolence in his attempt to protect these women from possible violence and abuse from British soldiers. As my research demonstrates, actions like this one were not only mentioned, but remarked upon throughout Lyons's statement.

In her statement, there is a moment in which Lyons makes a powerful judgement of propriety concerning her religious beliefs, after a British officer forced her to read aloud the following statement: "Sin no more lest a worse thing come unto thee." Lyons's response to this perceived humiliation captures the prominent role that religion played in the Easter Rising:

7. We have not committed any sin.

While the officer judges the Rising as a sinful act to be judged by God, Lyons invokes the same religious authority to assert the rightfulness and moral propriety of their actions against the British. This situation serves as an illustration of how "Catholicism functioned for the Irish not only as belief, rite and morality but also as defiance and as an alternative identity to that demanded by the British Empire" (O'Connor, 599). For Lyons and many of her comrades, the cause of Irish independence was intimately linked with religious fervour.

Lyons also makes numerous judgements on capacity and tenacity. Both categories present similar percentages (Table 5), as they often appear together in her witness statement. Because of the dangerous nature of the Rising, it was fundamental to have the necessary capacity, whether mental or physical, to help the Volunteers, and to be resolute enough to carry out the tasks and duties the rebellion entailed. In her statement, Lyons repeatedly praised the Volunteers' capacity and tenacity as they managed to take over a new post during the Rising (8), while also commending the couriers on their courage, ability and resolution to carry messages from one place to another (9):

8. I watched the Vols. taking over the Bridewell.

9. It proved very useful in getting him through the enemy line with messages.

At this time, being caught with a message from the enemy could mean imprisonment, torture and possible death.

In Table 6 below, we can see the percentages of use of the different appreciation categories. In its less strict definition (Benítez-Castro and Hidalgo-Tenorio), appreciation evaluates events, objects and people as well, whether aesthetically or from a social-valuation point of view:

APPRECIATION CATEGORY	%
Reaction	9.15
Composition	22.18
Social-valuation	68.66

Table 6. Appreciation categories in percentages.

Probably because the Rising involved a collective effort, in Lyons's statement the category that presented the highest rate of usage was social-valuation, which assesses how useful actions, objects or people are from a social point of view. Throughout her statement, Lyons referred to the Volunteers by their full names, as she did in relation to the organisations involved and the occupied buildings in the Rising. By choosing to refer to those entities by their full names, Lyons was reinforcing their social relevance (10). She is also explicit about the actions that Cumann na mBan members were supposed to carry out, such as helping the Volunteers and using their houses as safe houses, among other tasks that were socially valued. These beliefs can be observed in examples (11) and (12).

10. I met Frank Fahy and Peadar Clancy.
11. Then Barney Mellows came in and woke us.
12. Pauline Morkan invited us to spend the night at her house.

In (10) and (11) Lyons referred to the leaders by their full names. It is worth mentioning that these men were all actively involved in the Rising, and those who survived the rebellion continued to fight for an independent Ireland. In (12), Lyons used the same strategy and referred to a Cumann na mBan member by her full name, mentioning her comrade's act of group solidarity when she offered her own place for the recently released prisoners to spend the night safely – she "invited us."

Within the appreciation category, a subcategory that presents regular occurrence is that of composition (22.18%). This subcategory is used to evaluate the proportionality or balance and details of all types of entities and events. Lyons often used composition in order to describe the events that were taking place during the Rising, as in (13):

13. There was a great deal of noise of fighting, rumours and reports.

Here, Lyons pictures her involvement in the Rising by re-imagining the deafening ("a great deal of") noise of "fighting, rumours and reports." Though she seemingly prevents herself from expressing her own emotions, this passage transmits her confusion and, perhaps, fear, overwhelmed as she was by the situation. Another case of composition is (14), where Lyons reminisces about Ned Daly and Seamus O'Sullivan, two important Irish Volunteers:

14. They were the nearest approach to British officers in appearance and inspired us girls with feelings of enthusiasm and caused us many heart throbs.

Here, Lyons describes their appearance in terms of proportionality: there was more of the quality "British-looking" in Dally and O'Sullivan than in any other Irish Volunteer – most Irish rebels were not professional soldiers. Again, as in (13), Lyons transmits her emotions via composition, in this case through a positive appreciation of how these two Irish men were ready for combat, since they resembled British officers in their strength, disciplined appearance and skill. Lyons is, indeed, describing an emotional experience as she goes on to detail the emotions that Dally and O'Sullivan arose in young girls: "[They] inspired us girls with feelings of enthusiasm and caused us many throbs."

Finally, to reinforce the points previously made, the analysis now moves to the percentages of the appraiser and appraised categories (Table 7). The most noteworthy aspect here is that, within the category of appraised, which refers to what is being evaluated, the subcategory "other-appraised" presents the highest frequency.

APPRAISER CATEGORY	%	APPRAISED CATEGORY	%
Writer-appraiser	81.83	Self-appraised	18.69
Other-appraiser	4.01	Other-appraised	66.91
Non-applicable app.	14.69	Non-applicable app.	14.39

Table 7. Appraiser and appraised categories in percentages.

As an appraiser (81.83%), Lyons evaluated other people's actions and behaviour (66.91%), but hardly her own (18.69%), which supports the idea that she rejected a self-centred description of the Rising, preferring instead to focus on the collective struggle. In (15), through her use of appreciation and not of affect terms, Lyons praises her father because of his commitment to the cause of Irish nationalism:

15. He joined the Volunteers after their foundation in Roscommon, even though he was 65 years of age.

As stated earlier, during this crucial time in the history of Ireland, personal qualities of solidarity, loyalty and bravery were greatly admired among Irish nationalists. Furthermore, example (15) once again demonstrates how, even though Lyons seldom used affect terms about others and even less about herself, she did express her emotions eloquently through her appreciations and detailed descriptions of events and other people's actions.

Conclusion

An Appraisal Theory analysis of Brigid Lyons's statement reveals that she recalled her participation in the Rising via appreciation and judgement terms predominantly. Surprisingly for such a terrifying event, causing her much distress, insecurity and fear, Lyons hardly used affect terms to describe the Easter Rising. Even in those few cases where she did use affect terms, these expressions mostly concerned other people's emotions and her use of a language of proximity towards her relatives, friends and comrades. However, the scarcity of affect terms should not lead us to the wrong conclusion that Lyons remained emotionless, or emotionally detached, during the Rising. As I have argued drawing on Bednarek's concept of emotion talk, emotional experiences may be more vividly conveyed through terms that do not explicitly denote emotion. It is precisely because of Lyon's incessant use of judgement and appreciation expressions that emotions remain palpable in her statement. Had the traditional concept of emotional talk (which only considers words that explicitly express emotions) been applied, the nuances of Lyons's emotions would have been missed in the linguistic analysis.

Given her nationalist beliefs and feminist involvement in Cumann na mBan, I have argued here that Lyons may have channelled most of her emotional experience through her sense of collective commitment in her fight for Irish (including women's) emancipation. Limited only to one witness statement, my study will hopefully encourage the analysis of many other women's witness statements, in order to give a more complete account of how women experienced the Irish anti-colonial struggle, and how they contributed to, and fought for, Irish independence.

Appendix

Below is a number of relevant passages taken from Lyons's witness statement, as a complement to the analysis. In the social-valuation passages, the reader will notice how Lyons refers to people by their full names and how she names important Irish events and buildings, thus indicating their relevance. In the passages referring to capacity/tenacity, it can be observed that Lyons judged herself, other people and their actions in terms of the usefulness of their actions and their level of engagement in the activities. This Appendix closes with some excerpts about her reflections on religion and imprisonment.

Social-valuation

My earliest recollection of association with things national was my father's account of his period in Sligo Gaol for his connection with the Land League. He joined the Volunteers after their foundation in Roscommon, although he was 65 years of age. When I was 8 I went to live with my uncle on my mother's side, a brother of Joe McGuinness, in Longford.

One of my most vivid recollections before the Rising was a journey to a meeting in Athenry on an outside car. I was accompanied by M. Allen and the Nicolls. The meeting was addressed by The O'Rahilly.

With my uncle, Frank McGuinness and a man called Tom Bannon, a National Teacher, I motored up to Dublin on the Tuesday or Wednesday of Easter Week to take part in the Rising.

I was welcomed by Eamon Duggan whom I met for the first time. I cannot remember anyone else. I hastened on to the Four Courts and got in through a hole in the wall. Somebody may have come with us from Church St. My uncle Joe was delighted to see us and brought me to Ned Daly. I was thrilled with him and felt that although he was quiet he was very forceful. What I felt about him the first time I met him the previous summer, and also about Seamus Sullivan – they probably would not care to be told this – was that they were the nearest approach to British officers in appearance and inspired us girls with feelings of enthusiasm and caused us many heart throbs. I met Frank Fahy and Peadar Clancy. He was fascinating and epitomised for me all the attractive heroes in Irish history.

Capacity/Tenacity

My cousin Rose McGuinness was in the Four courts also, but she fell and cut her hands with a lemonade bottle she was carrying, so she was going around all the week with bandaged hands. She was then detailed for dispatch work. When my uncle Frank came back he had messages and the password "Antonio." So I and Mr. Bannon went down Bolton St., Church St. etc. hiding in doorways to escape the snipers' bullets. At the first barricade we were challenged and, having given the password, were allowed to pass through the cab that formed the centre of the barricade.

I went with Miss Derham, escorted by a Volunteer, I think Barney Mellows. It was a hazardous expedition over broken glass and with bullets flying; taking shelter from time to time, to No. 5 Church St., the home of a Mr. Michael Lennon. This was just before daybreak and we were barely able to make our way in the grey dawn. We got a fire going in the house. Mr. Lennon was there, but the family was gone. He did all the chores, bringing coal, etc. He was, of course, a Volunteer himself.

The Linenhall Bks. which was quite near was taken by the Volunteers and set on fire, and the British military seemed to have arrived in force and were heavily engaged by the Volunteers. There was deafening firing also from Ganly's and the Mendicity Institute. The sniping was uninterrupted.

Religion

The only really brutal individual we met during the whole time was a warder called Beatty. We were left standing in the hall for a time while he ranted and raved at us. Somebody directed him to take us to certain floors and he said "Bring them down this way first" and he marched us down an old corridor and held up his lantern and said "Read that" and I read out "Sin no more lest a worse thing come unto thee." I said "We have not committed any sin." He said "Shut up, it's to the 'drop' you should be taken, every one of you."

Surrender and Prison

I think it was on Saturday in the late afternoon the atmosphere seemed to change and things grew quiet. A Volunteer rushed in and asked me for a hatchet – we had been using it for chopping wood – and he started to hack the butt of his rifle rather than surrender it. Some others of the Volunteers tried to cut a hole through the wall of the backyard, though I don't know where that would have brought them to. Tom Walsh was among them and he and others cried bitterly. Three fellows came to me and gave me their revolvers to keep for them, thinking that I would get away. Eventually, quite suddenly, I found myself alone.

I went back to the Four Courts to the hole in the wall. I met Peadar Clancy coming towards me and, very politely, in spite of his distress, he helped me through the hole in the wall. I asked "what is happening?" He said "There is talk of surrender and they are all being taken to the Castle." He came back with me to No. 5 Church St. in the deep dusk and there I made sandwiches for him with the food I had taken back from the man, and wrapped them up for him. When I met him after his release in 1917, he told me they saved his life and those of some of his comrades who spent the night in the Rotunda Gardens, where I think they were taken.

About 10 a.m. we were all brought downstairs and herded into a lorry and brought to Richmond Bks. I met Lt. Lindsay again and told him he had broken his word. He did seem distressed about it. About eight of us were thrown into one room, the two Sullivan girls, Pauline Morkan, Flossie Mead and Carrie Mitchell – she was not Cumann na mBan. Winnie Carney was in the room with us too. The sentries outside threw us a few dog biscuits through the fanlight. That was all the food we had that day. During the day we were brought out one by one and interviewed by a couple of officers. About 7 p.m. we were all marched down to the barrack square where we found the Countess and a number of others lined up. During that day also we had had glimpses of Volunteers lined up there too. We were marched out the gate to Kilmainham and the crowds outside along the route gave us a mixed reception, cheering, jeering, boohing and making remarks, mostly uncomplimentary. The Countess was the only one in uniform and she attracted most of the attention. We were all a bedraggled lot after the week and certainly did not look our best. I'll never forget the dreariness, squalor and sordidness of Kilmainham when we came in there that lovely summer evening – Richmond Barracks had been bright.

We were there for all the executions. We used to hear the shots in the mornings. Every day fresh contingents of women were brought in and we used to see them when we were brought out for our short morning and evening exercise. The food was awful – a tin of slimy cocoa and a hunk of bread in the morning, the same tin with a sort of greasy stew and bad potatoes for dinner, the same tin with porridge in the evening. We got no implements of any kind to eat with. When we complained they told us they were not expecting so many visitors. We all got sick on the second or third day and the doctor ordered that we be put only two in a cell and we were given bed-boards and a blanket. Then Carrie Mitchell was released. I was assigned to a cell in which a street woman was huddled in the corner. I refused, young as I was, to stay in it and I was put in with a Miss Mulhall. She was a Town Councillor. I was alone a couple of nights. The Countess Plunkett, who got in a meal from outside, sent me in tea and an egg one night. That was the high light of my stay. We were interviewed a couple of times with a view to extracting any information we had about the Volunteers. We refused, of course, to give any. They were interested in the fact that I was a student in Galway and plied me with questions about it. On the Sunday we were let to Mass in the gallery with a heavy escort of soldiers. The Volunteers were down stairs and we saw Kent, Colbert and Houston going to Communion. These were executed the next day.

Works Cited

Primary Sources

Irish Military Archives
Military Service Pensions Collection (1916–1923):
"Lyons, Brigid." 24SP13615
UAM-Corpus Tool

Secondary sources

Bednarek, Monika. *Emotion Talk across Corpora*. Palgrave Macmillan, 2008.
Benítez-Castro, Miguel-Ángel and Hidalgo-Tenorio, Encarnación. "Rethinking Martin and White's Affect Taxonomy. A Psychologically-inspired Approach to the Linguistic Expression of Emotion." *Emotion in Discourse*, edited by J. Lachlan Mackenzie and Laura Alba-Juez, John Benjamins Publishing Company, 2019, pp. 301–32.
Crowe, Noelene Beckett. "Dr. Brigid Lyons Thornton. Physician/ Revolutionary." *Our Irish Heritage,* 30 December 2014, www.ouririshheritage.org/content/archive/people/101_mayo_people/military-revolutionary-activists/dr_brigid_lyons_thornton. Accessed 23 Feb. 2020.
"CumannnamBan Constitution." *South Dublin County Libraries,* www.source.southdublinlibraries.ie/bitstream/10599/10463/3/Constitution_OCR.pdf. Accessed 14 Nov. 2016.
Ferriter, Diarmaid. *The Transformation of Ireland, 1900–2000*. Profile Books, 2005.
Fontaine, Johnny J. R. "Dimensional, Basic Emotion, and Componential Approaches to Meaning in Psychological Emotion Research." *Components*

of Emotional Meaning: A Sourcebook, edited by Johnny J. R. Fontaine, Klaus R. Scherer and Cristina Soriano, Oxford University Press, 2013, pp. 1–26.
Gordon, Steven. "The Sociology of Sentiments and Emotion." *Social Psychology: Sociological Perspectives*, edited by Ralph H. Turner and Morris Rosenberg, Basic, 1981, pp. 562–92.
Griffiths, Paul E. *What Emotions Really Are: The Problem of Psychological Categories*. University of Chicago Press, 1997.
Halliday, Michael. *An Introduction to Functional Grammar*. Arnold, 1985.
Halliday, Michael and Christina Matthiessen. *Halliday's Introduction to Functional Grammar*. 4thed, Routledge, 2014.
Kee, Robert. *Ireland: A History*. Abacus, 1995.
Kiberd, Declan. *Inventing Ireland: The Literature of the Modern Nation*. Vintage, 1996.
Konstan, David. "Affect and Emotion in Greek Literature." *Oxford Handbooks Online*, Oct. 2015, www.oxfordhandbooks.com/view/10.1093/oxfordhb/978019 9935390.001.0001/oxfordhb-9780199935390-e-41. Accessed 27 Feb. 2020.
McGarry, Fearghal. *The Rising. Ireland: Easter 1916*. Oxford University Press, 2010.
———. "Helena Molony: A Revolutionary Life," *History Ireland*, vol. 21, no. 4, 2013, www.historyireland.com/18th-19th-century-history/helena-molony-a-revolutionary-life. Accessed 7 Feb. 2020.
Martin, James R. and Peter R. R. White. *The Language of Evaluation: Appraisal in English*. Palgrave Macmillan, 2005.
O'Connor, Thomas. "Religion and Identity: The Irish Dilemma." *The Furrow*, vol. 50, no. 11, 1999, pp. 596–603.
O'Malley, Cormac. *Modern Ireland and Revolution: Ernie O'Malley in Context*. E-book, Irish Academic Press, 2016.
Roseman, Ira J. and Craig A. Smith. "Appraisal Theory: Overview, Assumptions, Varieties, Controversies." *Appraisal Processes in Emotion: Theory, Methods, Research*, edited by Klaus R. Scherer, Angela Schorr and Tom Johnstone, Oxford University Press, 2011, pp. 3–19.
Sayers, Rachel. "Bridig Lyons Thornton, Rebel, Soldier and Doctor." *Women's Museum of Ireland*, 2013, www.womensmuseumofireland.ie/articles/brigid-lyons-thornton. Accessed 10 Feb. 2020.
Sebestyen, Amanda. *Prison Letters of Countess Markievicz*. Virago Press, 1987.
"Tagset." *Sketch Engine: Oxford English*, www.sketchengine.eu/oxford-english-corpus-tagset. Accessed 23 Feb. 2020.

5

Resurrecting the Rebellion: A Postcolonial Reading of Two Historical Documentaries on the Easter Rising

Paul O'Mahony

Introduction

The history of Ireland as a British colony is as contentious an issue today as it was one hundred years ago. In *A Pocket History Book of Ireland* (2010), Joseph McCullough explains how "the Norman invasion caused over eight centuries of English involvement in the governing of Ireland" (46). From almost the very beginning, once British rule was imposed on Ireland, the native Irish began to lose both power and wealth. In 1167, Henry II of England became the first King of England to come to Ireland. McCullough explains how, while Ireland did not change in any significant way at that time, once the king passed on control to his son John, the situation began to deteriorate quickly after he "took land" and "alienated most of the population" (49). From this significant juncture in history onwards, Ireland was treated as a colony of Britain, ruled by either royals or politicians from another country, usually with little or no input into the managing of its own affairs.

From the very beginning of occupation to the time of independence, there had been multiple uprisings against the forces of the Crown. All such attempts ended in bloody failure. Tim Pat Coogan explains how, after Theobald Wolfe Tone's revolt in 1798, it was one hundred and twenty years later, in 1916, before another serious attempt at dismantling British power was to occur. In the intervening years various famines had ravaged the country, but the most harmful one occurred in mid-nineteenth century, resulting in more than one million dead and a further two million being forced to emigrate to Britain, America, Australia and elsewhere. Coogan's analysis of the Great Hunger, as it became known, was that it re-enshrined "Wolfe Tone's philosophy of breaking the relationship by striking at England when she was involved with a foreign enemy" (13). For the rebels of 1916, the First World War would later provide such an opportunity.

In the years preceding the Easter Rising, the British government had promised to enact the Home Rule Bill, which would allow Ireland to govern itself while remaining loyal to the Crown. This promise, however, had been delayed and by 1916 many Irish were questioning whether it would ever arrive. A decision was made by the Irish Citizen Army – a paramilitary group of trained trade union volunteers –, and members of the Irish Republican Brotherhood (IRB) – an anti-constitutional physical-force Republican organisation. The plans for the attack were designed by Joseph Mary Plunkett who, according to Coogan, issued orders that "in Dublin, main buildings were to be seized and the roads and railways interdicted so that no military reinforcements could get into the city" (65). The group were well aware that their odds of a military victory against the British army were extremely unlikely. The Easter Rising, nevertheless, went ahead although its only real hope of success lay in the thought that it would encourage the native population to join in fighting for the right to independence. According to Roy Foster, "only about 1,600 members of the Irish Volunteers and Irish Citizen army turned out in Dublin" (*History*, 198). Foster further argues that "the main victims of the proclamation of the Irish Republic were thus unarmed civilians, whose suffering was compounded by the wreckage of central Dublin, widespread looting, disruption of employment, and the interruption of postal services" (198). It was not long before the vastly out-numbered and out-gunned rebels were defeated and the centre of Dublin lay in ruins. Within three days of the surrender by the rebels, news travelled through the country that the leaders had been shot for their roles in the rebellion. This was then followed by a continuation of executions of others involved. Fifteen revolutionaries in all were shot by a firing squad after a court martial, among them teachers and poets. These actions by the British government led to a change in public opinion. As sympathy for the rebels grew, so did anger against the actions of the British. As a result, the events that took place on Easter 1916 would ultimately lead to the founding of the Republic of Ireland and the partition of the island of Ireland.

Drawing on this historical scenario, the present chapter offers a comparative analysis of two documentaries released in 2016: *1916: The Irish Rebellion* by Ruán Magan and Pat Collins and the BBC documentary *Easter 1916: The Enemy Files*, directed by Andrew Gallimore. The analysis pays particular attention to the divergent representations of the rebels: as heroic martyrs in one film and as an unnecessarily violent crowd in the other.

Ireland and Postcolonial Theory

This study shall approach contemporary understandings of the Rising under the light of postcolonial theory. Postcolonial Studies entered the Irish scene in the early 1980s via the Field Day Project, set in Derry in Northern Ireland. This was an artistic, cultural and political project meant to overcome longstanding religious and political conflicts in Ireland, at the time still ruining many lives in the North. A further idea driving Field Day was to intervene in the contemporary heated debates between historical revisionism and nationalism via postcolonial criticism.[1] From the start, both through the plays and performances of the Field Day Theatre Company and through the Field Day Pamphlets (a series of fifteen critical pieces by Seamus Deane, Edward Said, Terry Eagleton, Richard Kearney and Seamus Heaney, among others), the project established its postcolonial credentials. Yet, even before the work of Field Day, one of the foremost international figures within the field of postcolonial criticism, Edward Said, had already referred to Ireland as a colony of the British Empire.

In his seminal work *Orientalism* (1979), Edward Said took over Franz Fanon's research into the construction of binary hierarchies while adding a Foucauldian touch of his own which emphasises the importance, for the West, of producing discourses on the East so as to construct an idea of the East which can be contained, policed and handled. Said examines how imperialism depends on a series of hierarchical binaries through which the East is categorised as uncivilised, feminine and dangerous, while the West is viewed as civilised, masculine and disciplined. "The essence of Orientalism," Said concludes, "is the ineradicable distinction between Western superiority and Oriental inferiority" (51). With specific relation to Ireland, Edward Said cited the Irish struggle for independence as a major influence on his work. He stated in an interview that, in relation to his research, he was "grateful to Ireland, especially for its literary and cultural example" (Whelan and Pollack, 13). Indeed, Said added that Ireland should be categorised as postcolonial, along with India and South Africa, as it is a place which offered a "spirit of resistance" which did not depend on arms alone (Whelan and Pollack, 13).

From the nineties onwards, some very prestigious Irish intellectuals and critics have published at least part of their work looking at Ireland from a postcolonial perspective. In this respect, the pioneering work of Declan Kiberd, *Inventing Ireland: the Literature of the Modern Nation* (1995), deserves mention, together with David Lloyd's *Anomalous States: Irish Writing and the Post-colonial Moment* (1993) and "Colonial Trauma/Postcolonial Recovery?" (2000), Joe Cleary's "Misplaced Ideas? Colonialism, Location and Dislocation in Irish Studies" (2003) and Richard Pine's *The Disappointed Bridge: Ireland and the*

---

[1] The discrepancies between historical revisionism, nationalism and postcolonialism will be explained in the following section.

Post-Colonial World (2014).

Yet, in spite of Ireland's sharing processes, circumstances, effects and affects with other colonies which amply justify a postcolonial approach, there are also certain factors that set the country apart: its European geographical location – so close to the imperial power – placed Ireland among western, civilised countries; or the racially unmarked nature of its population, among others. However, until 1922 Ireland was a British colony and its native people had historically been racialised and represented as having simian, monstrous, or black features. This is one of the many dislocations – Ireland's liminal position between civilisation and savagery – which may go to explain why, in 1996, Luke Gibbons defined the country as "a First World country, but with a Third World memory" (3), thus perfectly summarising the clash between the modern (colonial and postcolonial) and the pre-modern (native) that colonies experience (del Río).

Seamus Deane and David Lloyd have also provided definitions of Ireland meant to illustrate the country's postcolonial condition. In this respect, Seamus Deane considered Ireland a "strange country":

> The country remains strange in its failure to be normal; the normal remains strange in its failure to be defined as anything other than the negative of strange. Normality is an economic condition; strangeness a cultural one. Since Burke, there has been a series of strenuous efforts to effect the convergence of the twain, even though the very premises of their separation has been powerful enough in assuring that the twain will never meet. (197)

Similarly, David Lloyd referred to the "anomalous state" of Irish culture, marked

> ... by a self-estrangement which can take forms ranging from simple commodification to an almost formalist defamiliarization ... and which is the site of a profoundly contradictory and intensely political ambivalence. In the Irish context, that perception of self-estrangement, of being perceived and perceiving through alien media, has been expressed frequently and variously. (*Anomalous*, 1–2)

In Deane's case, as in Gibbons's definition above, Ireland is located in an in-between space – between the First and Third Worlds, normality and strangeness –, whilst Lloyd's remarks on Irish culture highlight a pervasive feeling of alienation suggesting a split and fragmented subjectivity: Ireland's liminality and divisive nature point towards the country's traumatic postcolonial legacy.

Critical and Cultural Background of the Documentaries

Before moving onto a postcolonial analysis of the Easter Rising documentaries, it is necessary to provide some background into the specific genre of documentary making. In *Introduction to Documentary* (2010), Bill Nichols defines the documentary as a genre which "draws on and refers to historical reality while representing it from a distinct perspective," a viewpoint which is "neither a fictional invention nor a factual reproduction" (6–7). Nichols goes on to explain that documentaries usually concentrate on the "historical world" that we, as human beings, share (7). A critical factor is that documentaries need to project and reinforce an appearance of objectivity, sustained by "verifiable evidence" (Nichols, 8). To do so, Sheila Curran Bernard remarks, directors engage in a "range of creative choices about a film's structure, point of view, balance, style, casting and more" (1). Bernard explains how, at the heart of a good documentary is the ability of the film to tell a story which engages with the audience and offers some type of a "credible resolution" (1). In *The Politics of Documentary* (2007), Chanan explains how "the documentary claim on reality is not just a question but a matter of practical concern to authority, at times a matter of law, and even state" (37). In other words, if a documentary intends to illuminate unknown facts to an audience, it may discomfit those in power whose interest is to maintain the status quo.

During 2016, and with the idea of commemorating the centenary of the Easter Rising, two documentaries were produced which presented very different viewpoints on a crucial Irish historical event. These documentaries can be said to illustrate separate historiographical tendencies in Ireland, and can be related to the disputes in the Ireland of the 1980s and 1990s between revisionist, nationalist and postcolonial historiography. Briefly, nationalist historiography – the official historical narrative in the south and for the nationalist Northern population until the late 1960s – has conventionally seen Irish history as the relentless heroic struggle of a dominated and colonised people towards independence and liberation. From this perspective, Irish history has continuously moved in that direction, through military failures, abortive rebellions and numerous deaths, just to achieve this rightful objective. The process culminated partially with the emergence of the Irish Free State in 1922 but is still to be achieved in the North, since the ideal of a single nation-state has not yet been realised. Nationalist history is a history of heroes and martyrs, a history that accentuates the personal and epic dimension of events and that relies heavily on the myth of an ideal unity of culture and a collective national identity. It is also a history that tends towards a dualistic, melodramatic and Manichean worldview, whereby the native Irish are cast as either innocent victims or romantic rebels, and the British as the all-powerful yet villainous victimisers.

Roy Foster, probably the most prestigious defender and practitioner of historical revisionism in Ireland, questioned the validity and truth-value of nationalist historiography on the grounds of the latter's treatment of history as narrative and its reliance on Irish myth, legend and folklore. These are Forster's words:

> Again and again in Irish history, one is struck by the importance of the narrative mode: the idea that Irish history is a "story," and the implications that this carries about it of a beginning, a middle, and the sense of an ending. Not to mention heroes, villains, donors, guests, plots, revelations and all other elements of the story form. And the formal modes of *Bildungsroman*, ghost story, deliverance-tale, family romance, all of which have lent motifs to the ways Irish history has been told. ("Lovely Magic," 4)

On the other hand, in Ireland historical revisionism emerged in the 1930s with historians T. W. Moody and R. Dudley Edwards and the founding of the journal *Irish Historical Studies*. Theirs was an attempt to professionalise Irish historiography, to turn it into a value-free, impartial and objective discipline by using empirical methodologies (a scientific model of history). In spite of its initial impetus towards an objective, empirical, scientific treatment of history, in time, and particularly with the outburst of violence in the North, revisionism came to be seen as a form of British nationalism, as simply a reaction to nationalist historiography, which many revisionist historians considered responsible for the resurgence of violence and hatred in Northern Ireland. By siphoning off the historical and political sources of the Troubles into ethnic, cultural and/ or religious arguments, revisionism tried to pass off as a disinterested cure for Northern evils.

Revisionism's aspirations to historical objectivity and political neutrality went against the poststructuralist and postmodern views on language and discourse (and their relationship with truth, reality and authenticity) which came to dominate the critical panorama after the "linguistic turn." In Ireland, Luke Gibbons addressed historical revisionism in the following terms, making explicit reference to historian F.S.S. Lyons's revisionist ideas:

> Thus, when Lyons protests that "myth" has obscured "reality" in our understanding of certain "symbolic" events, he does not seem to realize that the very existence of a *symbolic* dimension in human action requires a historical method that goes beyond literalist assumptions, and scientific norms of causality and certainty. For this reason, it is important not only to re-think but to *re-figure* Irish identity, to attend to those recalcitrant areas of experience which simply do not lend themselves to certainty, and which impel societies themselves towards indirect and figurative discourse – narratives, generic conventions, rhetorical tropes, allegory and other "literary" modes of composition. (Emphasis in the original; 17–18)

In a similar vein, Seamus Deane denounced historical revisionism on the grounds of its realist pretension to immediate and unmediated access to the truth and of its assumption of an impartial narrator, the historian, who claims that their historical discourse is absolutely free from rhetoric and ideological mystification. For Deane, these moves are nothing but ideological strategies meant to denounce nationalist and Republican myths and to conceal revisionism's defense of Britain's role in Ireland. From a revisionist perspective, at least from the implementation of the Union between the Kingdom of Ireland and the Kingdom of Great Britain (1801), Ireland cannot be considered a British colony, as S. Ellis affirms in the following quote: "The geographical proximity of Ireland and Britain and their long-standing economic interdependence encourage continual migration between the two islands, and consequently strong cultural ties, which cannot be described as colonial" (294).

As previously indicated in this chapter, in Ireland postcolonial approaches to Irish history and identity intervened with the intention of breaking up the confrontational slate-mate between nationalist and revisionist historiography. It did so first by internationalising the conflict: that is, by seeing it as related to many other colonial and postcolonial situations and processes around the world. Secondly, postcolonialism, while seen as deriving from nationalism, also tried to dismantle the monolithic, fixed and static narrative of the nation constructed by the Irish Free State. In this respect, Colin Graham states: "Post-colonialism's advantage over nationalism is that it has been able to move on with integrity to examine issues of class, gender and marginality which the 'nation' and its narratives cannot prioritize" (1109).

As for the Easter Rising more specifically, nationalist history would consider the rebellion as a necessary catalyst for the achievement of independence, whereas for revisionists there was never any need for the Easter Rising to occur: the violence, destruction and deaths that the Rising caused were completely unnecessary, just the result of irrational impulses, as Lyons in his *Ireland since the Famine* stated (33), and, more covertly, Yeats also suggested in "Easter 1916."

The confrontation in Irish Studies between the revisionist and the postcolonial school can be observed in the documentaries analysed here. Both documentaries, as will be revealed, had very different objectives and very different stories to tell about the 1916 Easter Rising. *Easter 1916: The Enemy Files*, a documentary made by the BBC (British Broadcasting Corporation), was released in 2016 in order to coincide with the centenary of the Rising. The documentary was directed by Andrew Gallimore, produced by Lucia Gavin and Mike Kean, and presented by Michael Portillo. The premise of the documentary, as one preview on *The Guardian* stated, was to reveal "how Britain saw – and crushed – the revolt" by "using cabinet papers, military orders and intelligence reports of the era" (Mueller *et al*).

The BBC's choice as presenter for *Easter 1916: The Enemy Files* was Michael

Portillo: a British journalist, broadcaster and conservative politician.[2] In addition to Portillo, the documentary invited a number of other commentators to share their opinion on the events surrounding the Rising. With the exceptions of Declan Kiberd and Robert Fisk, most, if not all of the other interviewees could be categorised as leaning towards the revisionist perspective on Irish history. The reception that *Easter 1916: The Enemy Files*[3] received could be best explained as mixed. On a webpage designed specifically by RTÉ, the documentary was described as both "challenging and controversial," adding that it threw "light on the difference between truth and fiction, offering an alarming glimpse at the many distortions that shape our history" ("The Enemy Files"). Billy Foley, of the *Irish News*, was glowing in his recommendation of the documentary, describing it as "a credit" to the national broadcasting company.

With twenty-five named donors for the project, including The American Ireland Fund and The President's Circle of Notre Dame, *Rebellion*, by Pat Collins and Ruan Magan, comes from a very different background to the BBC documentary. Produced by both the University of Notre Dame and COCO Television, the work had clear "artistic and strategic" objectives, according to the "1916 Project: A Preliminary Report" (Nic Dhiarmada and Fox). In this report, the artistic objective of the project is declared to be "to produce a landmark, three-part documentary that tells the story of Dublin's 1916 Rising and that will be broadcast nationally and internationally" (Nic Dhiarmada and Fox). The strategic objectives included raising the profile of the Keough-Naughton Institute for Irish Studies, engaging with the Irish diaspora around the world, and developing closer ties with a number of institutions and organisations, including the Irish Government and a number of Irish American organisations around the world. The intention of this documentary differs from that of the BBC documentary *Enemy Files*, the latter clearly stating in its introduction that its purpose is to tell the story of the Easter Rising using the words of "British politicians, soldiers, spies and bureaucrats" (00:01:15-00:01:30), that is, offering a primarily British perspective.

The creator and writer of *Rebellion* was Bríona Nic Dhiarmada, who, in a lecture titled "Screening the Irish Rebellion," explained the importance of the role that people from the United States played in the making of this documentary and expressed firmly the closeness of the relationship between Ireland and the USA both in 1916 and now. Central to this relationship was the fact that Irish people who had experienced civil and political freedoms in America had brought back that hope to Ireland, as well as the fact that the Easter Rising "appeared on the front page of the *New York Times* for sixteen

---
2   Michael Portillo was a member of Margaret Thatcher's political team in 1979 and served as junior minister under both Thatcher and John Major, entering Major's Cabinet in 1992.
3   For reasons of economy I will hereafter refer to the documentaries as *Enemy Files* and *Rebellion*.

consecutive days" (00:09:10-00:10:10). Nic Dhiarmada referred to her belief that the people who took part in the Rising "made a moral victory out of a military defeat," and that "without Irish American involvement, 1916 would not have happened" (00:08:30-00:12:15). Crucially, at least with regards to the premise in this chapter, Nic Dhiarmada described how she believed the documentary was critical not just with respect to Irish history, but also in the realm of world affairs, because of the fact that it reveals how "this tiny event in Ireland influenced places as far away as India" (00:15:27). Indeed, Nic Dhiarmada seemed to be drawing on Said's ideas when she stated that "Irish nationalism had a huge impact on Indian nationalism and later on in the 1960s on the whole decolonisation movement in Africa" (00:14:40-00:16:00). In order to gather the information needed for the documentary, Nic Dhiarmada explained that they had a team of researchers who went to Ireland to pour over the reams of newspaper headlines and academic articles in order to discover whether some historical facts had been missed. As well as the research carried out, she went on to describe how she and her team interviewed approximately forty historians over the course of two years. After this process was completed, the position of documentary narrator was then given to Liam Neeson, a well-known Northern Irish actor, who, as Nic Dhiarmada said, became "hugely supportive of the project" (00:41:30-00:42:30). Certainly, considering Neeson's leading role as Michael Collins in the 1996 eponymous Hollywood biopic, his participation in this project signalled this documentary's empathic approach to the Easter Rising.

Given the statements of intent of the two documentaries, the viewer can certainly expect that both representations of the Easter Rising incidents will be at variance. The following pages will discuss whether each documentary allowed for unbiased reporting and research into the events of Easter 1916 or, whether drawn by the echoes of history and by their respective interests, film makers decided on a tendentious view of history in order to please their separate audiences.

The Documentaries

The following analysis of both *Enemy Files* and *Rebellion* will concentrate on a number of particular scenes which will be examined from the perspective of postcolonial theory. In relation to *Enemy Files*, I will focus on specific details. The first such detail is the use of "infantalisation" by one of the interviewees, a usual colonial strategy based on the hierarchical binary adult/child, meant to demean the colonised. The second concerns the comparison of the rebels to contemporary Islamic extremists, and the third looks at how the language used in the film attempts to shape the viewers' opinion. Following this, I will provide an analysis of *Rebellion*. In this case, I will analyse how the rebels are portrayed throughout the three episodes and also their use of violence, which seems to fit Franz Fanon's views on the relationship between the oppressor and the oppressed. I will also refer to the connection made in the documentary between the Irish fight for freedom, the American Dream and the French Revolution. The last point in the analysis relates to how the documentary uses the letters of the dead rebels to frame them as martyrs.

1. *1916: The Enemy Files*

1916: The Enemy Files is a one part documentary which includes a minimal use of music and uses a narrator in much the same way as *Rebellion*. In formal terms, it can be considered a more traditional type of documentary, if compared to *Rebellion*, aimed mainly at a domestic (British) audience rather than an international one. In order to provide a background to the 1916 Rebellion, Portillo invites Prof. Roy Foster, a leading revisionist historian, to give a historical background on events preceding the Rising. The documentary uses military files, government documents and interviews to shape a revisionist version of the events which surrounded the Rising.

On hearing Foster's words in the documentary talking about the Easter Rising, the argument could be made that the historian is engaging in a process of "infantalisation."[4] The discursive strategy of figuring the colonised as children and the colonisers as adults had already been identified by Said as a common process of Orientalist thinking. The colonised is categorised as helpless or incompetent and therefore in need of help from the older, wiser, coloniser. In *Inventing Ireland*, Declan Kiberd refers to this tactic directly when he speaks of Britain's "imperial strategy of infantilizing the native culture" (102). Such a process is seemingly undertaken again by Foster in his explanation of events in Easter 1916. Foster, framing the rebels as if they were a group of teenagers, claims that "in some ways they are warring against their parents and their parents' generation as much as against the British State" (00:12:00-00:13:00). Figuring the Rising in terms of a generational confrontation, if even only partially, diffuses the political implications of the rebels' rightful fight for the independence of their country. Placing the Irish as rebelling teenagers, as Foster does, suggests that the British government was the parent or guardian of a wild, unruly lot. An explanation of why Foster came to this conclusion is conspicuous by its absence. Drawing on Said's *Orientalism*, it is hard not to conclude that Foster behaves here as "the spectator, the judge and the jury, of every facet of Oriental behaviour" (109).

The use of such Orientalist methods to attribute British power over the

---

4   I draw here on the definition given by *The Cambridge Online Dictionary*, which states that infantilisation involves the treatment of "someone as if that person were a child, with the result that they start behaving like that" ("Infantilize").

colonised is exemplified again after Portillo introduces Robert Fisk. Fisk is a renowned journalist who covered events in the Middle East and devoted a number of years of his journalistic career to report on the Troubles in Northern Ireland. Fisk has written widely on the Middle East and Ireland and is widely known as an unbiased reporter who is unafraid to challenge authority. Indeed, Fisk has often been a thorn in the side of both British and American governments. His book *The Great War for Civilisation: The Conquest of the Middle East* (2007) is among the most comprehensive historical accounts of the history of the Middle East and has often been critical of the crimes of the West. It might come, then, as a surprise that Fisk compares the Irish rebels to modern Islamic extremists. As Fisk explicitly declares, there is a

> ... very odd parallel between the kind of cult of blood and martyrdom which we can read about in the proclamation itself and another cult that exists today in the Middle East, which I don't even need to name, which also has a cult of blood sacrifice. Other people's blood too. (00:26:00-00:27:00)

The comparison is somewhat startling and we may wonder if it is necessary and accurate at all. Fearghal McGarry has also registered this simile. In his words: "Recent commentators have drawn comparisons with Al-Qaeda – another conspiratorial minority willing to sacrifice their lives in a spectacular act of symbolic violence against a superpower in a fanatical attempt to awaken the apathetic masses" (291). Then McGarry adds that the Islamic extremists "would be appalled by the egalitarianism of the Proclamation," although they would surely admire "their [the Easter 1916 revolutionaries'] tremendous success in legitimizing the violence that their iconic act of self-sacrifice would subsequently inspire" (291).

Far from merely endorsing a "cult of blood sacrifice," as Fisk bluntly puts it, the Irish freedom fighters sought to liberate their country from British rule and create a more egalitarian society.[5] On the contrary, the Islamic cults to which Fisk refers – which are popularly regarded as cruel, blood-thirsty and the most prominent threat to Western civilisation since 9/11 – pursue no democratic goals and use religious fundamentalism to justify their terrorist attacks. Aside from being biased, Fisk's identification of Irish freedom fighters with Islamic jihadism somehow sanitises British colonial oppression. By emphasising that those combating British rule claimed "other people's blood too," Fisk delegitimises the Easter Rising rebels' anti-colonial struggle since their use of violence is compared with the fear that Islamic terrorism provokes today on a global scale.

Fisk's word-choices merit further attention, as when he uses the term "cult."

---

5   Nonetheless, as became clear later on with the Civil War, within the Irish revolutionaries there were also different ideas of what kind of nation they wanted.

For Irish freedom fighters, religious symbolism was indeed important: blood sacrifice and martyrdom lie deep in Christianity, and the choice of Easter Week for the Rebellion allowed them to see themselves as Christ-like figures who were giving their lives to save their country. Yet they also drew on Celtic mythology through the figure of the legendary hero Cuchulainn, who defended the province of Ulster against the invading armies of queen Medb of Connaught. And they also considered their rebellion as establishing a historical continuity with the 1798 rebellion of the Society of United Irishmen, the 1848 Young Ireland Rising and the 1867 Fenian Rebellion. Fisk, of course, obviates such cultural referents, and rather offers a de-contextualised interpretation that equates the "cult" of Irish rebels to that of "dangerous" Islamic groups in the Middle-East.

What emerges from Fisk's interpretation is that, when analysing a rebellion like Easter Rising, one central question must be "whether violence, as a principle, could be a moral means to just ends" (Benjamin, 236). Whereas the second documentary, as we shall see, resolves such dilemma by establishing parallels with culturally celebrated episodes of national liberation such as the American Revolution, Fisk in *Enemy Files* clearly perceives no "just ends" in the Irish rebels' use of violence, likening it to Islamic extremism.

Because of the ways in which terms like "cult" and "blood sacrifice" are used in the documentary, we must then conclude that "language is a fundamental site of struggle for post-colonial discourse because the colonial process itself begins in language" (Ashcroft, Griffiths and Tiffin, 283). As an example, an interesting moment in the documentary occurs when Portillo uses the word "plot." This word is mentioned four times to describe the Easter Rising. One of these is the final scene, which zooms in on the word "plot," carved in the graveyard of Dublin's Glasnevin cemetery, the resting place of many of those involved in the Rising. The word itself is used in the documentary to define two significant events. One meaning of "plot" is "a secret plan made by several people to do something that is wrong, harmful, or not legal, especially to do damage to a person or government" ("Plot"). This meaning is used in the opening section of the documentary in which Portillo describes "a secret plot in the heart of the mighty but distracted British Empire" (00:03:00-00:04:00). This sentence is critical in the shaping of the viewer's opinion of the conditions which existed at the time of the rebellion. The rebels are consequently portrayed as sneaky, criminal and morally corrupt. The British Empire, meanwhile, is displayed as mighty, an adjective which conveys a sense of greatness. This in turn may lead to assumptions by the audience that orders carried out by those who represented the Empire attained a certain moral justification against the actions of the lesser, morally corrupt rebels. Moreover, the allusion to the Empire's distractedness adds additional distaste towards the rebels' activities. It marks them as people unwilling to fight a fair battle. Such a suggestion could barely hold much weight given the shortage of man power or weaponry the rebels had, especially when compared to the wealth and manpower of the British army.

The second meaning assigned to the word "plot," which is recalled in the documentary, is that of a piece of land marked for a particular purpose. In the documentary, this word is used at the very last moment as the camera zooms over the graves of the dead rebels in Glasnevin Cemetery in Dublin while focusing on the words "Republic Plot" (00:37:00-00:38:00). The inclusion of this moment as the final scene in the documentary is extremely significant, especially when taking into account how the word was used earlier on. The suggestion is that those rebels who "plotted" at the beginning to take on the British Empire lay dead now in this Republican "plot" as a result. This use of language is only an illustration of how a seemingly objective genre, like the documentary, can create subtle associations that convey negative judgements, in this case, about the Rising.

2. *1916: The Irish Rebellion*

My analysis of *1916: The Irish Rebellion* will concentrate on issues such as language, the representations of Irish rebels as martyrs, the use of violence as a means of acquiring freedom from oppression, and the framing of the Easter Rising as an international event being watched closely by many abroad, particularly in the United States. The immediately noticeable difference between the BBC documentary and *Rebellion* is that the latter is much longer. In fact, with three episodes of fifty-two minutes each, entitled "Awakening," "Insurrection" and "When Myth and History Rhyme," this documentary is almost three times as long. As a result, *Rebellion* offers a version of events which has both the room and the scope to delve deeper into the causes and the effects of the Easter Rising. The documentary begins by reviewing the history of British rule in Ireland, an evaluation which is important in order for the audience to appreciate the scale of the timeline of events leading up to the Rising. Its retelling of the Rising is done, in part, by interviewing modern day historians and academics. In addition, the documentary draws heavily from the letters of the dead rebels, many of which were written to family members and loved ones as they awaited execution. Central figures discussed in the documentary include Patrick Pearse, whose beliefs and actions, as will be seen, can be closely linked to the writings of both Fanon and Said. In addition, there is much reference to the influence of Irish America on the Rising, framed as a seminal moment, not only in Ireland, but also internationally.

The need for the Easter Rising to gain support from the world was indeed an objective of those involved. In episode two, the documentary quotes from the witness statement of Jim Ryan, a member of the Irish Volunteers. Ryan declared that, as the fighting went on, there was an "atmosphere of subdued excitement and determination," adding that they "talked of maybe making enough noise to draw the attention of the outside world" (00:29:50-00:30:19). The documentary then goes on to explain the importance of *The New York Times*. Robert Schmuhl explains how the paper "devoted fourteen days to coverage of the Easter Rising on its front page" (00:30:40-00:30:52). The connection between the Irish hope for freedom and America's realisation of their own freedom is reinforced as the words "all men are created equal" are written in large letters across the screen. The point being made, then, is that Ireland, like the United States in the past, was being governed by a foreign power against its will. Irish men and women who travelled to the United States and lived the American Dream were inspired by such an ideal of political freedom, and sought to gain the same degree of liberty for themselves in Ireland.

In order for such a dream to be realised it first needed to be dreamt. As Edward Said explains "within the nationalist revival, in Ireland and elsewhere, there were two distinct political moments, each with its own imaginative culture, the second unthinkable without the first" (*Culture*, 221). Indeed, many of the rebels of the Easter Rising declared their own personal visions for Ireland in the letters they wrote from their jail cells as they awaited execution. The third episode of the documentary, which deals mainly with the Rising itself, precisely focuses on these letters. Among the letters read are those of Thomas MacDonagh, Tom Clarke, Patrick Pearse and Seán Mac Diarmada. In Pearse's letter to his mother, he explains that "this is the death I should have asked for, if God had given me the choice of all deaths: to die a soldier's death for freedom" (00:08:00-00:08:27). Pearse's words, spoken as the camera zooms slowly in a candle lit cellar, encourage the idea of romantic martyrdom. This belief that a man must put his country and his freedom ahead of his own life was also mentioned by Fanon when he declared that "the colonized man ... must take part in action and throw himself body and soul into the national struggle" (232). This belief system was shared by many of those involved in the rebellion. In a letter to his family, for example, Sean Mac Diarmada states that "the cause for which I die has been re-baptised during the past week by the blood of as good a men (sic) as ever trod God's green earth and should I not feel justly proud being numbered amongst them and feel a lasting pride at my death. I die that the Irish nation may live" (00:14:35-00:14:56).

It is interesting that the rebels sought to manufacture a vision of themselves as martyrs. Indeed the decision to hold the rebellion at Easter further emphasises the fact that the men wished to equate their dying for their country with the redemptive act of Jesus dying for the sins of men. It offers their actions as the ultimate sacrifice and places them not only as heroes, but also in a closer relationship with God than ordinary men. In Mac Diarmada's letter, as in Pearse's, there is a sense that he considered to be dying for some mystical and transcendental principle.

5. RESURRECTING THE REBELLION: A POSTCOLONIAL READING ...

Throughout *Rebellion*, as has been discussed earlier, the idea of using violence as a means of attaining freedom is constant. Fanon himself remarks on the unfortunate but inevitable use of violence involved in anti-colonial struggles, when he relates that "the proof of success lies in a whole social structure being changed from the bottom up"; in order for this to happen, it must be "willed, called for, demanded" (35). Unless change is forced, Fanon explains, the colonised is kept outside of the circle of power because "in the colonies it is the policeman and the soldier who are the official, instituted go-betweens, the spokesman of the settler and his rule of oppression" (38).The call for violence is echoed in the documentary by Pearse, as he declares: "We must accustom ourselves to the thought of arms, to the use of arms. We may make mistakes in the beginning and shoot the wrong people but bloodshed is a cleansing and a sanctifying thing" (00:28:55-00:29:50). Pearse seems to share Fanon's views on how the oppressed, Ireland, needs to act in order to bring about change. His defence of violent struggle is certainly an attempt by the oppressed to change the nature of the relationship between the coloniser and the colonised.

Evidence of Pearse's belief in the necessity of the Irish to use force to enact change is woven throughout the documentary. Pearse is said to be one of the leaders of "a small band of rebels, including poets and teachers" (00:00:01-00:00:20). This statement reinforces the disparity of forces between the two sides and sees the rebels as romantic idealists, as poets and teachers. The documentary shapes the story in such a way that the audience is encouraged to view the rebellion as akin to the biblical fight between David and Goliath.[6]There is of course much reason to frame the moment in such a way. A few thousand badly trained, non-professional soldiers had little or no hope of ever matching the firepower of the British Empire. The documentary reveals how Pearse, though keenly aware that the odds for a military victory were stacked against the rebels, was unafraid to meet the British army in a fight. In the first episode, Liam Neeson explains how Pearse used every opportunity to speak to the masses of Irish people. One such critical moment occurs at the graveside of "O Donovan Rossa, leader of London bombing campaign in the 1880s" (00:41:30-00:42:30). Over photos of Pearse at the graveside, we hear his warning that "they think that they have pacified Ireland but the fools, the fools, the fools, they have left us our Fenian dead and while Ireland holds these graves, Ireland unfree will never be at peace" (00:41:30-00:41:47). Scenes such as this present a theme of continuity in both life and death. As Fanon said, "the practice of violence binds them [the colonised] together as a whole, since each individual forms a violent link in the great chain, a part of the great organism of violence which has surged

---

6   David and Goliath are characters from the Bible. Goliath was a giant expected to defeat David easily in order to reveal that the latter was not man enough to be king. David, however, defeated the giant and took his place as king of Israel. The story is often used as a means of encouraging people to overcome seemingly impossible odds (Gladwell, 17).

upward in reaction to the settlers' violence in the beginning" (93).

In summary, *Rebellion* seems to transmit the moral that violence was a useful tool which helped to force change to come at a quicker pace in Ireland than it would have done otherwise. This is especially apparent in the third part of the documentary, when Dr. Fearghal McGarry of Queens University Belfast states that "five days of violence seems to have been more effective than several decades of constitutional agitation" (00:25:00-00:25:15). Unlike the other documentary, *The Enemy Files*, *Rebellion* opts to depict the failure of the Easter Rising as a moral victory for the Irish in their anti-colonial struggle.

Conclusion

In analysing these two documentaries, it is clear that the views that were held by the opposing sides on 1916 have changed very little, if at all. It can be argued that both films set out to create a counter-history in order to challenge the version of events put forward by the other. While *Enemy Files* uses official government and military documents to achieve its goal, *Rebellion* draws from the letters of the imprisoned rebels in order to present its perspective. The revisionist approach to Irish history, which *The Enemy Files* represents, continues to perpetuate the idea that the Easter Rising was an error of judgement which began a circle of unnecessary violence in Ireland. The documentary insinuates, again echoing Yeats's "Easter 1916," that Britain would have handed Ireland its freedom eventually, once the distraction of the First World War was over, without any bloodshed. On the other hand, in *Rebellion*, there is the continuation of the belief that the relationship between the US and Ireland was critical in bringing about the Easter Rising. Indeed, the fact that *Rebellion* is an Irish American production reinforces the feeling that, even after a hundred years, the influence of America in helping the Irish tell their history is just as important today as it was in 1916.

Another significant finding is that both documentaries rely, in different ways, in the set of binaries coloniser/colonised described by postcolonial theory. As has been remarked *The Enemy Files* approximates Orientalist thinking by infantilising Irish rebels and demeaning them by comparison with Islamic extremists. On the contrary, English soldiers feature as innocent men who must contend with the unjustifiable violence of Irish rebels. The documentary *Rebellion*, by contrast, portrays the rebels as martyrs who died for the cause of freedom for Ireland. It creates a discourse which views their actions as both necessary and successful and the argument for the rebellion is laid out in simple terms: the poets, teachers and dreamers of a small nation brought about the end of occupation in (part of) their country by demanding justice through physical force. By comparing the Easter Rising to the French Revolution and the American War of Independence, and by describing those involved in the

Easter Rising as selfless heroes, the documentary romanticises the events which took place during the Easter Rising and caused the deaths of many, including the loss of possible future Irish leaders such as Pearse and Connolly.

As James Joyce famously wrote in *Ulysses,* "history is a nightmare from which I am trying to awake" (4). Many strides have been made in recent years to place the wounds of the bloody history between Ireland and Britain firmly in the past. Nations and people can neither be equal nor enjoy a true and lasting peace as long as one continues to seek dominance over the other. As the analysis of these documentaries reveals, while the violence of yesteryear has dimmed, the struggle to control the story of the past continues unabated.

Works Cited

Ashcroft, Bill, Gareth Griffiths and Helen Tiffin. *The Post-Colonial Studies Reader.* Routledge, 1995.
Benjamin, Walter. "Critique of Violence." *Selected Writings Volume 1, 1913–1926,* edited by Marcus Bullock and Michael W. Jennings, Harvard University Press, 1996, pp. 236–52.
Bernard, Sheila Curran. *Documentary Storytelling: Making Stronger and More Dramatic Nonfiction Films.* Focal Press, 2007.
Carroll, Clare and Patricia King. *Ireland and Postcolonial Theory.* University of Notre Dame Press, 2003.
Chanan, Michael. *The Politics of Documentary.* British Film Institute, 2007.
Cleary, Joe. "Misplaced Ideas? Colonialism, Location and Dislocation in Irish Studies." *Theorizing Ireland,* edited by Claire Connolly, Palgrave, 2003, pp. 91–104.
Coogan, Tim P. *1916: The Easter Rising.* Weidenfeld & Nicolson, 2010.
Deane, Seamus. *Strange Country: Modernity and Nationhood in Irish Writing since 1790.* Clarendon Press, 1997.
Del Río, Constanza. "Postconial Legacies: Trauma and Irish Identity." Unpublished keynote lecture delivered at the Irish Itinerary 2018 (EFACIS), University de la Rioja, Spain, 12 February 2018.
Ellis, S. "Representations of the Past in Ireland: Whose Past and Whose Present?" *Irish Historical Studies,* vol. 27, no. 108, 1991, pp. 289–308.
Fanon, Franz. *The Wretched of the Earth.* Grove Press, 2004.
Fisk, Robert. *The Great War for Civilisation: The Conquest of the Middle East.* Vintage, 2007.
Foley, Billy. "TV Review: *The Enemy Files* Shows how we have Matured in our View of the 1916 Rebellion." *The Irish News,* 26 March 2016, www.irishnews.com/lifestyle/2016/03/26/news/tv-review-the-enemy-files-shows-how-we-have-matured-in-our-view-of-the-1916-rebellion-462323/. Accessed 2 Jan. 2017.
Foster, Roy F. *The Oxford History of Ireland.* Oxford University Press, 1992.
——. "The Lovely Magic of its Dawn: Reading Irish History as a Story." *Times Literary Supplement,* 16 December 1994, pp. 4–6.

Gallimore, Andrew, director. *Easter 1916: The Enemy Files*. BBC, 2016.
Gibbons, Luke. *Transformations in Irish Culture*. Cork University Press, 1996.
Gladwell, Malcolm. *David and Goliath: Underdogs, Misfits, and the Art of Battling Giants*. Little, Brown and Company, 2013.
Graham, Colin. "Rejoinder." *Irish Writing in the Twentieth Century: A Reader*, edited by David Pierce, Cork University Press, 2000, pp. 1107–12.
"Infantilize." *The Cambridge Online Dictionary*, dictionary.cambridge.org/es/diccionario/ingles/infantilize?q=infantilising. Accessed 1 Feb. 2020.
Joyce, James. *Ulysses*. Wordsworth Classics, 2010 (1922).
Kiberd, Declan. *Inventing Ireland*. Jonathan Cape, 1995.
Lloyd, David. *Anomalous States: Irish Writing and the Post-Colonial Moment*. Lilliput Press, 1993.
———. "Colonial Trauma/Postcolonial Recovery?" *Interventions* vol. 2, no. 2, 2000, pp. 212–28.
Lyons, F.S.L. *Ireland since the Famine*. 2nd revised ed., Harper Collins, 1973.
McCullough, Joseph. *A Pocket History of Ireland*. Gill & Macmillan, 2010.
McGarry, Fearghal. *The Rising. Ireland: Easter 1916*. Oxford University Press, 2010.
Magan, Ruán and Pat Collins, directors. *1916: The Irish Rebellion*. Performance by Liam Neeson and Declan Kiberd, COCO Television, 2016.
Mueller, Andrew, John Robinson, Hannah Verdier and Ben Arnold. "Friday's Best TV: *Easter 1916: The Enemy Files*, Billy Connolly's Tracks across America and Boomers." *The Guardian*, 1 April 2016, www.theguardian.com/tv-and-radio/2016/apr/01/friday-best-tv-easter-1916-enemy-files-billy-connolly-tracks-boomers. Accessed 1 Feb. 2017.
Nic Dhiarmada, Bríona. "1916: Screening the Irish Rebellion – Briona Nic Dhiarmada (Saturday Scholar Series)." University of Notre Dame College of Arts and Letters. *Youtube*, 10 Aug. 2016, www.youtube.com/watch?v=0lIEH83MIuQ. Accessed 4 Jan. 2017.
Nic Dhiarmada, Bríona and Christopher Fox. "The 1916 Project: A Preliminary Report." Keough-Naughton Institute for Irish Studies, December 2016, https://1916.nd.edu/assets/220403/kni_1916_report_rev_v5.pdf. Accessed 1 Feb. 2020.
Nichols, Bill. *Introduction to Documentary*. Indiana University Press, 2010.
Pine, Richard. *The Disappointed Bridge: Ireland and the Post-Colonial World*. Cambridge Scholars, 2014.
"Plot." *The Cambridge Online Dictionary*, dictionary.cambridge.org/es/diccionario/ingles/plot. Accessed 3 Feb. 2020.
Said, Edward W. *Culture and Imperialism*. Vintage Books, 1994.
———. *Orientalism*. Pantheon Books, 1978.
"The Enemy Files." *RTÉ*, 1916.rte.ie/risingonrte/the-enemy-files/. Accessed 3 March 2017.
Whelan, Kevin and Andy Pollak. "Interview with Edward Said." *Postcolonial Text*, vol.3, no. 3, 2007, pp. 1–15.

Part Two
Social Transformations

6

Politics, Sex and Land through the Lens of Exile in the Novels of Edna O'Brien

María Amor Barros-del Río

Introduction

In his illuminating study on Edna O'Brien's use of epigraphs, Bertrand Cardin detects a high recurrence of the words "mother" and "house" (68–69), two terms that in the Irish context acquire a paramount significance and address wider issues within the frame of gender and space. Overall, the semantics of O'Brien's oeuvre converges towards the precarious status of women in the Republic of Ireland, although critics and reviewers have not always duly acknowledged the political nature of her work.

Edna O'Brien's prolific career includes novels, collections of short stories, poetry, plays, screenplays, biographies and two memoirs; yet, despite this variety of texts and genres, her production, frequently linked to her stage persona, has for long been associated with women's fiction and romance. If the early reception of her work alternates between the polarities of "fame and infamy" (Kersnowski, ix), recent criticism has now recognised her oeuvre as "an important testimony to socio-political realities in twentieth-century Ireland" (D'hoker, 272).[1] Hence, while acclaimed writer Anne Enright affirms that "O'Brien is the great, the only, survivor of forces that silenced and destroyed who knows how many other Irish women writers" ("Review"), Fiona McCann asserts that Edna O'Brien's most recent fiction is "a counter-narrative of the Republic" (69). Likewise, Sinéad Mooney concludes that "O'Brien, in fact, was

---

1 Since her début in 1960 with probably her best-known novel, *The Country Girls,* her work has received numerous awards, although her relevance in the Irish contemporary canon has only gained ground more recently. In 2001 O'Brien was awarded the Irish PEN Award; then in 2015 she was bestowed Saoi by the Aosdána; in 2018 she was conferred the PEN/Nabokov Award for Achievement in International Literature, and in 2019 she received the UNESCO One City One Book Award for *The Country Girls Trilogy.*

always a political writer" ("Edna O'Brien Wins").

This chapter focuses on the increasing and more explicit political stance present in the novels of Edna O'Brien and on how, through the eyes of her female protagonists, these fictitious stories serve to highlight the most significant milestones of Irish women's contemporary history. In her work, O'Brien gives voice to the silenced and subdued effects of legal, social and religious boundaries upon Irish women's bodies and lives. By so doing, the author not only subverts the female stereotypes imposed by the nationalist and Catholic Irish Republic – an oppressive situation thoroughly studied by Gerardine Meaney (41–44) –, but also challenges the structural and institutional borderlines that have traditionally limited women's agency. O'Brien's most recent work guides the reader through the notable changes her country, and the world, have undergone by using the feminine perspective that is characteristic of her writing.

But to understand Edna O'Brien's production in the context of the young Irish Republic up to the present, it is necessary to acknowledge the paramount role of space in her life as much as in her work. Both vital experience and literary production run parallel in the search for an identity that attempts to shirk off limiting physical and ideological boundaries. At the same time, both in her life and her work she sought to reconcile herself with what being an Irish woman entails. In this regard, her non-fiction works, *Mother Ireland* (1976) and *Country Girl, a Memoir* (2012), stand out as the author's personal reflections on her own experience as an exiled Irish woman and give light to a deeper explanation of her works of fiction. As O'Brien has admitted, writing could only happen from a distance "because one needs the formality and the perspective that distance gives in order to write calmly about a place" (Eckley, 26). In a way, exile becomes "a revealing metaphor" (George O'Brien, 43), an idea that the author confirmed in a radio interview as follows: "In the crossing of the sea both emotionally and geographically I found my voice" (Pat Kenny, 00:10:25–30), and that Tony Murray would later expand upon by stating that "the process of migration … plays an important structural role in O'Brien's work by framing and contextualising the often dramatic shifts in perspective and identity" (86). Through this lens, her fiction and, most particularly, her non-fiction works guide Edna O'Brien's reader through this quest, and elucidate through her work the evolution of Irish women's status. Initially, her production confronts the reader with a frank depiction of Irish women's romantic experiences. However, moving beyond romance, a more nuanced approach unfolds wider issues that address female emancipation and sexuality, land and exile, and the political and legal framework that regulates them all.[2]

---

2   Interviewed in 2014 and following her admired James Joyce, Edna O'Brien highlighted nationality, language and religion as the main concerns of her production, adding gender as a fourth focal point (Kersnowski, xv). In my opinion, female emancipation and sexuality, land and exile, and the political and legal framework that regulates them, are more suitable and updated concepts to approach the author's interests.

Early Work: The Personal is Political

Tailoring this analysis to the previously mentioned guidelines, O'Brien's extensive production has often been classified chronologically in two distinctive phases (Ingman, 253), an arrangement that has overshadowed a continuous and broader line of thought. Her early books focus on Irish women's struggles and desires with a noticeable subjective stress on love and sexuality within the legal framework of the young Irish Republic. Among them, we can include *The Country Girls* (1960) and its sequels, *The Lonely Girl* (1962), renamed *Girl with the Green Eyes* two years later, and *Girls in their Married Bliss* (1964) plus an *Epilogue* added to the trilogy in 1986, together with *August is a Wicked Month* (1965), *Casualties of Peace* (1966), *Night* (1972) and *The High Road* (1988). In broad terms, this first literary period has "its own inherent or latent sense of politics" (Moloney and Thompson, 200), as it addresses different forms of female emancipation and failure in the psychological, emotional and physical domains.

At first reading, these novels seem to pivot around the issue of growing up and becoming a woman under the dictates of De Valera's Ireland. During the decades following the Civil War, Ireland's governments concentrated on reconstructing a nation that had been a colony for several centuries. The postcolonial pursuit of a distinctly national identity entailed rigid ideological principles and strict gender roles (Crowley and Kitchin, 369). Symbolic endorsement by the Catholic Church, a protectionist national policy, and a vigorous legal and moral control over the Irish population, founded on traditional patriarchal values, secured the authenticity and autonomy of the newly born nation. This combination contributed to a severe limitation in access to work and public spaces for women, and the imperative of submitting to marriage and procreation for the sake of the country, as the 1937 Constitution would outline.

The Country Girls Trilogy and Epilogue is a paradigmatic example of truncated female *Bildungsheld* (Mansouri, 236). Through formal experimentation and thematic transgression, the trilogy typifies resistance to and deviance from the normative behaviour for women in the Irish Free State and beyond (Barros-del Río, "Thematic Transgressions", 86). In this and subsequent novels, Edna O'Brien illustrates common practices of the Irish peasantry that destabilised the ideological foundations of the nation. Her ultimate betrayal to the nation was the candid representation of everyday Ireland in her first writings, where watchful families and claustrophobic rural settlements cohabited with normalised alcoholism among the male population. Women's feelings and sexuality were overtly discussed as Ireland's comely maidens had love affairs, with some women developing venereal diseases and others openly acknowledging sexual dissatisfaction in wedlock (*August*), and recounting experiences of domestic violence (*Casualties*). In general, women's feelings and sexuality were openly aired, unwanted pregnancies (*Night*) and lesbian desire included (*The High Road*). In writing about stigmatised social issues, O'Brien called into question the founding nationalist principles outlined in the 1937 Constitution, such as the concept of "Irishness" as a symbol of identity (Gray and Ryan), the idealisation of rural Ireland, female identification with the land and women's confinement to the home in support of the family and the State.

As a response to Article 41 of the aforementioned Constitution, Baba, one of the protagonists of *The Country Girls*, refers to herself on her wedding day as "the sacrificial lamb" (*The Country and Epilogue*, 386), hence acknowledging the bleak destiny that awaited Irish women at that time. The irreverence apparent in O'Brien's writing was immediately condemned in her homeland, especially among her relatives, as she recalls in her memoir, *Country Girl*: "In her letters my mother spoke of the shock, the hurt and the disgust that neighbours felt" (141). In such a suffocating social context as that in which Edna O'Brien was born and raised, it is no surprise that these early works were banned and burned, evidencing how undesirable her protagonists' behaviour was at the time.[3] In *Country Girl*, the author recalls her mother's anger and her threat to burn the book she was reading (91), a scene she would also fictionalise in her first novel, *The Country Girls*. This typification of the repression of female emancipation extends into other areas among which female sexuality is prominent. Her experimental novel *Night* explores the protagonist's deepest and most carnal desires where lust, longing and punishment intertwine. In this novel, Mary Hooligan's candid and heady journey to her most intimate feelings and experiences epitomises transgression and challenges the passive and pure icons of Mother Ireland and the Virgin Mary that sustained women's submission for the sake of the young nation (Innes, 42). In general terms, these novels focalise on exploring "a compromised female subjectivity amid the conventions of a denatured or destabilized romance plot," as Mooney has concluded ("Edna O'Brien," 245). Furthermore, the singularity of O'Brien's work led writer and critic Andrew O'Hagan to affirm that "not since James Joyce's Molly Bloom has a woman in literature spoken up for the true properties of her sex."[4]

---

3   The Censorship of Publications Act, passed in 1929, exerted an increasingly tight control on publications and particularly on sensitive topics amongst which contraception and abortion were included. Added to this, lack of information on a matter that specifically affected women contributed to the male monopolisation of public debate. Authors Edna O'Brien and John McGahern were banned in the 1960s by the Irish Censorship Board, generating much controversy. In 1967, Mr. Brian Lenihan introduced a new censorship law that limited the censorship period of a book to twelve years. For more information on Irish censorship, see the works of Adams and Mary Kenny.
4   As many scholars have noted, the critical reception of Edna O'Brien's production has too often been unfairly interspersed with her personal reputation as an exiled female woman writer. Special attention should be drawn to her account of her divorce and fight for custody in her memoir *Country Girl*, where she laments that passages from her novel

Her first memoir, *Mother Ireland*, dwells on these topics. In this non-fiction volume, O'Brien fuses the personal and the historical in a nostalgic and lyrical narrative focusing on the influence of nationalist iconography upon the real lives of Irish women. Over a decade after her departure from Ireland, the author examines her past through the lens of her exile in London. As Altuna-García de Salazar notes, this iconic work "engages in the exposition of the fossil and stagnant traditional Ireland in a nostalgic way but also advances, albeit timidly, the much needed revision and revisit of the female and eternal feminine" (199). Hence, it is her physical and (to a lesser degree) emotional distance from her mother land, together with the social and economic changes occurring throughout the 1970s, that facilitate O'Brien's detachment from a claustrophobic past, as the following passage suggests: "I looked at one of the many pictures of the Virgin Mary along the wall and realized that she no longer spoke to me as she used to when I was a child" (*Mother Ireland*, 107). Distance from "home" brings some liberation of social norms and taboos.

Later Work: The Political is Personal

During the 1970s and 1980s, most of Edna O'Brien's production utilises the short story form, a genre she masters and for which she has received much praise (Grogan; Peggy O'Brien; Shumaker). But at the dawn of the twenty-first century, O'Brien amplifies the specific struggles of her female Irish protagonists and makes the transition to a more open and critical account of Ireland's topical subjects in her novels. This turn is intimately related to the legal and economic changes the Republic of Ireland underwent in the final decades of the twentieth century. When in 1973 Ireland joined the European Economic Community, new opportunities for change became available. The country's economy, previously over-dependent on agriculture, slowly strengthened in other sectors such as services, tourism, pharmaceuticals and, more recently, ICT. The communications market was progressively liberalised and external influences infiltrated the Irish socio-cultural autarchic policies, causing an undeniable change in the cultural and ideological foundations upon which the Irish Republic was built. A slow turn in the Irish arena for women would begin in 1972 with the publication of the First Commission on the Status of Women. Second-wave feminism also became significant in that decade, particularly with the efforts of the Irish Women's Liberation Movement. In 1973 a group of feminists set up the Council for the Status of Women, leading eventually to the establishment of the National Women's Council of Ireland in 1995. In 1973, an out-dated marriage bar for women in public service jobs was abolished, and two Employment Equality Acts were subsequently passed in 1977 and 1998.

August is a Wicked Month were used against her to prove her unsuitability as a mother (165). For a comprehensive review on the matter, see Thompson.

The Family Home Protection Act, passed in 1976, had real import on the lives of ordinary women but it was not until 1995 that the Fifteenth Amendment of the Constitution Act removed the prohibition on divorce.

The reproductive rights of Irish women would have to wait much longer. In 1979 the sale of contraceptives was made legal in Ireland, but in 1983 the Eighth Amendment of the Constitution of Ireland established that abortion could only be conducted if the life of the mother was at risk. In 1992, the X Case became a landmark in the right to abortion. Again in 2012, the death of a pregnant woman after miscarriage resulted in international outrage. Finally, in 2016 abortion became a central issue and a focal point in the general elections, and in March 2018 the government announced a Referendum that would take place in May of that year. The Thirty-sixth Amendment of the Constitution of Ireland, that would permit the Oireachtas to legislate for the regulation of termination of pregnancy, obtained 66.40% of votes in favour and the Repeal of the Eighth Amendment came into force on 18 September 2018.

In light of these changes, O'Brien's later novels show a more explicit political stance, always emphasising the effects of life and politics in modern Ireland upon her female characters. This stage includes what has been called her "second trilogy" (Thompson, 85) and it comprises *House of Splendid Isolation* (1994), *Down By the River* (1997) and *Wild Decembers* (1999), to which her most recent novels, *The Light of Evening* (2006) and *The Little Red Chairs* (2015), could be added.[5] These novels reflect much of Ireland's political situation and amplify the underlying ideologies explored earlier in her work to pursue "a more explicit examination of the national culture that shapes the individual" (Mooney, "O'Brien," 254). Now, the concepts "mother" and "home" acquire a more symbolic significance and expand into wider domains, the former encompassing womanhood, pregnancy and maternity, and the latter including land, country and diaspora. Hence, her plots tackle issues that surpass the individual experience, situate their characters at precise historical moments, and incorporate politics at national and international levels.

This is particularly visible in O'Brien's approach to the issue of land. Formerly, her perspective was limited to the rural possessions of the peasantry, identified with the country as a whole. Now, that nationalistic perspective is doubly challenged with regard to its physical integrity and its ideological foundations as a nation, as stated in *Wild Decembers*: "Fields that mean more than fields, more than life and more than death too" (1).[6] In this novel, the author introduces the Irish diaspora as a destabilising element, impersonated

---

5   The first three novels have been described as "state-of-the-nation novels" due to their political content (O'Hagan).
6   With this sentence, O'Brien refers to the pastoral ideal of rural Ireland contained in the traditional folk song "Four Green Fields." The writer also invokes the mythical symbolic significance of Cathleen Ní Houlihan with the purpose of underlining the topicality of the binary land-woman, an ever-present issue in her works.

in Michael Bugler, an Australian immigrant of Irish descent, who returns to Ireland after inheriting a piece of land. The plot centres around the friendship and eventual hatred between two neighbours, Joseph Brennan and Michael Burgler. By intertwining this story with the love affair between Burgler and Breege, Joseph's sister, O'Brien subtly situates fear of the outsider at the core of the tragedy. This becomes evident in the novel when, after having shot Michael to death and being interrogated by the guards, Joseph confesses: "'I was afraid of him.' ' How come?' 'Twas him or me'" (228).[7] Although the novel is open to other readings and analyses (Colletta and O'Connor; Lindahl-Raittila), the author certainly emphasises the destabilising effect of external influences on rural Irish contexts.

At this stage, Edna O'Brien ventures into issues of diaspora and exile in a more determined way, a topic that would later play out more extensively in *The Light of Evening*. At a time when Ireland became an international economic force, *The Light of Evening* presents the opposition between home and abroad by means of memory. The experiences of migration impersonated by Dilly, who travels to the USA at the beginning of the twentieth-century, and by her daughter Eleanor, who departs for Great Britain several decades later, characterise the gendered Irish diaspora as a chain process that threatens what the Irish call "a sense of place," understood as "a component of identity and psychic interiority" (Martin, 92).[8] Furthermore, O'Brien incorporates the tensions between the Irish cultural space and the actual space of opportunities abroad, to the conflict inherent in the mother–daughter story. Far from being a new topic in O'Brien's production, her approach in *The Light of Evening* confirms the persisting ideological construction of Ireland as a land of exclusion, but now this construction colludes with women's diaspora. The conflict causes an emotional tension between mother and daughter that blocks a much-desired intergenerational dialogue. The effects of migration on the fates of Willa McCord in *Casualties of Peace*, Nell Steadman in *Time and Tide*, Mary MacNamara in *Down by the River*, and Dilly and Eleanora in *The Light of Evening*, are equally notable and signify a sustained preoccupation with the subject on the part of the author.

At a more overtly political level, in *House of Splendid Isolation* O'Brien

---

7   The story, immediately criticised for being "out of touch" with Ireland's actual situation (Hayden, 40), had sadly become true two years prior to the novel's publication. Psychiatrist Seamus Dunne had walked the short distance to his neighbours' house and shot the Cullys to death. Differences of opinion over trees and bushes and a leaky septic tank had been reported to the Gardai in the previous months.

8   Note that the topic is not exclusive of Edna O'Brien's. Contemporary Irish literature shows a strong tendency to look backwards and evoke Irish migrants' experiences, an issue that has met with considerable success in the form of the fictionalised lives of Irish migrant women. For a more extended review of female migration in contemporary Irish novels, see Barros-del Río ("Recalling Female Transgression").

addresses the Troubles in Northern Ireland between Unionists and Republicans from an authentically human perspective, forcing an encounter between Josie O'Meara, an elderly widow confined to her big house, and McGreevy, an IRA gunman. This novel, which was written after a blank-page period and required several visits to Northern Ireland according to the author (*Country Girl,* 235), shows how personal relationships are marred by the course of historical events and, at the same time, how these events can become insubstantial in the face of the deepest of human feelings. *House of Splendid Isolation* is the novel that Edna O'Brien "both did and did not want to write" (*Country Girl,* 235), fearing the harsh criticism that would (and did) come later, and the immense pain caused by violent confrontation and bloodshed. In any case, this novel illustrates the complexity of and pathos in a war among Irish people and vindicates the latent humanity under the horrors of conflict.

Down by the River is, together with *House of Splendid Isolation*, one of O'Brien's most political novels, and some critics have called it "the heart of the trilogy" (King, 150). Here, the author addresses the issue of incest and abortion bringing to the fore the cultural impact of the then recent X Case on Irish society and abroad. It could be argued that it is in *Down by the River* that the author best incorporates her criticism of Ireland's masculinist nationalism and its control over women's bodies. In this book – O'Brien's "most scalding critique of patriarchal Irish society" (Lindahl-Raittila, 82) – underage and motherless Mary MacNamara is sexually abused and subsequently gets pregnant by her own father. This "Magdalene," as the media call her, becomes the centre of a dispute between pro-life and pro-choice parties, and the scandal drags her through courtrooms and psychiatric wards. The protagonist, who eventually miscarriages, is represented again, though differently, as the "sacrificial lamb" of O'Brien's first novels, yet surrounded by an ideological and political debate that cannot reach a settlement. As late as 1992, Ireland was still not prepared to face the abortion issue. As a result, the pregnant body, when it does not submit to social and moral norms, remains stigmatised and problematic in Irish society, as *Down by the River* demonstrates.

Her eighteenth novel, *The Little Red Chairs*, echoes the Balkan war and represents a step further into the international perspective O'Brien has infused in her most recent works. Present-day Ireland has become a hybrid society but, in O'Brien's configuration, it still retains a degree of insularity, which reflects the emergence of what has been named as "glocal Ireland" (Morales Ladrón and Elices Agudo, 1–2). The "spirit" of glocal Ireland is clearly represented in the refugees, migrants and displaced workers that appear in the novel.[9] In *The*

---

9   In their introduction to the volume *Glocal Ireland: Current Perspectives on Literature and the Visual Arts*, Morales Ladrón and Elices Agudo refer to a continuum of interaction between the global and the local. For these scholars, the term "glocal" encompasses the tensions between a search for an identity and the negotiations inherent in a postmodern and multicultural country. In sum, they conceive the glocal as a "dialogic point"

Little Red Chairs, the rural peasants of Cloonoila, like Fifi, have emigrated to Australia, and travel regularly on holidays to other European countries, as Fidelma's family does. Yet, they all fall for Dargan's lie, a Balkan-wanted criminal now pretending to be a faith healer. However, when the fraud is uncovered, the wrath of the rural community is directed towards its women. Fidelma, pregnant with Dargan's child, is raped and forced to leave her hometown and her country. As she struggles to survive in a hectic and merciless London, O'Brien's character suffers the discrimination of being a single mother and an exiled Irish woman, her experiences mirroring the lives of other women in similar situations. In the end, the novel shifts from contemporary rural Ireland to London's dark underworld of social instability and emotional longing for the homeland, thus highlighting the fallout of globalisation in two different settings that remain very familiar to the author.

Edna O'Brien's latest novel, *Girl* (2019), ventures into the abduction and marriage of a Nigerian young girl to Boko Haram. The author's growing interest in landscapes beyond her native island is hereby confirmed, as well as her drive to keep exploring the complexity of female identity in hostile environments. In sum, O'Brien's latest works show her unique ability to detect and explore women's traumatic experiences, and their relation with female body abuse and land domination, beyond Irish borders.

Conclusion

Internationally recognised Irish author Edna O'Brien has devoted much of her literary career to voicing female experiences in a country whose upheavals in the twentieth and twenty-first centuries have made a deep impact on Irish people's lives. As a novelist, memoirist, playwright, poet and short story writer, Edna O'Brien portrays Ireland's historical evolution through the eyes of her female protagonists, always challenging the social and structural barriers that limit their agency. Hence, the whole of Edna O'Brien's work focuses on the (im)possibilities of female emancipation in the Republic of Ireland, from the mid-twentieth century to the present.

Praised and criticised in equal parts, her work illustrates the silenced and subdued effects of legal, social and religious boundaries upon Irish women's bodies and lives over time, and portrays their problematic negotiations with the concepts of womanhood, motherhood and identity (Barros-del Río "Translocational," 12). But the exploration of these notions can only be done prior to the acknowledgment of space as an axis that vertebrates O'Brien's stance. Place, locality, movement, travel, exile and diaspora articulate her perspective on a feminine and endless search. Hence, this leads to the conclusion that the

---

(2) where homogeneity and heterogeneity meet and where contemporary Ireland strives to find itself.

guiding thread of O'Brien's oeuvre is space and the place women inhabit both physically and symbolically.

Her early works concentrate on the exploration of sexuality, emotions and the difficulties of female emancipation in the context of a young Irish Republic. Within the female universe explored by the author, the discovery of female sexuality, the idealisation of marriage, the emotional upheavals of love affairs and divorce, coexist in permanent tension with the oppressive atmosphere of rural settings, a tension that can only end in punishment for her protagonists. The legal and moral imperatives imposed by the 1937 Constitution and the Catholic Church incited the most obscure and unthinkable forms of behaviour. Thus, only from the physical and emotional distance that exile in London allows can the author bring to light the social strictures that neither the law nor the creed recognised. Through her fiction, O'Brien lays bare her negotiations and those of her female protagonists' in relation to a progressive escape from the recreated physical and ideological spaces she had inhabited in rural Ireland. The political essence of these works is undeniable as her fiction is a counter-narrative that challenges the trivialities of society and the structural and institutional limitations in Irish women's daily lives.

Her later fiction evolves at the pace of the country's most relevant political and economic milestones. Now, the author tackles topics that transcend the personal experience and resonate at higher levels. The opening up of frontiers, Ireland's membership of the EU and the effects of globalisation are clearly reflected in her novels. Pregnancy and abortion, land property, the Troubles and other international issues like the Balkan War and migratory processes populate the pages of these novels, integrating the political, economic and social changes of contemporary Ireland. In this way, her oeuvre provides a continuous and evolving line of thought that positions their characters at particular historical moments. By doing so, Edna O'Brien's fiction presents a continuous line of thought that addresses the political dimensions of Irish womanhood in an increasingly explicit political tone. Her personal biography intertwines with her production, as the author attests both in *Mother Ireland* and in *Country Girl*. These two memoirs epitomise the physical and ideological journey of an Irish writer exiled from rural conservative Ireland to international settings.

Transformed into a revealing metaphor, exile allows and shapes the author's evolution from the intrinsic mother and house to the extrinsic woman, land, nation and country. At the same time, distance becomes a necessary requisite to subvert the concepts of Irish women and the Irish nation as unitary and immutable entities. It expands the author's scope and elevates her focus from the personal to the political. It is only through detachment that she can affirm that politics, sex and land are important themes to herself and, most of all, to Ireland (Moloney and Thompson, 200). The nature of her most recent works unveils O'Brien's concerns with international affairs. Her novels keep on denouncing the harm inflicted upon women all over the world, their bodies rendered as sites of control and metaphors of land possession. Her former Irish landscapes have given way to remote locations, but the spirit that moves her writing remains intact: for Edna O'Brien, women's emancipation is very much an ongoing issue, both in Ireland and elsewhere.

Works Cited

Adams, Michael. *Censorship in Ireland*. Scepter Books, 1968.
Altuna-García de Salazar, Asier. "Edna O'Brien's *Mother Ireland* Revisited: Claire Keegan's '(M)Other Ireland.'" *Revista Canaria de Estudios Ingleses*, vol. 68, 2014, pp. 195–206.
Barros-del Río, María Amor. "Recalling Female Migration in Contemporary Irish Novels: An Intersectional Approach." *Women on the Move: Body, Memory and Femininity in Present-day Transnational Diasporic Writing*, edited by Silvia Pellicer-Ortín and Julia Tofantshuk, Routledge, 2019, pp. 141–57.
——. "Thematic Transgressions and Formal Innovations in Edna O'Brien's *The Country Girls Trilogy and Epilogue*." *Estudios Irlandeses*, vol. 13, no. 2, 2018, pp. 77–90.
——. "Translocational Irish Identities in Edna O'Brien's Memoir *Country Girl* (2012)." *Gender, Place and Culture*, vol. 23, no. 10, 2016, pp. 1496–507.
Byron, Kristine. "In the Name of the Mother ...: The Epilogue of Edna O'Brien's *Country Girls Trilogy*." *Women's Studies*, vol. 31, no.4, 2002, pp. 447–65.
Cardin, Bertrand. "Words Apart: Epigraphs in Edna O'Brien's Novels." *Edna O'Brien: New Critical Perspectives*, edited by Katryn Laing, Sinéad Mooney and Maureen O'Connor, Peter Lang, 2006, pp. 68–82.
Colletta, Lisa and Maureen O'Connor, editors. *Wild Colonial Girl: Essays on Edna O'Brien*. University of Wisconsin Press, 2006.
Crowley, Una and Rob Kitchin. "Producing 'Decent Girls': Governmentality and the Moral Geographies of Sexual Conduct in Ireland (1922–1937)." *Gender, Place and Culture: A Journal of Feminist Geography*, vol. 15, no. 4, 2008, pp. 355–72.
D'hoker, Elke. "Edna O'Brien." *The Encyclopedia of Twentieth-Century Fiction*, edited by Brien W. Shaffer, vol. 3. Blackwell PA History of Modern Irish Women's Literature Publishing Ltd., 2011, pp. 272–75.
Eckley, Grace. *Edna O'Brien*. Bucknell University Press, 1974.
Enright, Anne. "*Country Girls* by Edna O'Brien-review." *The Guardian*, 12 Oct. 2012, www.irishtimes.com/culture/books/edna-o-brien-i-have-a-ferocity-in-me-but-i-m-also-fearful-1.3992871. Accessed 14 May 2018.
Gray, Breda and Louise Ryan. "(Dis)Locating Woman and Women in Representations of Irish National Identity." *Women and Irish Society. A Sociological Reader*, edited by Anne Byrne and Madeleine Leonard, Beyond the Pale Publications, 1997, pp. 517–34.
Grogan, Maureen L. "Using Memory and Adding Emotion: The (Re)Creation of Experience in the Short Fiction of Edna O'Brien." *The Canadian Journal of Irish Studies*, vol. 22, no. 2, 1996, pp. 9–19.

Hayden, Joanne. "Unveiling Naked Truth of Rural Life." *Sunday Business Post*, 26 September 1999, p. 40.
Ingman, Heather. "Edna O'Brien: Stretching the Nation's Boundaries." *Irish Studies Review*, vol. 10, no.3, 2002, pp. 25–65.
Innes, Catherine Lynette. *Woman and Nation in Irish Literature and Society, 1880–1935*. University of Georgia Press, 1993.
Kenny, Mary. *Goodbye to Catholic Ireland*. Sinclair-Stevenson, 1997.
Kenny, Pat. "Interview with Edna O'Brien on 'Today with Pat Kenny,' Part 1." *RTÉ Radio1*, 17 Oct. 2011, tcg2011.blogspot.com/2011/10/. Accessed 22 May 2019.
Kersnowski, Alice Hughes. *Conversations with Edna O'Brien*. University Press of Mississippi, 2013.
King, Sophia H. "On the Side of Life: Edna O'Brien's Trilogy of Contemporary Ireland." *Wild Colonial Girl. Edna O'Brien*, edited by Lisa Colletta and Maureen O'Connor, The University of Wisconsin Press, 2006, pp. 143–161.
Lindahl-Raittila, Iris. "Negotiating Irishness: Edna O'Brien's 1990s Trilogy." *Nordic Irish Studies*, vol. 5, 2006, pp. 73–86.
McCann, Fiona. "'The Right of the People of Ireland to the … Unfettered Control of Irish Destinies': Edna O'Brien, Wilful Subjects, and Counter-narratives of the Republic." Études Irlandaises, vol. 41, no. 2, 2016, pp. 69–84.
Mansouri, Shahriyar. *The Modern Irish Bildungsroman: A Narrative of Resistance and Deformation*. 2014. University of Glasgow, PhD dissertation, theses.gla.ac.uk/5495/. Accessed 25 June 2019.
Martin, Angela K. "The Practice of Identity and an Irish Sense of Place." *Gender, Place and Culture: A Journal of Feminist Geography*, vol. 4, no.1, 1997, pp. 89–114.
Meaney, Gerardine. *Gender, Ireland and Cultural Change: Race, Sex and Nation*. Routledge, 2010.
Moloney, Caitriona and Helen Thompson. *Irish Women Writers Speak Out. Voices from the Field*. Syracuse University Press, 2003.
Mooney, Sinéad. "Edna O'Brien Wins 2018 PEN/Nabokov Award." *Irish Humanities Alliance*, 6 April 2018, www.irishhumanities.com/blog/edna-obrien-wins-2018-pennabokov-award/. Accessed 29 Aug. 2019.
———. "Edna O'Brien." *A History of Modern Irish Women's Literature*, edited by Heather Ingman and Cliona Ó Gallchoir, Cambridge University Press, 2018, pp. 244–59.
Morales Ladrón, Marisol and Juan F. Elices Agudo. "Introduction." *Glocal Ireland: Current Perspectives on Literature and the Visual Arts*, edited by Marisol Morales Ladrón and Juan F. Elices, Cambridge Scholars Publishing, 2011, pp. 1–10.
Murray, Tony. "Edna O'Brien and Narrative Diaspora Space." *Irish Studies Review*, vol. 21, no.1, 2013, pp. 85–98.
O'Brien, Edna. *Casualties of Peace*. Penguin, 1968.
———. *August is a Wicked Month*. Penguin, 1973.
———. *Night*. Penguin, 1973.

———. *Mother Ireland*. Penguin, 1976.
———. *The Country Girls Trilogy and Epilogue*. Penguin, 1988.
———. *House of Splendid Isolation*. Weidenfeld and Nicolson, 1994.
———. *Down By the River*. Weidenfeld and Nicolson, 1997.
———. *Wild Decembers*. Weidenfeld and Nicolson, 1999.
———. *The Light of Evening*. Mariner Books, 2007.
———. *Country Girl. A Memoir*. Faber and Faber, 2012.
———. *The Three Little Chairs*. Back Bay Books, 2015.
———. *Girl*. Faber and Faber, 2019.
O'Brien, George. "The Aesthetics of Exile." *Contemporary Irish Fiction. Themes, Tropes, Theories*, edited by Liam Harte and Michael Parker, MacMillan Press, 2000, pp. 35–55.
O'Brien, Peggy. "The Silly and the Serious: An Assessment of Edna O'Brien." *The Massachusetts Review*, vol. 28, no. 3, 1987, pp. 474–88.
O'Hagan, Sean. "Edna O'Brien: 'I Want to Go Out as Someone who Spoke the Truth.'" The *Guardian*, 25 August 2019, www.theguardian.com/books/2019/aug/25/edna-obrien-interview-new-novel-girl-sean-ohagan. Accessed 29 Aug. 2019.
Shumaker, Jeanette Roberts. "Sacrificial Women in Short Stories by Mary Lavin and Edna O'Brien." *Studies in Short Fiction*, vol. 32, no. 2, 1995, pp. 185–98.
Thompson, Helen. *The Role of Irish Women in the Writings of Edna O'Brien: Mothering the Continuation of the Irish Nation*. Edwin Mellen Press, 2010.

7

Evelyn Conlon's "What Happens at Night" (2014): Revolution, Art and Memory Practices

Melania Terrazas

Introduction

This chapter examines Evelyn Conlon's short story "What Happens at Night," published in *Lines of Vision: Irish Writers on Art* (2014), a beautifully illustrated anthology of new poems, essays and short stories by a wide range of Irish writers – 56 in total, including John Banville, Roddy Doyle, Seamus Heaney and Jennifer Johnston. The anthology was inspired by pieces in the National Gallery of Ireland, Dublin, on the occasion of its 150th anniversary.[1] Novelist, short story writer and essayist Conlon is the only contributor in the collection to engage with two works: Edwin Hayes' *An Emigrant Ship, Dublin Bay, Sunset* (1853) (Figure 7.1) and Sarah Purser's *A Lady Holding a Doll's Rattle* (1885) (Figure 7.2). Conlon uses these two paintings as starting points to explore ideas about art, loss, women's voices, dreams, change and memory. In engaging with two very different pieces of art, which Conlon nevertheless brings together, her literary response is wonderfully diverse in subject matter and tone. This essay not only explores Conlon's role as a mediator, but also the author's representation of women's thoughts and feelings, past and present. Conlon's story, as shall be explained, pays tribute to female mobilisation through memory and art.[2]

---

1   *Lines of Vision: Irish Writers on Art* was edited by Janet McLean, Curator of European Art 1850–1950 at the National Gallery of Ireland. McLean also set up the accompanying exhibition, formally opened by President Michael D. Higgins, himself a poet, on 7 October 2014.

2   The research on which this paper is based was funded by projects APPI16/13 and APPI17/06 and the research group grant EGI16/31, and is in tune with the aims of the

Figure 7.1: Edwin Hayes, *An Emigrant Ship, Dublin Bay, Sunset* (1853).[3]

Revolution

In its depiction of women's oppression and capacity for rebellion, Conlon's short story addresses two specific types of revolution in Ireland: first, the "devotional revolution," which ran from 1850 to 1875, the decades after the Great Famine, when these two paintings were created; and, second, the gender and sexual revolutions of first-wave and second-wave feminisms. As a feminist, Conlon herself was involved in the 1970s struggle for women's rights. In what follows, I will show not only the relevance of the devotional revolution to the later sexual and gender revolutions, but also how these revolutions relate to issues of culture and memory in Conlon's short story and the two paintings that inspired it.

While discussing the devotional revolution, in 1972 Larkin asserted that it

> satisfied more than the negative factors of guilt and fear induced by that great catastrophe [the Great Famine] ... The Irish, after all, had been gradually losing their language, their culture and their way of life for nearly a hundred years before the famine ... The Irish were being effectively Anglicized ... The Irish before the famine had nearly all become cultural

Centre of Irish Studies Banna/Bond (EFACIS). I wish to express my deepest gratitude to Dr. Constanza del Río, Irish writer Evelyn Conlon, and Alwyn Harrison for their helpful thoughts, comments and suggestions.
3   Edwin Hayes (1819–1904), *An Emigrant Ship, Dublin Bay, Sunset*, 1853, Oil on canvas, 58 x 86 cm, Presented, Miss Mary S. Kilgour, 1951, NGI.1209, National Gallery of Ireland Collection, Photo © National Gallery of Ireland.

7. EVEYLYN CONLON'S "WHAT HAPPENS AT NIGHT" (2014)

Figure 7.2: Sarah Purser, *A Lady Holding a Doll's Rattle* (1885).[4]

emigrants ... In a word, then, Irishmen who were aware of being Irish were losing their identity, and this accounts in large part for their becoming practicing Catholics. The devotional revolution ... provided the Irish with a substitute symbolic language and offered them a new cultural heritage with which they could identify and be identified and through which they

---

4   Sarah Henrietta Purser (1848–1943), *A Lady Holding a Rattle,* 1885, Oil on canvas, 41 x 31 cm, Purchased, 1975, NGI.4131, National Gallery of Ireland Collection, Photo © National Gallery of Ireland.

133

could identify and be identified with one another. This is why, for example, Irish and Catholic have become almost interchangeable terms in Ireland, despite the attempts of Nationalists to make Irish rather than Catholic the inclusive term. (649)

The devotional revolution – which involved the homogenisation of Catholic practice and the penetration of the Church's power into the homes and private lives of parishioners – can be associated with the simultaneous social phenomenon of "familism," which emerged in rural Ireland, and was then transferred to cities due to heavy migrations from the countryside. Both the devotional revolution and familism firmly contributed to the modernisation of agriculture on the one hand, and, on the other, to the regulation of sexual practices and marriage patterns, which were necessary for the development of an increasingly powerful class of Catholic tenant farmers. Drawing on Arensberg and Kimball's study on familism, Cairns and Richards considered that the main purpose of the social and sexual practices known as familism was the progressive consolidation and extension of landholdings, which implied the control and regulation of inheritance, sexuality and marriage within the family (42). Cairns and Richards then defined familism as follows:

> Familism consisted of a number of procedures to control access to marriage, including the imposition and perpetuation of strict codes of behaviour between men and women, general endorsement of celibacy outside marriage and postponement of marriage in farmers' families until the chosen heir was allowed by the father to take possession of the farm. (42)

The devotional revolution and familism became active collaborators in the regulation of sexuality, transforming the socio-cultural practices and values of Catholic tenants at the forefront "in the struggle to create the sense of national identity necessary for the birth of the Irish Free State" (del Río, 209). Del Río explains that "[f]amilism brought about changes in social behaviour, the most relevant being the widespread practice of matchmaking, the endorsement of strict chastity outside marriage and pressure on superfluous sons and daughters to emigrate," all of which "acted as preventive checks whose main purpose was to secure the property and avoid the division of the land" (210). The presence of the Catholic priest in the homes, surveying people's everyday lives and habits, including their sexual and reproductive patterns, became overwhelming. Such a strict scrutiny of family matters and, particularly, of sexual behaviour, increased religious and moral pressures on women. The situation before the Famine and emigration had been oppressive for Irish women mainly in material terms (hunger, poverty, lack of expectations, etc.). After the Famine, the devotional revolution, coupled with the material practices of familism, burdened women with the symbolic task of becoming the preservers of the essence of the Irish race and nation by stressing the crucial role and reproductive function of the female body for the whole nation. In Horgan's words:

> Women in the post-famine period were offered the role said to be the most important in society – bringing up children in the Catholic faith. To a large extent women had little choice in this. There was nothing else on offer and, in return for embracing the new morality, they received a level of respect, of status, even authority, which they could not otherwise have expected, given their changed economic role ... All over the country shrines of devotion to Mary sprang up. The Virgin Mother was the model for Irish women. The alternative was the convent or emigration. (3)

It is also true that one of the effects of the Great Famine, due to the scale of deaths and emigration, was the clearance of the land: that is, there was now more land for fewer people. Rural Ireland started a process of modernisation and entered the capitalist system of land exploitation. The native Irish may now be less poor, yet all this came at the cost of their relinquishing a historical and cultural dimension of their identity – remnants and adaptations to the colonial situation of ancient Gaelic socio-cultural practices that had endured under colonial pressure for more than seven centuries.

The Great Famine had profound and long-term effects: Ireland's drastic demographic and social changes, the end of traditional Gaelic practices, the great Irish diaspora between 1847 and 1860, and the implementation of the devotional revolution and familism, which worked together to indoctrinate Irish women into "decency" and obedience. Yet the transit from the 1880s to the 1970s was not a desert either. Some feminist movements emerged in the last two decades of the nineteenth century, at the time of Sarah Purser's portrait, when the stirrings of first-wave feminism reached Ireland. It was mainly (Protestant) upper-middle-class women, such as the "Lady holding a rattle" or Purser herself – well-educated and wealthy women with a convenient safety net of social relations –, who mostly led the activism of the period.

Born in 1848, Purser decidedly transcended the isolationism of her privileged socio-cultural milieu. She was an educated Protestant woman with a very dynamic personality who managed to open up the provincial Dublin art world. She was very interested in making art education available to women, and became a key figure in the Irish art revival of the late nineteenth century. As Hepburn puts it, Purser was an artist with "more than a streak of the revolutionary," who did what she did not in spite of being a woman, "but because of it" (130). This may be why, in Conlon's story, the lady empathises with a poor emigrant woman and wants to help her "because I would like to" (52) – this may have also been Conlon's wish.

Conlon's involvement with Irishwomen United makes of her a kindred spirit to feminist demands, which in the 1970s were made through publications such as *Banshee*, a seminal feminist magazine and the mouthpiece of Irishwomen United, which spoke for all Irish women who took a stand against the Catholic Church's intervention in the State and its staunchly repressive measures against women (Connolly, 130). Some of their demands were the removal of all legal and bureaucratic obstacles to equality, free and legal contraception, the recognition of motherhood and parenthood as social functions, equality in education, and equal pay for equal jobs. Together with other organisations, such as Irish Women's Liberation Movement (1971), Women's Political Association (1971) or Irish Women's Aid (1975), Irishwomen United was there at the start of the "sexual revolution" in Ireland, and saw the legalisation of contraception and divorce in the 1990s. In 2015, Ireland legalised same-sex marriages, and the constitutional ban on abortion (Eighth Amendment) was removed in May 2018, a removal joyfully celebrated around Ireland and the world, placing the country, which had its first openly gay, mixed-race Prime Minister in 2017, at the vanguard of a social revolution.

Conlon's short story "What Happens at Night" recreates an imaginary scenario of the "What if ..." kind: "What would happen – which conversations, exchanges, alliances, gestures and postures – would occur if the figures in the paintings at the National Gallery came alive at night and started to converse with one another?" A flight of imagination is precisely what Conlon offers her readers in the short story, where an upper-class lady – the one holding the doll's rattle in Purser's painting – addresses contemporary viewers while reporting a conversation with a poor woman about to migrate to America because of the Famine. The poor woman is the one portrayed in Hayes' painting, sitting at the back of the boat closest to the emigrant ship. Conlon's short story fictionalises the concerns of these two women about to part from each other with great intimacy, and at times with irony, as she does here:[5]

> You think, looking at me, with my toy and my blue eyes, that I have nothing to dream about ... You think I'm the same each day ... But that's not how it is at all. At night, when the last of the uniformed men go home, we ... prepare to tell each other what we can ... But something went wrong ... last night ... A woman from one of the small boats called out to me ... shouted that she had seen the future. She said that ... her own particular one worried her, she hoped it was not going to be true. She shouted that the world was full of sharks ... determined not to let some of us speak and that's why she was telling me. ... She said it was important to believe that the future she had seen could be changed ... She asked me to keep true to her ... This is why I dreamt the wrong dream last night, seeing all the dangers that she meant, seeing her future before it happened

---

5   For a detailed analysis of Conlon's use of irony and the rhetoric of satire in her fiction, see Terrazas ("The rhetoric").

7. EVEYLYN CONLON'S "WHAT HAPPENS AT NIGHT" (2014)

> ... Now I will have to wait all day to find out how she thinks I can keep faith with her, because I would like to. And if she thinks that knowing the pitfalls will save us. A woman with a future like hers is bound to know. I hope she's not already on board by the time this evening comes ... Maybe they [the visitors contemplating the paintings in the gallery] will not hear what she calls back to me – it might alarm them if they did ... Yes, maybe I'll be able to do this to-day and then it will be possible for me to dream the right dream to-night. (50–52)

The passage above is an example of ironic literature as cultural reaffirmation, as a means of relating to public life, and is characterised by the search for a female identity that is confrontational rather than tragic or victimised. The irony of the text not only resides in the binary opposition between "the wrong dream" experienced by the lady in Purser's painting and "the right dream" that she wants to have, but also in the way she addresses the reader–viewer. Here, the narrator hints that bonding and dialogue across history and the social-class and religious divide are crucial in Ireland for Irish women's self-definition and reassurance, because they will all have to cooperate to forge a positive Irish female identity, one that is self-assertive and free from external impositions.

Conlon's short story rewrites the past and, in so doing, explains the present. As a result, "What Happens at Night" provides a sense of liberation from hard times for these two women. In crafting a story about two women in ironic dialogue, Conlon hints that women were aware of more issues than seemed to be the case, and that by joining forces and crossing the class and religious divide they could make things happen and pave the way for progress. This may explain why the text begins with the words, "[L]ast night I dreamed the wrong dream" (48), the "wrong dream" being an example of irony because it refers perhaps to the false belief that emigration is the answer to Ireland's social problems. In other words, emigration might not benefit those emigrants who set out to find solutions for their plight elsewhere. It may also point to the uncertain destiny of the emigrant woman on the boat, and by extension of all the others who left Ireland in the wake of the Famine, as well as to the decades of surveillance, oppression and repression of the female body and sexuality that still lay ahead for Irish women.

The narrator in Conlon's short story uses verbal irony to suggest that, in spite of the prevalent image of post-Famine Irish women as submissive and confined to the home, Irish women in the second half of the nineteenth century stayed silent in public because that is what was expected of them, though they had other ways and strategies, unknown to men, to discuss things and exchange opinions:

> You think I'm the same each day. But that is not how it is at all ... we take some moments to ourselves ... and then prepare to tell each other what we can ... There are some who remain passive, aloof, too wrung out with

experience to venture small talk. There are some who burst into blazes of noise, full of excitement and glee, flying this way and that, making no sense at all, but enjoying themselves doing it. I am somewhere in between. (48)

This is a liberal woman projecting her own strength and character onto an illiterate and uneducated woman raised in rural Ireland's oral culture. As a literate, upper-class urban woman, Conlon's narrator occupies a position between post-Famine oppression and the modernity of Irish womanhood. She is thus able to reflect upon the lives of those women who depart, those who stay, those who talk and those who remain silent. However, as a master of rhetoric, the author takes neither one side nor the other. To a certain extent, "What Happens at Night" revisits a concern that is constant in all of Conlon's work: the tension between how women are perceived and what they are really like. The following quotation exemplifies the narrator's self-consciousness as for the discursive rules governing social exchanges in the Ireland of the 1880s. Though aware of them, Conlon's narrator chooses to disregard some of these rules, like the interdiction on intimacy and contact across social classes and religious faiths:

> That's not a usual thing – certainly from those quarters. In fact it's a rare thing for most of us to speak – we tend to use subtler ways for trading thoughts. We're good secret keepers too, hearing the most extraordinary things as people drop their guards in front of us and let out the most precious of free thoughts. (50)

Conlon's narrator obliquely faces the conventional understanding of how the mind of the Other is conceived and may be conceived. Yet, above all, she conveys the importance of effective communication among women from different social classes as a means to change their future for the better. Otherwise, social circumstances may lead to a "wrong dream," a future as bleak as that of the Irish emigrants captured in Hayes' painting. Conlon presents the barriers to verbal communication between women, particularly highlighting the rarity, and the necessity, of women's interactions breaching class and religious divides.

Sarah Purser and Evelyn Conlon on Art

It is perhaps because Conlon has always been extremely concerned with gender issues, has written many radio essays about the value of galleries and public art, and is a regular visitor to the National Gallery that her creative response to the two paintings invites us to look at art in a new light and from a different angle. Breathnach describes Conlon's choices thus:

7. EVEYLYN CONLON'S "WHAT HAPPENS AT NIGHT" (2014)

"A Lady Holding a Doll's Rattle" is an example of Sarah Purser's mastery of portrait painting. While this work captures the intimacy of art and the style of 19th century Parisian high society, Edwin Hayes' painting is of an altogether different world. The image of an emigration ship at anchor in the mouth of the Liffey in the wake of the Great Famine captures so much of Ireland's history. (2)

Despite their differences, the conjunction of these two paintings through Conlon's imagination breathes life into a singular idea: the relevance of women's drive and dialogue in order to accomplish revolutions that may provide wide-reaching and radical changes in their situations, lifestyles, beliefs and attitudes and, thus, improve their social circumstances and prospects.

Sarah Purser's situation must have been very different from that of the woman in Hayes' painting and much more similar to the lady's in her own painting. She was born into a wealthy Protestant County Dublin family in 1848, a year of revolution and famine. Purser quickly made her mark as an artist. After Irish independence in 1922, she became a good friend of the new leader of the Irish Free State, W. T. Cosgrave. Purser took control of her destiny. She exhibited work at the Royal Hibernian Academy in her early twenties, and in 1923, at 85, became the first female member of the Royal Hibernian Academy.[6] Purser was unmarried, held strong opinions, and remained stubbornly self-sufficient to the end. Inevitably, given her personal dynamism and wide range of contacts, she became heavily involved in attempts to open up the Dublin art world to broader horizons. Finding the art education available in Dublin either inadequate or closed to women, she headed for Paris and the prestigious Académie Julian. On her return to Ireland, Purser became a key figure in the Irish art revival. She was a successful society portraitist, and founded the stained-glass workshop *An Túr Gloine* (The Tower of Glass), which operated in Dublin from 1903 to 1944. The work that was produced there, which is displayed in many Irish churches, remains her finest memorial.[7]

Edwin Hayes, another Anglo-Irish Protestant artist, studied drawing and painting at the Dublin Society Art School and soon set his sight on becoming a marine painter. Like Purser, he exhibited at the Royal Hibernian Academy, doing so for the first time in 1842, at the age of 22, after which he continued to paint in Dublin over the next decade before moving to London. Hayes continued to submit work to the Academy, and was elected an associate member in 1853 and a full member in 1871. His vast knowledge of and "eye" for the sea allowed him

---

6 The Royal Hibernian Academy is an influential institution, an artist-based body founded in 1823 along the lines of the London Royal Academy. Although not always conspicuous, historically, for its recognition of women artists, or of those who deviated from conventions, the Academy has made an enormous contribution to Ireland's fine arts heritage.

7 For more on Purser's life, see Chilvers and Glaves-Smith.

to capture all aspects of marine activity and scenery, and he is considered an outstanding exponent of marine visual art in Ireland ("Edwin Hayes").

Irish art of this period could scarcely have taken shape as it did without a core of remarkable women like Purser and men like Hayes. As art critic Brian Fallon argues, the history of Irish art over the last hundred years (at least) is filled with women who were hardworking committee members, efficient secretaries and organisers, canvassers of patronage and funding, hunters of publicity, seekers-out of new talent (1). Some posed in the limelight, others hid from it, while still others were content to work away at the essential chores that most either rejected or had no time to do. Fallon particularly called attention to Sarah Purser's significance when he wrote: "Irish women artists owe [Purser] a debt for fighting the good fight during the years when most art institutions seem to have felt that a woman's place was in the home and not the studio" (2). When Purser painted the portrait that inspired Conlon's short story, there were already signs of the changes in gender roles that would be consolidated in the following decades, due to the first-wave of feminism in Ireland (Connolly, 57). Purser had to fight to make her voice heard and establish herself as a painter. Conlon's text reads, "You [the visitor to the gallery] do not see that I am hiding the things that I know … You don't think of me talking and sleeping and dreaming. You think I'm the same each day. But that's not how it is at all" (48). This passage is very interesting, because, as Conlon claimed in an interview conducted by Brendan Rooney, Head Curator of the National Gallery of Ireland, the lady with the rattle apostrophises viewers to draw their attention to the remarkable female artwork created by women (Rooney), like this portrait by Purser, who was a talented artist and made a living from her art. Yet Conlon's short story also hints at the covert, secretive ways in which women were frequently forced to communicate among themselves.

In her choice of painters and paintings, Conlon seems to have wished to visualise and give voice to Irish women across history while trying to demolish the barriers between them. She has claimed in interview that she chose "the portrait by Purser" because it "was about the outside world, about how the woman being portrayed examines something inside herself in her world" (Rooney). The lady holding the doll's rattle functions on two levels in Conlon's story. First, the lady reflects upon Hayes' painting, which depicts poor women emigrants, and thinks about them and their journey. Then, through her character's gaze, Conlon reflects upon women's experience of emigration from an external perspective. Her rhetoric of irony does not aim to bring any comfort, but to expose and explore the sharing of women's experiences.

By focusing with irony on topics that are of special interest to the contemporary Irish woman, Conlon provides new perspectives on the issues she deals with, at the same time revising the predominantly realist mode of the Irish short story. By eradicating established perceptions of women, and presenting the reader with a new image of Ireland, Conlon paves the way for a more liberal yet less idealised vision of women in Ireland. Conlon's rhetoric of irony highlights important cultural questions, while situating the short story as a platform for imagining ways in which aspects of Irish society might have changed or might still have to change. As a study of women's lives, this narrative enacts what Avery Gordon calls a "confront[ation of] the ghostly aspects" of social life (7). This short story becomes an inclusive space where past, present and future meet. The subaltern are allowed to express themselves, and social barriers are blown up.

One subversive aspect of the story is the narrator's enthusiasm and optimism. In fact, both the woman on the boat and the lady holding the rattle intuitively know that their own belief in the possibility of change is fundamental, that faith and loyalty between women across time is absolutely vital. The woman on the boat seems to be asking the lady to stay loyal to feminist ideals of equality, to have faith in womankind and sisterhood, and she implicitly invites the lady to cross the historical and class divide and remember her.[8] The woman wants to be remembered, and she is remembered in Hayes' and Purser's paintings and in Conlon's short story. As Draaisma remarked:

> Memory seems to be something that we need to make concrete; that we need to *realize* in the world. It is so vital an idea to our notions of ourselves as humans, so utterly indispensable to all we do, that memory has been transformed over and over from an ether, an energy, into a tangibility that we want to see. (cit. in Frawley, *History*, xxiv)

This quotation is relevant for the purposes of my analysis since, in response to a question about her latest novel *Not the Same Sky* (2013), a story that revolves around the emigration of orphan girls from Famine Ireland to Australia, Conlon said: "I imagined these women [the protagonists of her novel] as illiterate, poor, and hungry, and obliged to dig a mental hole and bury their memories in it" (Terrazas, "I Have Always Been," 213; "Questioning," 68). I believe that Conlon chose Hayes' painting as it allowed her to delve into the theme of memory. In "What Happens at Night," the woman with the rattle reflects upon this moment of rupture in which the mechanics of emigration will perhaps bury the poor woman's grief. The lady is determined to keep watch and wait patiently for the night to come so that she can resume her dialogue with the emigrant woman: "I can keep watch with him, the big emigrant ship, as he waits for the small boats with the small people, as his sailors prepare for departure, as the noise of him and them mix into one thing, seldom letting us

---

8   In her review of *The Glass Shore* (2016), Sinéad Gleeson's edited collection of twenty-five short stories including one by Conlon, Elizabeth Day notes that one can perceive a shared "concern with identity and borders, both physical and imagined" (Day). "What happens at Night" also reflects such concern.

hear any weeping" (50).

In the following section, historical events, works of art and socio-cultural practices will be gathered together as diverse manifestations of "Irish cultural memory" (Frawley, *History*, xvii). First, I will explain the meaning of the phrase "Irish cultural memory" and the concrete forms that cultural memory acquires. This introduction will serve to frame the consideration of Hayes' and Purser's paintings, Conlon's short story, the Great Famine, the great Irish Diaspora in the second half of the nineteenth century, the first and second waves of Irish feminism, and the feminist journal *Banshee* as "memory practices" (Frawley, *Diaspora*, 129). In doing so, I will try both to illustrate how these forms of Irish cultural memory serve as "ways of cultural remembering that result from and are shaped by particular cultural forms" (Frawley, *Diaspora*, 129) and to assert the great social value of literature and art.

Oona Frawley's Concepts of "Irish Cultural Memory" and "Memory Practices"

In the first of the recent four-volume *Memory Ireland* series, entitled *Memory Ireland: History and Modernity*, Frawley explains "Irish cultural memory" as

> a broad, classificatory term that indicates a body of memories, which allows us to discuss memorial processes from philosophical and ideological points of view, and which, crucially, allows for the expression of an array of Irish cultural memories by different groups, at different times, and in different places. (xvii)

Frawley's claim enables the exploration of this convergence of particular forms of Irish cultural memory and Conlon's concerns in "What Happens at Night." The idea of cultural memory is developed in great detail by Frawley in the second volume of *Memory Ireland*: "Cultural memory can be analyzed not only ... through groups of people – like those in the diaspora ... – but also through particular forms: organizations of individuals, cultural mediums such as photography, architecture, music, literature" (*Diaspora*, xxii). Following Frawley's ideas, Conlon's story and the two paintings which inspired it can certainly be considered forms of cultural memory, which shall be analysed in light of the devotional revolution and the more recent sexual revolution of 1970s Ireland.

The analysis that follows aims to answer a diversity of questions related to the memory practices that this essay has been considering so far. For example, as I will further argue, what is the memorial impact of painting on Conlon's sense of the past?; how do the paintings by Hayes and Purser which inspired "What Happens at Night" evoke, capture and represent cultural memory?; how

7. EVEYLYN CONLON'S "WHAT HAPPENS AT NIGHT" (2014)

do other cultural practices, such as the devotional revolution that followed the Famine, foster memory practices through the rehearsal of a specific identity?; finally, what is the relationship between consciously organised groups, such as Irishwomen United and their seminal journal *Banshee*, and Irish cultural memory? Frawley argues that:

> Many of these cultural forms are embodied materially – through, for instance, language, music, photography – and, because of their distinctive expressions of culture, give rise to distinctive memory practices. There are other cultural forms that develop their own memory practices through the rehearsal of an identity. That is often the case among particular subsets of the population: minority groups, those who speak a particular language or dialect ... there is an almost endless possibility for identifying oneself not only as Irish, but also as something else, with that "something else" often providing a distinctive way into a wider body of what I have been calling Irish cultural memory through a memory practice. Each of these memory practices embodies a particular memory discourse, and, perhaps more important, transmits a particular memory discourse. (*Diaspora*, 129)

As suggested in the quotation above, the way in which memory is shaped results in distinct types of cultural transmission, for example, the art of painting. Partly due to the artist's "disappearance" behind the canvas, paintings become powerful transmitters of collective memory, as they "capture a moment and bring that moment from the past to us directly, seemingly unmediated" (Frawley, *Diaspora*, 133). To analyse a painting, viewers draw on their cultural memory, on their previous experiences and cultural knowledge as the painting bears and impacts on their lives as part of a community. The interpretation of the painting thus becomes an act of memory practice. Following this line of argument, Hayes' and Purser's paintings, Conlon's short story and the *Banshee* magazine constitute cultural practices distinctively embodied. Gaelic social practices, the Famine, the Great Irish Diaspora, familism, the devotional revolution and the first and second waves of feminism in Ireland constitute, as quoted above, "cultural forms that develop their own memory practices through the rehearsal of an identity." Notions and discourses of identity became central to both the first and second feminist waves. If in Ireland first-wave feminism, due to historical circumstances, was intimately linked to the national question, the second-wave, starting in the 1970s, attacked restrictive definitions of Irish identity, which constrained women's personal freedom. By placing both contexts together, Conlon provides new routes into Irish cultural memory.

In her analysis of the relationships between particular memory practices and the Irish diaspora, Frawley draws attention to Benedict Anderson's seminal work and his definition of the idea of "imagined communities" in *Imagined Communities: Reflections on the Origin and Spread of Nationalisms* (1991), which "demonstrated just how forcefully collective senses of belonging

143

influence the development of powerful nationalisms. That the imagination explicitly participates in this process is significant; the projections managed by imagination can bridge generations and all manner of differences" (*Diaspora*, 3–4). Frawley then concludes that "[t]his aspect of Anderson's work is particularly interesting in relation to the diaspora, which constructs its sense of community through imagination, but also through memory" (4). This feature of Anderson's work and Frawley's appreciation of it are crucial to understanding not only the significance of Conlon's imaginative exercise in "What Happens at Night," but also the issues touched upon by the two women in the story – one who migrates because of the Famine and another who has stayed, yet wants to remember the former and "keep faith with her" (50). Diasporic memory has passed across generations, which may be why it is represented with such intimacy in some cultural forms like Conlon's "What Happens at Night." This is so because, according to Chamberlain, "a collective, diasporic memory has distinctive features – such as the need to 'tell' and the need to 'connect'" (177). Yet the need to tell and to connect are mediated in different ways: first the codes and conventions of the material embodiment (be it a painting, a song, an academic lecture or a TV ad) should be taken into account since they condition the memory's final shape; second, memory is not meant to, and cannot, give us access to what actually happened, for it always distorts and filters reality. Memory does not so much keep faith with the past as rewrite it, and, in this sense, Conlon's story can be interpreted as an act of "memory practice." Though fallible, memory can become, as this short narrative shows, both a conduit to the past and a reinterpretation of it which articulates contemporary and future concerns.

So, what is the significance of memory to the Irish Diaspora and what role does it play in Conlon's short story? "What Happens at Night" not only reimagines two paintings and the historical, social, political, and economic circumstances of their time, but also their details, which are then magnified and presented in a new light. Conlon seeks to reconsider the past aesthetically and critically by using literary and artistic tools. When asked in an interview about her interest in migration as a topic in her fiction, Conlon answered:

> There was a huge level of emigration in my family, to England, Canada, and the USA. And I have dealt with that in the novel *A Glassful of Letters* … emigration … fascinated me for two reasons: one, the thought of [the women] and their journey, and two, that so few people had examined it … That is why I got into the whole subject of memory, because I feel that they dug a hole and put their memories in it. (Terrazas, "I Have Always Been," 213)

"What Happens at Night" makes readers reconsider their own ideas about the connection between Irish cultural memory, Irish memory practices, famine, diaspora, class, gender, revolution, literature and art. Conlon makes Hayes' and Purser's paintings talk; she makes the story talk, confides in the reader, hoping s/he will grasp the subtlety and irony in the text and, instead of casting off the emigrant from her memory, thus eliding this emigrant's memory of Ireland, Conlon's narrator chooses to speak for her.

"What Happens at Night" is a good example of the mediating role of the writer in reconstructing women's difficult past lives so as to pay tribute to their strength and resilience. It also conveys the central role played by painting and literature in giving rise to distinctive memory practices. The lady with the rattle becomes the creator of her own fictional existence within the museum at night – "Just as I was curling into my silence a woman from one of the small boats called out to me" (50) – and reflects upon how women portrayed in art, such as herself, and real women by extension, "use subtler ways for trading thoughts" (50). While the paintings allow visitors and viewers to imagine the lives of these women as portrayed by the artists, Colon in her story positions herself as "the subject's consciousness" (Hagen, 1). This seems to suggest that, in order to transcend their circumstances, women must not only be aware of past pitfalls, that is, the dangers, penury and traps suffered by the woman on the boat before her departure and very likely again at her destination, but also stay loyal to themselves, and have faith in themselves and in one another to improve their situation.

Second-wave feminism was undoubtedly a formative experience for Conlon, one that partly shaped her cultural memory. As the seventh issue of *Banshee* (1977) shows, Irishwomen United worked through general meetings (discussions and action planning every week in Dublin), joint actions (pickets, public meetings, workshops on women in trade unions, contraception, social welfare, and political theory), and consciousness-raising groups. As the number of feminist publications such as *Banshee* increased, the ways in which women's movements and publications were remembered started to change. Despite long-term impediments to progress, Irish women's associations can now enjoy their own memory practices. In fact, when asked to recall *Banshee* and to reflect upon what Irishwomen United achieved, Conlon asserted that they "saw amazing things achieved, such as the legalization of contraception and divorce" (Terrazas, "I Have Always Been," 209).

Throughout these pages I have tried to show that, more often than not, different cultural discourses and socio-cultural practices are historically linked, so that they constitute a constellation that is born at a certain time and continues through generations. In this sense, Conlon's engagement with a group of radical activists had a significant impact on her own cultural memory, and this legacy helped her maintain a spirit of revolution for the sake of women's liberation. In my view, progress towards gender equality and solidarity are likely to feature in "the right dream" to which Conlon's narrator refers at the end of "What

Happens at Night." Taken together, all the distinct cultural forms and groups examined in these pages produce various and diverse memory practices, which feed one another and come to fill in historical and cultural voids and silences, or, as Frawley states, to compensate for historical fractures that may appear in other narratives (*Diaspora,* 136). A whole historical constellation can be recovered from the past through a painting, a feminist magazine, a group of people emigrating to a far-away territory, or the struggle for women's liberation. In this way, memory practices are always subjected to constant revision and change.

Conclusion

This chapter has shown how Conlon's "What Happens at Night" brings together two artistic traditions, painting and literature, and fictionalises powerfully two crucial moments in the history of Irish women captured by the paintings of Purser and Hayes. Both artists were recognised by the Royal Hibernian Academy, an institution well known for its long history of supporting women artists like Purser, herself a cultural emigrant to Paris, and of those who deviated from the canons of conventional art, like Hayes. Perceptive and at times deeply intimate, Conlon's short story calls not only for remembrance of those who departed because of the Famine, but also of those who stayed, and of women of all social strata to join together in dialogue and collaboration to achieve progress.

"What Happens at Night" confronts gently and obliquely the conventional understanding of how the mind of the Other, here, of other women from different social classes and cultural traditions, may be conceived. Such a rhetoric differs from, but is not inconsistent with, the aforementioned charter of demands made by Irishwomen United in publications like *Banshee,* to which Conlon was a contributor. Conlon's short story constitutes an attempt to imagine a process of potential transformation in the lives of women in Ireland in the second half of the nineteenth century, that is, the "right dream" that Irish women temporarily had during the first-wave of feminism, to be continued in the second-wave from the 1970s onwards. Conlon reinterprets Irish history from an aesthetic position that seeks to use the past to explain the present, creating a short story inspired by two paintings; these three different art works together provide a sense of release from difficult pasts. "What Happens at Night" explores the role of the rhetoric of irony as a means not only to exteriorise women's inner energies to an outside world, but also to suggest the country's changing socio-cultural map.

The three artistic works discussed in this study embody Irish cultural memory. These distinctive expressions of culture give rise to distinctive memory practices, just like the diasporic memory of the Irish in the second half of the nineteenth century or the Irishwomen United (and their feminist banner magazine *Banshee*) in the late twentieth. They are different ways of touching upon the cultural memory of Ireland. In this regard, through Conlon's short story, this article has tried to highlight the relationships between historical events, cultural forms and memory practices in the Irish context, and to encourage reflection upon the workings of memory in Irish studies. In sum, I have tried to open new pathways into this body of cultural memory, demonstrating how memory may be shaped by the negotiations of individuals like Hayes, Purser, Conlon, or the two women in the paintings, individuals who nevertheless also pertain to different social formations and discourses and who have inherited other forms of collective memory. This analysis has attempted to offer insights into the intersections of Irish cultural memory, the Famine, the Irish Diaspora, and particular cultural forms concerned with gender and revolution. Ultimately, my reflections on the characters' emotions and feelings in Conlon's "What Happens at Night" highlight important cultural questions about what women are really like, while situating Conlon's fiction as a means of exploring different ways to remember culture that are the outcome of, and are moulded by, specific forms of cultural discourses.

Works Cited

Anderson, Benedict. *Imagined Communities: Reflections on the Origin and Spread of Nationalisms*. Revised edition, Verso, 1991.
Breathnach, Ronan. "Art and Politics as Inspiration for Writing." *News Talk*, 14 March 2015, www.newstalk.com/Art-and-politics-as-inspiration-for-writing. Accessed 22 Dec. 2015.
Cairns, David and Shaun Richards. *Writing Ireland: Colonialism, Nationalism and Culture*. Manchester University Press, 1988.
Chamberlain, M. "Diasporic Memories: Community, Individuality, and Creativity: A Life Stories Perspective." *The Oral History Review*, vol. 36, no. 2, 2009, pp. 177–87.
Chilvers, Ian and John Glaves-Smith. "Purser, Sarah." *The Oxford Dictionary of Art and Artists*, edited by Ian Chilvers, Oxford University Press, 2009, pp. 505–06.
Conlon, Evelyn. "What Happens at Night." *Lines of Vision: Irish Writers on Art*, edited by Janet McLean, Thames and Hudson, 2014, pp. 48–52.
Connolly, Linda. *The Irish Women's Movement: From Revolution to Devolution*. The Lilliput Press, 2003.
Cusack, Christopher and Lindsay Jansen. "Death in the Family: Reimagining the Irish Family in Famine Fiction, 1871–1912." *New Voices, Inherited Lines: Literary and Cultural Representations of the Irish Family*, edited by Yvonne O'Keeffe and Claudia Reese, Peter Lang, 2014, pp. 7–33.
Day, Elizabeth. "*The Glass Shore* Review: A Further Feast of Female Voices." *The Irish Times*, 1 October 2016, www.irishtimes.com/culture/books/the-glass-

shore-review-a-further-feast-of-female-voices-1.2802050. Accessed 20 Dec. 2016.

Del Río, Constanza. "Misogyny in Flan O'Brian's *The Third Policeman*." *Gender, I-deology: Essays on Theory, Fiction and Film*, edited by Chantal Cornut-Gentille D'Arcy and José Angel García Landa, Rodopi, 1996, pp. 207–24.

"Edwin Hayes RHA (1820–1904)." *Encyclopedia of Visual Artists in Ireland*, www.visual-arts-cork.com/irish-artists/edwin-hayes.htm. Accessed 10 May 2015.

Fallon, Brian. "A Painter and a Fighter." *The Irish Times*, 17 December 1996, www.irishtimes.com/culture/a-painter-and-a-fighter-1.116821. Accessed 17 Dec. 2016.

Frawley, Oona, editor. *Memory Ireland: History and Modernity*. Syracuse University Press, 2011.

———. *Memory Ireland: Diaspora and Memory Practices*. Syracuse University Press, 2012.

Gleeson, Sinéad, editor. *The Glass Shore: Short Stories by Women Writers from the North of Ireland*. New Island, 2016.

Gordon, Avery. *Ghostly Matters: Haunting and the Sociological Imagination*. University of Minnesota Press, 2004.

Hagen, Patricia. "Review: *Lines of Vision: Irish Writers on Art*, edited by Janet McLean." *Minneapolis Star Tribune*, 15 November 2014, www.startribune.com/review-lines-of-vision-irish-writers-on-art-edited-by-janet-mclean/282640111/. Accessed 10 May 2015.

Hepburn, Allan, editor. *Listening In: Broadcasts, Speeches, and Interviews by Elizabeth Bowen*. Edinburgh University Press, 2010.

Horgan, Goretti. "Changing Women's Lives in Ireland." *International Socialism Journal*, no. 91, Summer 2001, pubs.socialistreviewindex.org.uk/isj91/horgan.htm. Accessed 10 May 2015.

Irishwomen United. *Banshee*, no. 7, 1977. *Irish Left Archive*, www.clririshleftarchive.org/document/1894/. Accessed 10 May 2016.

Larkin, Emmet. "The Devotional Revolution in Ireland, 1850–75." *The American Historical Review*, vol. 77, no. 3, 1972, pp. 625–52.

McLean, Janet, editor. *Lines of Vision: Irish Writers on Art*. Thames and Hudson, 2014.

Rooney, Brendan. "Public interview with Evelyn Conlon at the Irish National Gallery." 13 October 2014.

Terrazas, Melania. "The Rhetoric of Satire in Evelyn Conlon's *Telling* (2000)." *Clepsydra: Revista de Estudios de Género y Teoría Feminista*, vol. 12, 2013, pp. 81–97.

———. "'I Have Always Been a Writer': An Interview with Evelyn Conlon." *Atlantis: Journal of the Spanish Association for Anglo-American Studies*, vol. 39, no. 1, 2017, pp. 207–19.

———. "Questioning Women's Lives: Famine, Migration and Memory in Evelyn Conlon's *Not the Same Sky*." *Nordic Irish Studies*, vol.16, no. 1, 2017, pp. 5–74.

8

The Changing Status of Wounded Masculinity in Colm Tóibín's Ireland[1]

José M. Yebra

Introduction

In the last three decades, the transformation of Ireland from an ultra-conservative country in social and, particularly, sexual terms into a much more liberal and tolerant society has become evident. In relation to progress in human rights, gender equality and legal recognition of alternative sexualities and marriages, much of what has been achieved has been the result of years of women's struggles in multiple organisations, associations and institutions. If slowly, the sexual revolution brought about by second-wave feminism quite logically reached Ireland. With the reconfiguration and displacement of the categories of gender and sexuality that feminist activism promoted, whereby the location of women was no longer the home and a woman's body stopped being the asset shared by Church and State, the theory and practice of a taken-for-granted heterosexual, patriarchal masculinity had to accommodate themselves to the new situation. Consequently, in very different social and cultural venues – from the Academy to Hollywood, to TV and other scenarios – talk of the contemporary "crisis of masculinity" has been discussed for some decades now.

In Ireland, women were also responsible for the first outcries against the Catholic Church's interventions in and power over state policies, its control of health and education, and a tremendously restrictive and disabling consideration of women: their bodies, minds, appearance, behaviour, decency, function, etc. With modernisation and progressive policies usually also come

---

[1] The author gratefully acknowledges the support of the Spanish Ministry of Economy, Industry and Competitiveness (MINECO) and the European Regional Development Fund (DGI/ERDF) (code FFI2017-84258-P); the Government of Aragón and the ERDF 2014–2020 programme "Building Europe from Aragón" (code H03_17R), for the writing of this essay.

society's demands for institutional transparency, and it is in this terrain that the Irish Catholic Church has contributed to its own decline in religious, social and political power. From the 1990s onwards, numerous cases of sadism, sexual abuse, paedophilia and exploitation perpetrated by priests and nuns in religious schools, Magdalene Laundries, orphanages and industrial schools have been made public.

The following are some of the achievements towards a more egalitarian and inclusive society reached in Ireland from the 1990s onwards: the decriminalisation of homosexuality in 1993 – recently endorsed and/or validated by referenda on divorce (1995), children's rights (2012), marriage equality (2015), abortion (2018) and blasphemy (2018). At the moment, Ireland's *Taoiseach* (President) is Leo Varadkar, from Indian origins and the first Irish politician to come out as gay. It looks as if Ireland were in an ever-increasing headlong plunge into the future while trying to terminate a secular Catholic tradition.

Colm Tóibín was born in 1955, so his childhood and adolescence would have been informed by a strictly Catholic morality, and he published his first novel, *The South*, in 1990. His career and production would seem to be socially and sexually located between the crisis of traditional gender roles starting in the 1970s and the outburst of new discourses, policies and laws in the last three decades. For Christine St Peter, Ireland has often been mapped as a female space appropriated by the Other; hence the trope of body as map and map as body (16–17). However, in St Peter's view, recent writers have explored the boundaries of the human body "in various transgressive journeys across forbidden borders, particularly those that attempt to contain and discipline gender and sexuality" (16). Tóibín's discourse is a case in point: it deconstructs the male body as a cultural artefact that bears witness to recent Irish sexual politics, particularly the representation of same-sex desire. And yet, despite his being a leading voice in Irish gay writing, Tóibín proves a transitional figure.

He was raised in a country that criminalised homosexuality and alternative non-Catholic life styles. Hence, his approach to same-sex desire, albeit frank, is rather Jamesian. In fact, the writer has confessed to still feel uneasy and melancholic about his sexuality (Walshe, "Queering History," 143). Tóibín's problematic engagement with gayness is traceable in his writings, which swing between sexually explicit accounts of same-sex desire in short stories like "Three Friends" (2007) and "The Street" (2010) to homoerotic texts like *The Master* (2004) and narratives on AIDS like *The Blackwater Lightship* (1999). The country (and Tóibín with it) is decidedly moving forward in sexual politics although Tóibín's literary discourse is still complex and problematic for aesthetic, historical and/or socio-cultural reasons. Unlike non-Irish literary gay voices such as Alan Hollinghurst's, Tóibín usually withdraws from the excesses of sexuality and corporeality conventionally granted on gay bodies. In his case, gay bodies are often decorporealised as an effect of AIDS, historical and religious repression or personal restraint and melancholy. Masculinity is either absent (most fictional fathers being dead) or wounded, with the numerous cases of paedophilic priests being a powerful metaphor for castrating fatherhood. These men are sexual predators, but also (before their crimes are known) national father figures that replace actual fathers while wounding idealised Irish masculinity itself in different ways: in Tóibín, children bear witness to their actual fathers' funerals (*The Blackwater Lightship*), cope with often emasculating mothers ("The Use of Reason" [2006] and "The Name of the Game" [2006]) and are victims of sexual assaults from the clergy ("A Priest in the Family" [2006] and "The Pearl Fishers" [2010]).

With all the above in mind, this paper aims at exploring the discourse of change in Ireland, particularly concerning dissident, non-normative masculinities in trauma contexts, like paedophilia and AIDS, in Tóibín's short stories "A Priest in the Family" and "The Pearl Fishers," and his novel *The Blackwater Lightship*. To do so, I will delve into the underlying discourses that trigger and help explain these traumas: in the first place, the "Perfect Clerical Celibacy" model whereby the Church Hierarchy has constrained its members into an impossible masculinity, trauma and self-hatred in all three texts. Closely related to this concept, Eve Sedgwick's notion of the "Homosocial Continuum" will be addressed to envision masculinity in "A Priest in the Family." Finally, AIDS as a political and aesthetic trope will serve to frame gayness as sacrifice and renovation.

Trauma as Trigger of Change or Change as Trigger of Trauma

Jennifer Jeffers argued some years ago that "Irish culture is in a state of becoming ... and we must consciously create new contexts and new ways of understanding texts, historical situations and cultural change" (6). The idea and reality of change has thus become a mantra in recent Irish history as concerns the economy, politics, culture and very especially religious practices and belief. Catholicism has been a traditional distinctive feature of Irish identity, one that has set Ireland apart from its coloniser, hence the "resonance between the Catholic religion and the national identity in the psyche of many Irish people" (Williams, 317). Yet this centuries-old alliance between Catholicism and Irishness has come to an end. There are many different socio-cultural aspects that evince Ireland's transformation, but, for reasons of space, I will focus on the decline of Catholicism as a result of the discovery of so many cases of paedophilia among the clergy and of the consequent tepid reaction of the Hierarchy; and I will also refer to the effect of AIDS on the gay community and society at large.

As for the many cases of paedophilia and sexual abuse among the Irish clergy, the Church has attempted to detach itself from this unremitting number of sexual scandals by arguing that, rather than the institution, it is individual homosexual priests that must be blamed. In other words, it is homosexuality that poses a threat on both the country and the Church, the institution claims (Bowyer, 814). In this vein, in Kathryn Conrad's words, gays are "the foreign at home, the free-floating moral contaminant" (127) in Catholic Ireland. Beyond the specificity of Ireland, the country's religion-inflected position on gayness as threatening and exogenous instinctively draws on Abraham and Torok's much wider concept of the "crypt" and encryption of the dead or foreign body that must be expunged to overcome trauma (1994). After this logic, Ireland has constructed its identity as a response to the foreign coloniser, yet incorporating its own traumas as if they were foreign as well. In this sense, Irish homosexuals have been constructed as contaminants that bring foreign (moral and health-related) threats and eventually death, and incorporate them to the Irish DNA. They are somehow dead "objects," "enclosed in an isolated part ... sealed by ... repression" (Yassa, 87). It is as if homosexuality was (in Abraham and Torok's terms) a phantom that had been encrypted by the Irish political and religious Establishment to be later expelled. The resulting loss is not properly mourned in an introjecting process whereby gayness would be ideally assimilated into Irishness. Instead sexual dissidence is incorporated in phantasmatic terms; in other words, it cannot be mourned and remains encrypted in melancholia. Tóibín's texts seem to respond to this process of encryptation.

1. Whose Wound?

There seems to be a current debate around the problematic relation between gayness and Irishness. As Susanna Bowyer points out, critics like Kieran Rose argue that "lesbian and gay equality in Ireland was generated through an appeal to 'real and positive traditional Irish values'" (801). Others, like Conrad, defend that equality legislation is less related to "traditional Irish values" than to the fact that "the Irish state has opened its doors to both the European Community's laws and its economic opportunities" (134). Be it as it may, gay decriminalisation (and similar civil rights advances) has paradoxically advanced, at least in part, as a consequence of the clergy's abuse of (mostly) young boys. In trying to answer "What is wrong with the Irish male?" Patsy McGarry concluded that the Church's control of sexuality after the great Famine of 1845 led to a reification of celibacy, which changed the country's mapping of desire and self-regulation. Once celibacy became a national asset to prevent overpopulation and against foreign moral contamination, the Church's tenets turned into the country's flagship. Yet, despite the alleged moral superiority of abstinence, "Irish male sexuality in particular didn't go away. It was simply redirected into areas where its expression was least likely to be found out" (McGarry). Since women were,

8. THE CHANGING STATUS OF WOUNDED MASCULINITY IN COLM TÓIBÍN'S IRELAND

McGarry says, "a no-no" and the clergy had access to children and boys who were likely to keep the secret in a repressed and repressive society, the numerous cases of abuse coming out are no surprise. That is, sexual repression triggered out a national dysfunctionality that concealed a collective or cultural trauma. That is what was wrong with the Irish male. Who is responsible for this collective trauma scattered over many individual traumas? Is it the Catholic Church, itself a foreign invasion, as Father Doherty has argued? (Bowyer, 813). Is it the effect of a "discipline [and] surveillance and sexualisation of the body" that were imported, in Doherty's view, by French and Italian Jansenism? (813). In short, an increasing number of voices argue that Ireland's national discourse of repression is exogenous. They emphasise "the idea of an essentially healthy Irish sexual identity" and even "an early Irish culture accepting ... of homosexuality and ... sexuality in general" (813). This view allegedly gains ground since, with the weakening of Catholicism, Ireland has rapidly embraced major reforms in the moral and legal codes. Yet, there is an alternative reading, which, it seems to me, is more reasonable than the essentialist consideration whereby the Irish are more or less prone to the repression of sexuality. Current trans-culturalism, whereby national identity is constructed and reconstructed through contact with the Other, informs the changes of the country. In other words, change is both an endogenous and exogenous phenomenon.

Marie Keenan's analysis of sexual abuse in the Catholic Church is particularly illuminating because she moves away from classic individualistic perspectives that disregard the institution's implicit responsibility in these men's crimes. Keenan rejects the Church's self-exculpatory discourse as an institution. It is not these priests' homosexuality that explains their crimes. There are, Keenan argues, a number of circumstances that the institution has urged and upheld that have constituted the breeding ground for the sexual abuse of minors by members of the Catholic clergy. Hence, "there is a need to move from individualistic perspectives to a relational perspective, which incorporates cultural, theological and organizational factors" (66). Keenan's considerations on the construction of clerical masculinity shed new light on the problem. The balanced hydraulics of masculinity and purity/chastity has favoured an extreme hegemonic model on the part of the hierarchy whereby the social power of the Church depends on its self-control and is conveyed in what Keenan calls "Perfect Celibate Clerical Masculinity" (67). This institutionally-promoted model "avoided and effectively denied their [priests'] sexuality and sexual desire"; they tried, she continues, "to become 'holy and detached' and 'sexless'" (68). The clergymen who embody this introvert discipline model learn "to live in 'no man's land,' a place where gendered identity was to be avoided, [where they] intellectualised [their] emotions ... [and] internalised shame and personal failure" (68).

A major point in Keenan's argument is that, contrary to widespread opinions, many priests abusing minors "do not fit the psychiatric classification of paedophilia" (69). In other words, it is their transmutation into Perfect Clerical Celibate priests "losing their personal selves and integrity in the process" (69) that would often trigger their crimes. Within the different adaptation strategies that the different models of priesthood require, Perfect Clerical Celibate priests undergo a transitional "conversion." This transition from "ordinary" to "holy" men implies withdrawing one's self and behaving instead according "to the institutional role and identity" (70). In other words, in the name of holiness, these men are required unbending obedience to dogma. The conflict that these men suffer is particularly traumatic because the model they aspire to is impossible to accomplish. Indeed, "the failure to achieve such an impossible life has been internalised as personal failure and shame-based priestly existence, out of which the sexual abuse of minors arise" (71). It is obvious that Keenan is not exonerating individual sexual abusers. She is just refocusing the problem as an organic one. In inducing traumatic (i.e. unfeasible) masculinities on its members, the Church is co-responsible with these criminals' acts, albeit vicariously. If the institution distances itself from its individuals pretending that those of them who abuse are just deviant cases, "out of keeping with the dominant organizational church ethos" (72), the problem is far from being solved.

As happens with trauma poetics as a whole, sexual abuses by the clergy are often a systemic issue as well as one of (im)possibility. It is impossible to bear witness to the traumatic event as it happens, its consequence being that it haunts the victims of the episode itself. As Caruth expressed, "[w]hat returns to haunt the victim, these stories tell us, is not only the reality of the violent event but also the reality of the way that its violence has not yet been fully known" (19). Likewise, in enforcing an impossible masculinity on its members, the Church furthers a traumatic dead-end that may result in the dissociation between these men's original sense of masculinity and the one imposed upon them when joining the institution. The impossibility of coming to terms with this aporia is occasionally the trigger of the abuse. These abusers are victims of this aporia but also the perpetrators of a trauma they unflinchingly produce on vulnerable minors. In likewise terms, Slavoj Žižek addresses the problem, arguing that the "*institutional unconscious* designates the obscene disavowed underside that, precisely as disavowed, sustains the public institution" (Emphasis in the original; 142). In disavowing human drives, the institution affirms itself by sacrificing its members, no matter the social effect that the resulting pathologies or deviancies may produce. Thus, the Church reinstates the original trauma that gave rise to the Judeo-Christian tradition. In this sense, Cathy Caruth argues that the repetition and acknowledgment of the murder of the primal father by rebellious sons "explains both Judaism and its Christian antagonists" (18). When Christians narrate Christ's death as the atonement for the original sin, they are vicariously raising Moses's murder, which still haunts them (18). Caruth speaks of an Oedipal conflict that engages both Jews and Christians within a same original conception of traumatic sin; hence, "the traumatic nature of history means that events are only historical to the extent that they implicate others. And it is thus that Jewish history has also been the suffering of others' traumas" (18).

I do not think Caruth's discourse can literally be applied to Irish history and the abuses of the clergy. Yet, it can be illuminating in accessing Tóibín's discourse. Ireland has been mapped as wounded, being deprived of its original Irishness when "raped" by the British invader. Likewise, minors are the victims of members of a religious institution whose ideology pretends to be endogenous while having been imported from abroad. Irish history – like that of the Jews, as seen above – also encompasses the suffering of others' traumas; that is, Irishness is edified on the vicarious pain of wounded and dying gays like Declan in *The Blackwater Lightship* and the narrator of "The Pearl Fishers," and of suffering mothers like Molly in "A Priest in the Family" and Mary in *The Testament of Mary* (2013). From the 1990s onwards, the discourse and figuration of change in Ireland have become a cultural beacon that both describes a reality and a yearning to come to terms with an original Oedipal trauma. Yet, it can be argued that this yearning is the symptom of the (im)possibility of uttering change because it would imply a rejection of the traumatic undertones of Irish culture and history that Tóibín's texts recall. Atonement, particularly Christ's crucifixion, has been a national trait, repression being its performative vehicle. The question is whether the change that the country is undergoing is a mere metamorphosis or (using Catholic terminology) a transubstantiation that may modify the very foundations of national identification. The issue is far too ambitious for this paper. That is why the focus is on how Tóibín's writing – the novelist being widely considered a voice of change – bears witness to the redefinition of masculinity after the outburst of AIDS and the clergy's paedophilic crimes.

The Texts. The Poetics of Sacrifice

Tóibín's discourse is a revision of how the poetics of sacrifice in Ireland has been reified to construct a normative masculinity which has brought about traumatic impossibility and exclusion. The poetics of masculine sacrifice is not only related to the Catholic repression of sexual drives. It is also related to the performativity of male bodies in the context of foreign invasions. Irish males' reaction to the invader often took the form of aggressiveness, but also, as Ashe and Harland point out, the form of "the bodies of men and the ideals of masculinity, bravery, sacrifice and stoicism [that] could be deployed through the practices of suffering and martyrdom to expose the cruelty and corruption of the enemy" (753). Tóibín's texts reflect on the multiple faces that sacrifice and repression adopt to reify and deconstruct Irish manliness. This is patent in the characters that kidnap Mary, the protagonist of *The Testament of Mary*. According to Rychter, "[t]hey have favoured a re-enactment of the traumatic event, a monstrous rehearsing of cold cruelty and dark brutality" (45). In other words, the Catholic canon has edified masculinity on the restraint and cruelty implicit in Christ's crucifixion as the event that resurfaces the original trauma of sin. This is Tóibín's raw material so as to deconstruct Irish manliness.

1. *The Blackwater Lightship*

The Blackwater Lightship[2] turns around Declan's return home when he is about to die of AIDS. Back there, he is cared for by his sister Helen, mother Lily and grandmother Dora. Although the novel mostly deals with these women's disengagements and rivalry in a nuanced (albeit insightful) tone, I will focus on Declan's diseased body as a map of atonement and, allegedly, of (im) possible change. I have addressed elsewhere the cultural significance of Declan's death as a catalyst for national transformation; be it from the perspective of transgenerational trauma (Yebra, "Transgenerational") or the liminality of gayness in the 1990s (Yebra, "Interstitial Status"). Drawing on this last point, Declan's diseased body "constitute[s a] redemptive force for Ireland to overcome its atavism without it being fully rejected" ("Interstitial Status," 98). It is in this sense that Declan, like Christ, is sacrificed to redeem Ireland (98), a "casualty of the Irish modernization process" (99); a return in sum. Yet, if the novel bears witness to the youth's "return to the chora ... his oneness with his (m)others" ("Interstitial Status," 101), the question is whether the problem remains. In other words, is Declan's death worthy if it barely structures change?

As already said, homosexuality was decriminalised in Ireland in 1993, ironically the time in which the novel is set. However, those nearby do not seem ready to come to terms with Declan's disease and identity. His grandmother's neighbours cannot even figure out that his physical deterioration is due to AIDS, that he is gay and that he is not going to marry a girl (*TBL* 246). Even his family seems more concerned with coming to terms with its own discord than fully addressing the implications of Declan's illness and sexual orientation. Indeed, in *The Blackwater Lightship*, the actual politics of liberation never seems to occur in Ireland, but in Europe. Likewise, AIDS has been largely regarded "not likely to become indigenous but imported by homosexuals and unlikely to be problematic in a traditional Catholic country like Ireland" (Nolan, 115). The disease obviously reached the country and triggered an overall change in gay politics. Nevertheless, in Tóibín's texts inclusive social measures always appear to come from elsewhere, particularly Europe. Declan's friend Paul recalls his love affair with François, a French guy, in rather nostalgic terms, not to claim

---

2   Henceforward referred to as *TBL*.

8. THE CHANGING STATUS OF WOUNDED MASCULINITY IN COLM TÓIBÍN'S IRELAND

his youth in Ireland but his Arcadian coming-out in France: "François' father always said what he meant and normally that was something quite gentle and straightforward. I loved how straightforward they all were ... It was a sort of pure happiness" (166). That is, against Rose's and Doherty's arguments, homophilic change in *The Blackwater Lightship* comes from elsewhere. Tóibín's Irish fathers still die before sons come out because "normative" masculinity keeps being irreconcilable with explicit gayness. If there is room for some reconciliation between mothers and sons, heterosexual men are virtually excluded or dead.

In *The Heather Blazing* (1992), published and set just before gay decriminalisation, Judge Eamon Redmond recalls his father's death as he ponders if a pregnant girl must be expelled from school. The tension in Redmond's masculinity – which swings between his problematic adolescence due to his mother's death and his relationship with his father, and his decision on the pregnant girl when his own daughter is a single mother – is further problematised in Declan's sacrificial demise in *The Blackwater Lightship*. Despite the prospective changes *The Heather Blazing* forecasts, Redmond keeps faithful to the traditional hard masculinity embodied by his father and De Valera's Fianna Fail, disallowing the pregnant girl to go back to school. However, Declan surrenders when he decides to die at home – the women of the family holding a vigil and praying for him – rather than in a Dublin hospital (*TBL*, 257). Unlike Christ, who claims for his Father's help, Declan asks for his mother's assistance, who utters something inaudible or unintelligible to the others (258). The unfathomable of the mother's discourse when the son is about to die is especially significant. In fact, her words can only come in the form of a lullaby; a mumbling that escapes symbolic language and belongs to a primal communication between mother and son, Ireland and its people: "October winds lament around the Castle of Dromore. But peace is in the lofty hall, *a pháiste bán a stór*,[3] / Though autumn winds may droop and die, a bud of spring are you" (264). The poem Lily chooses to "lullaby" Declan with, "the Castle of Dromore," merges Christian references to Holy Mary grieving in Heaven, with the renewing spirit of nature ("Castle of Dromore"). No matter that youth is about to die, as autumn winds do, and announce he is still a birthing bud for his mother (land).

Eibhear Walshe says that *The Blackwater Lightship* is pedagogical, especially in its treatment of AIDS ("Particular Genie," 119). In this sense, the novel recalls that "the covert and ambiguous approach adopted by both Church and State to policymaking for AIDS enabled Ireland to transition peacefully through a challenging period of social change" (Nolan, 123). However, the novel is also an allegory of painful (if peaceful) evolution. Hence, the metamorphosis from a conservative to a more open-minded country is not for free or complete. Some people, like Declan, keep behind while pain remains a distinguishing feature of

---

3   These Gaelic words could be translated as "Darling fair-haired child."

the transformation. Yet, the poem of the Castle of Dromore is aimed at solving deep-rooted conflicts, merging the English and the Irish, the voices of Lily and Helen, Christianity and Paganism.

When Helen walks the seashore of Wexford, she bears witness to how the cliff is "eaten away by the weather, washed away by the sea" (260). In other words, the seashore is transformed slowly but inexorably. For Walshe, this erosion and "the defunct lighthouse all reflect the mutability, loss and death of the men of her family" ("Particular Genie," 125). The symbol of erosion is, in my view, even more eloquent and pungent, as Anne Fogarty hints (171). It embraces but transcends the death of these men, as Helen's nihilism conveys (260). The land is eroded, just like Declan's de-corporealised body and Irish mores are. Nonetheless, it is a gradual metamorphosis rather than a radical change. The substratum remains; it is only that so-called realities take a different shape.

2. "A Priest in the Family"

"A Priest in the family" – a story from the *Mothers and Sons* collection (2006) – and "The Pearl Fishers" – from *The Empty Family* (2010) – deal with sacrifice and masculinity drawing on children's abuse by Catholic priests. The visibilisation of these cases has been a catalyst in the changing moral climate in Ireland in the last decades. In both short stories, this change (apparently a transubstantiation) is just nuanced but climactic. Fogarty refers to how Tóibín reverts the logic of normative Oedipal relations to accommodate motherhood and the articulation of the sons' same-sex desire: "The eerie, absent space that she [the mother] occupies becomes the locus in which crucial aspects of male identity are negotiated and reconceived" (170). It is not that the Oedipal is transubstantiated; that is, mother and son do not exchange roles, although the images Tóibín supplies feature "unappeased, homeless sons and rancorous, needy mothers conjoined in a symbolic alliance with death and destruction" (181). It is rather that the (dis)engagement between mother and son is regulated in unconventional terms.

This anti-Oedipal reformulation of desire is particularly complex in "A Priest in the Family," the mother–son bond being inscribed in the problematic articulation of masculinity in the Irish Church. Molly is an old woman who bears witness to and participates in the social changes in Ireland. Years ago, she says, "the old women spent their lives praying. Now, we get our hair done and play bridge and go to Dublin on the free travel, and we say what we like" (152).[4] A strong woman takes a strong son. Nevertheless, strong does not mean forward-looking in Frank's (Molly's son) case. Molly's grit to change a woman's role is the locus where Frank's religious fervour is allegedly negotiated and conceived. He stands for the "Perfect Celibate Clerical Masculinity" mentioned

---

4   References to the text will be to the 2006 *Mothers and Sons* Picador edition.

8. THE CHANGING STATUS OF WOUNDED MASCULINITY IN COLM TÓIBÍN'S IRELAND

above, as Molly points out: "I have to be careful what I say in front of Frank, he's very holy" (152). Frank's status implies introvert discipline, which results in the internalisation of shame and self-emasculation. It does not follow from the above that Molly is responsible for her son's personal failure. His is a systemic failure of which the mother is simply a passive agent and witness. Obviously, it does not mean either that Frank is not to be blamed for the abuses he has committed. Yet, holiness is too heavy a burden and goal altogether, Frank being both a perpetrator and a vicarious victim: a perpetrator for the horrible crimes he has committed, and a victim of an unfeasible masculinity whose traumatic acting-out looms large along the story. That Frank's crimes are systemically-induced is intimated rather than stated. The role of the Church as an institution that forces on its members unachievable masculine models remains silenced, as when Father Greenwood informs Molly of the events in a reticent fashion: "He's in trouble … There's going to be a court case" (159). This proves how restrained language is to engage and disengage from the facts uttered. It is not only the implication of the Church in Frank's crime and fall that the story addresses. Molly's insightful analysis of a society whose mores change ascertains that such change is merely a cosmetic one. Moreover, if the Church, as an institution, is co-responsible for the priests' abuses, socially systemic surveillance also affects her family. Indeed, she assumes that her neighbours' malicious gossip about Frank will eventually affect them all (161).

The story features two transformative processes, almost a transubstantiation of roles and realities. Frank is no longer holy, no matter that he has embodied "Perfect Celibate Clerical Masculinity" for years. He is careful when reversing and turning his car, "not to drive on her [Molly's] lawn" (170) even after holding the most difficult conversation with his mother. Yet, this exactness, formerly a symptom of his holiness (i.e. perfect male celibacy/restraint), gives him away now. Unlike Declan's, though, Frank's social sacrifice is justified. After the traumatic revelation, first by Father Greenwood and later by Frank himself, Molly's everyday life transubstantiates into an uncanny hostile territory:

> The town during the next week seemed almost new to her. Nothing was as familiar as she had supposed. She was unsure what a glance or a greeting disguised, and she was careful, once she had left her own house, never to turn too sharply or look too closely in case she saw them whispering about her. (165)

Although the passage above delves into Molly's sense of loss, her change from strong eerie mother to frightened object of social scrutiny confirms the systemic nature of change itself.

3. "The Pearl Fishers"

"The Pearl Fishers," which is "perhaps the best story in the collection [*The Empty Family*]" (Prose), leaves the Oedipal behind, exploring masculinities in an allegedly new Ireland from a different perspective. Indeed, although the story revisits the abuses of members of the clergy, it focuses on the case of a female, Gráinne, when she was an adolescent. The internal narrator is, however, a middle-aged gay man who unwillingly accepts his school partners', Gráinne and husband Donnacha's, invitation for dinner. The meeting is revelatory of sexual abuse and same-sex bonds at school, and of a new Catholic rhetoric; these are three issues the story frames from the viewpoint of the Girardian triangle that the three protagonists make up. Gráinne has become a religious leader, "a fierce believer in the truth" (63) who calls for national renewal.[5] Through her active role in the media, she addresses "the state of the Church and the soul of the nation" (63), a message that, far from cajoling the narrator, sickens him even further. His reasons to keep away from her are various, one of them being his loss of "interest in arguments about the changing Ireland" (63), and another that he fell in love with Donnacha at school (65). Yet the narrator especially loathes her because the change she announces, he feels, is more of the same. Rather than a rebirth, her militancy is a coup d'état against the hierarchy to build up an analogous regime of alleged purity. "Are you still in daily touch with the Virgin Mary?" (65), the narrator asks, ironising on Gráinne's renewed "Perfect Clericalism," which is implacable with – yet thrives on – "Perfect Celibate Clerical Masculinity." She articulates this change around humility and truth: "There is a new humility among the Hierarchy ... They know they are ... servants of the truth" (77).

In claiming for "Perfect Celibate Clericalism," Gráinne keeps an idealised image of the clergy, an image which, as analysed above, can be the source of (im)possibility, trauma, self-hatred and abuse. In this process of truth-unveiling, she decides to account for her own abuse. For her, the change of Ireland is not essentially economic or even sociological, but one of religious and ethical dimensions, the truth being its central value. Religious and socio-political institutions have failed, she believes, because truth has been disregarded. That is the transubstantiation she yearns for, from secrecy to truth. Gráinne's conception of secrecy is obviously one of illicitness and silence, which has eventually triggered abuse. However, she forgets the other side of secrecy, that which has helped emerge subaltern and hybrid identities, particularly Irishness and gayness when the former was suppressed by British rule and the latter by criminalisation. In other words, assuming Gráinne is right in denouncing the clergy's abuses, she reifies the very strictness that straitjacketed the institution's

---

5   Further references to this text will be to the 2010 Penguin edition of *The Empty Family*.

members in the first place. Moreover, in narrowing truth as one and only, her discourse is misleading and often biased.

"There has been a great change and I wanted to write about that" (77), Gráinne confesses. If the personal is political, for her, the political is personal. That is why she feels she has to speak out (78). While at school, she had sex with Father Moorehouse, to the narrator's surprise. And the reason why Gráinne invites the narrator is that she wants him to be her witness. In view of his reluctance, for he confesses never to have witnessed any misbehaviour on the part of the priest, she reminds him: "We were in that room ... we knew him, and we were vulnerable" (79). The story is once again very inconclusive. Whether Gráinne was forced to have sex is never confirmed, although the many cases of children being abused tilt the scales in her favour. Yet, the narrator keeps at a distance for unrevealed reasons. He may not believe her, or he may dislike her because she married Donnacha in the end, or simply consider her radical beliefs a threat to his newly acquired rights as a gay man. That is why, when she avows she is "going to tell the story of [her] life" (80), he eludes the issue, only interested in knowing his role in the story. Indeed, her zeal for truth only raises new secrets, particularly the narrator and Donnacha's teenage love affair. Unlike Father Moorehouse's alleged abuse of Gráinne, this affair constitutes a different kind of secret that is both a symbol of sacrifice, and of freedom and contestation. For Donnacha, secrecy is a sacrifice forcing him to keep his sexual orientation at bay and fulfil heteronormative masculinity. Ironically, when he asks the narrator to keep their teenage secret, the latter cannot help recalling their sexual activity in explicit terms: "I remembered that nothing made him happier ... than to have me lie on my back while he knelt with his back to me and his knees on either side on my torso. He would bend as I pushed my tongue hard up into his arsehole while he sucked my cock and licked my balls" (76).

Paradoxically, the narrator recalls, Donnacha remains "part of the culture that produced him"; a restrained social order where the body is disavowed, no nudity allowed and doors locked (76). For the narrator, however, their secret is still erotic, the source of his queer identity. In a context of repression, their affair contested established rules, hence its sexual thrill and political magnitude. The narrator stands for a new Ireland which has moved away from hackneyed discourses. As a teenager, he conflated religious devotion with sexual pleasure: "It was more or less at the time I began to have sex with Donnacha that I became deeply religious" (71). Likewise, he avows, his "interest in Patrick Moorehouse's mind, and [his] fascination at the points he made and the terms he used and the writers he quoted from, were entirely sexual" (73). That is the paradoxical circuit of desire and contestation that makes up the narrator's alternative libidinal discourse. In other words, in pre-gay-decriminalisation Ireland, he conjures up secrecy as a metaphor for the pleasures it hides. As an adult, and as pointed out above, he is not only openly gay, but an Irish gay man inhabiting a transcultural world: "I make enough money from the grim, almost plotless thrillers with gay sub-plots I produce, which are popular in Germany and in Japan, and from overwrought and graphically violent screenplays" (63–64). The narrator puts forward new forms of articulating masculinity. He does so by revising the underneath of sexual repression in Catholic Ireland as a teenager and taking up gay subculture as an adult.

The climax of the story coincides with the narrator and Donnacha's love affair, more specifically the scene when they attend the dress rehearsal of Bizet's opera *The Pearl Fishers*. As mentioned above, the story turns around the Girardian triangle made up by the two boys and Gráinne. To understand the triangular logic that structures the story, Eve Sedgwick's recasting of Girard's triangle comes handy. Both in *Between Men* (1985) and *Epistemology of the Closet* (1991), Sedgwick delves into a socio-cultural pattern deeply rooted in the articulation of sex, gender and sexual orientation. In her view, there is a continuum between homosociality, homophobia and homosexuality that explains how identity, libidinal positions and power are constructed. Within a homosocial framework, "social bonds between persons of the same sex" are privileged (Sedgwick, *Between Men*, 1). Indeed, "there is a special relationship between male homosocial (including homosexual) desire and the structures for maintaining and transmitting patriarchal power" (*Between Men*, 25). In other words, the homosocial is complicit with heteronormativity, though underpinned by homosexual undertones. If the balance between the homosocial and the homosexual breaks down and hence heteronormativity is menaced, homophobia comes into play. This frail stability is nowhere better represented than in the Girardian triangle in which two males engage with each other in homo-social/erotic terms through a female. In other words, the woman is merely an exchange value that disguises a homosocial status quo and normalises a relation between men that, otherwise, would be unnameable. Both "The Pearl Fishers" story and Bizet's opera address this triangulation of identity and desire. And although Gráinne does not know about the narrator and Donnacha's love affair, her figure and presence are necessary in order to understand and articulate the male characters' post-gay bond.

Bizet's opera tells the story of the life-long friendship of Zurga, the leader of fishermen in ancient Ceylon (current Sri Lanka), and fisherman Nadir. The famous duel is a re-enactment of a former oath whereby they promised to be faithful to each other until death. They did so when they glimpsed beautiful Leila, a young priestess. That is, they set up their bond on its being menaced and reassured by a woman. She thus becomes both a galvaniser of their love and of their rivalry according to complex, contradictory and dominant homosocial conventions. For Sedgwick, in homoerotic, gay and queer texts, the Girardian triangle recasts itself by replacing the woman, as the third vortex of the triangle, with a third man. Yet, Tóibín's "The Pearl Fishers" keeps to Bizet's original.

8. THE CHANGING STATUS OF WOUNDED MASCULINITY IN COLM TÓIBÍN'S IRELAND

The story is metafictionally engaged with the opera, their intertextual relation being a metaphor of gays' discrimination, isolation and invisibility in pre-decriminalisation Ireland. In "The Pearl Fishers" we can read: "The men's duet was about eternal friendship sworn between them as they knew they were in love with the same woman. By the end of the opera that same melody would be sung as a duet by the tenor and the woman, who had found love, thus leaving the baritone alone and miserable" (81). The triangle in the short story, homoerotic at first, eventually turns homosocial and heteronormative to comply with social norms. Moreover, the narrator is a baritone, a liminal voice range between bass and tenor, Donnacha standing for the tenor. In other words, the narrator is the one in the middle, the hybrid, the man who is not a "full" man, the redundant figure. Yet, the socio-sexual stereotypes their voices stand for (sexual ambiguousness in the narrator's case and ultra-masculinity in Donnacha's) break down during the opera's performance:

> I was overwhelmed when the two men began to sing. When we were told about the difference between a baritone and a tenor I had understood it but it had not meant much to me. Now the tenor's voice seemed vulnerable and plaintive, and the other voice masculine and strong ... You could hear each voice clearly when it came to the duet and when the voices finally merged in harmony I was almost in tears. I could not take my eyes off the two men. What they had done together in that aria was the beginning of a new life for me. (82)

The aria is the climax both of the opera and the story. The narrator is simultaneously an actor in and witness to the dramatic display. In particular, he addresses the transubstantiation on stage as long as the gender roles of vulnerability/femininity and strength/masculinity are contested and finally merged in an indivisible whole. While other students loathe or, like Gráinne, do not care about the opera, the narrator feels transfixed and changed forever. This could be taken as symbolic of a then upcoming new Ireland. However, he confesses that the music that "had seemed like a great new beginning [had become] within a decade ... sweet and silly" (84). The narrator's epiphany is thus a teenage dream, the illusion of a new beginning, a coming-out to himself. However, although the epiphany is just a delusion from the viewpoint of the adult narrator, its effects are still evident. His sarcasm towards Gráinne's new Church and her memoirs/confession is both an effect of his coming out and of that of the country: "Dublin, no matter what remained, was new with gay men in twos or threes or hungry ones alone on their way to the Front Lounge or GUBU or some new joint that I have yet to hear about. If I know them, we nod or smile" (88). Like Molly's Dublin in "A Priest in the Family," the narrator of "The Pearl Fishers" features a city arranged in layers, the outer one revealing a society in transformation.

Conclusion

Tóibín is an author of change, or rather of transition. An active writer since the 1980s, his literature has been witness to and part of the so-called transformation of Ireland from a deeply Catholic isolated insular country into the Celtic Tiger, a modern and much wealthier country. This process, Tóibín's writing proves, has not always run smoothly. In analysing a novel and two stories ranging from the 1990s to 2010, this chapter claims the change of Ireland to be more a metamorphosis than a radical transformation or transubstantiation of values and ways of life. The effect of traumatic events like AIDS – related chronologically to gay liberation in Ireland – and the abuse of children by members of the clergy have changed the articulation of masculinity. In Tóibín's texts, fathers are mostly absent or dead,[6] which clears the way for sons to concoct new ways of experiencing masculinity. AIDS kills Declan and many of his generation. However, his death may be redemptive and his nephews are likely to profit from it. If this is so, the change from a country that criminalised sexual dissidents to one that grants them full citizenry seems to have been fulfilled. Yet, the fact that the change results from an act of redemption makes it into a metamorphosis rather than a total transformation. That is, the rules of the game are not completely overturned, if that is possible at all. The same holds for the stories analysed here. The social impact of the clergy's abuse of minors is undeniable. Silence in "A Priest in the Family," and the narrator's and Gráinne's will to contest the Church and its hierarchy respectively in "The Pearl Fishers" bear witness to a self-contested country: whether religion is a foreign body "poisoning" pre-Catholic Irishness or a genuine Irish feature against British Anglicanism is contentious. Be it as it may, Tóibín's texts address how old discourses need revising to accommodate new realities.

Religion is not and cannot be the only socio-cultural referent, especially when civil rights movements and political activism have thrived in the country and the "Perfect celibate" model has proved unrealistic and problematic. More recently, in *The Testament of Mary*, Tóibín puts forward a more radical account of change than appears in the texts analysed in this study. As Rychter argues, the Virgin's "gothic romance exposes the suppressed, darker, trauma-inducing side of the Christian religion" (46), for which Christ's crucifixion is the climactic moment. Thus, this novella addresses an overall transformative event, a metaphor of transubstantiation that is only hinted at in Tóibín's previous texts.

---

6 This is by no means an exclusive characteristic of Tóibín's fiction but a recurrent feature in Irish novels. Yet, in Tóibín's case it is closely related to the articulation of gay identity.

Works Cited

Abraham, Nicolas and Maria Torok. *The Shell and the Kernel: Renewals of Psychoanalysis*. Translated and with an Introduction by Nicholas T. Rand. Chicago University Press, 1994.
Ashe, Fildelma and Ken Harland. "Troubling Masculinities: Changing Patterns of Violent Masculinities in a Society Emerging from Political Conflict." *Studies in Conflict & Terrorism*, vol. 37, 2014, pp. 747–62.
Bowyer, Susanna. "Queer Patriots: Sexuality and the Character of National Identity in Ireland." *Cultural Studies*, vol. 24, no. 6, 2010, pp. 801–20.
Caruth, Cathy. *Unclaimed Experience: Trauma, Narrative, History*. The Johns Hopkins University Press, 1996.
"Castle of Dromore." *King Laoghaire*, www.kinglaoghaire.com/ lyrics/862-the-castle-of-dromore. Accessed 2 Nov. 2018.
Conrad, Kathryn. "Queer Treasons: Homosexuality and Irish National Identity." *Cultural Studies*, vol. 15, no. 1, 2001, pp. 124–37.
Fogarty, Anne. "After Oedipus? Mothers and Sons in the Fiction of Colm Tóibín." *Reading Colm Tóibín*, edited by Paul Delaney, The Liffey Press, 2008, pp. 167–82.
Jeffers, Jennifer. *The Irish Novel at the End of the Twentieth Century: Gender, Bodies and Power*. Palgrave, 2000.
Keenan, Marie. "Masculinity, Relationships and Context: Child Sexual Abuse and the Catholic Church." *Irish Journal of Applied Social Studies*, vol. 15, no. 2, 2015, pp. 64–77.
McGarry, Patsy. "An Irish Disease?" *The Irish Times*, 4 May 2002, www.irishtimes.com/news/an-irish-disease-1.1056148. Accessed 15 Oct. 2018.
Nolan, Ann. "The Gay Community Response to the Emergence of AIDS in Ireland: Activism, Covert Policy, and the Significance of an Invisible Memory." *The Journal of Policy History*, vol. 30, no. 1, 2018, pp. 105–27.
Prose, Francine. "Stories from an Irish Master." *The New York Times*, 14 January 2011, www.nytimes.com/2011/01/16/books/review/Prose-t.html. Accessed 18 Oct. 2018.
Rychter, Ewa. "Romancing the Crucifixion in Biblical Rewritings by Phillip Pullman and Colm Tóibín." *Sciendo*, vol. 10, no. 1, 2018, pp. 39–49.
Sedgwick, Eve. *Between Men: English Literature and Male Homosocial Desire*. Columbia University Press, 1985.
———. *Epistemology of the Closet*. University of California Press, 1991.
St. Peter, Christine. "Border Crossing with 'no Proper Maps.' Éilís Ní Dhuibhne, Colm Tóibín, and Anne Enright Attempt the Art of Cartography." *Rewriting Boundaries. Critical Approaches in Irish Studies*, edited by Asier Altuna and Cristina Andreu, PPU, 2007, pp. 15–26.
Tóibín, Colm. *The Heather Blazing*. Pan Books, 1992.
———. *The Blackwater Lightship*. Picador, 1999.
———. *Mothers and Sons*. Picador, 2006.
———. *The Empty Family*. Penguin, 2010.
———. *The Testament of Mary*. Penguin, 2013.

Walshe, Eibhear. "Queering History: Contemporary Irish Lesbian and Gay Writing." *Re-writing Boundaries. Critical Approaches in Irish Studies*, edited by Asier Altuna and Cristina Andreu, PPU, 2007, pp. 141–50.

———. "'This Particular Genie': The Elusive Gay Male Body in Tóibín's Novels." *Reading Colm Tóibín*, edited by Paul Delaney, The Liffey Press, 2008, pp. 115–30.

Williams, Kevin. "Faith and the Nation: Education and Religious Identity in the Republic of Ireland." *British Journal of Educational Studies*, vol. 47, no. 4, 1999, pp. 317–31.

Yassa, Maria. "Nicolas Abraham and Maria Torok – The Inner Crypt." *The Scandinavian Psychoanalytic Review*, vol. 25, no. 2, 2002, pp. 82–91.

Yebra, José M. "The Interstitial Status of Irish Gayness in Colm Tóibín's *The Blackwater Lightship* and *The Master*." *Estudios Irlandeses*, vol. 9, 2014, pp. 96–106.

———. "Transgenerational and Intergenerational Family Trauma in Colm Tóibín's *The Blackwater Lightship* and 'Three Friends.'" *Moderna Språk*, vol. 109, no. 2, 2015, pp. 122–39.

Žižek, Slavoj. *Violence*. Profile Books, 2009.

9

Direct Provision and Asylum Archive: Power and Surveillance

Vukasin Nedeljkovic

Memory, for migrants, is almost always the memory of loss. But since most migrants have been pushed out of the sites of official/national memory in their original homes, there is some anxiety surrounding the status of what is lost, since the memory of the journey to a new place, the memory of one's own life and family world in the old place, and official memory about the nation one has left have to be recombined in a new location.

(Appadurai, 21)

Rhythm of the wheels, stronger than hunger or tiredness; until, at a certain moment, the train would stop and I would feel the warm air and the smell of hay and I would get out into the sun; then I would lie down on the ground to kiss the earth, as you read in books, with my face in the grass. And a woman would pass, and she would ask me "Who are you?" in Italian, and I would tell her my story in Italian, and she would understand, and she would give me food and shelter. She would not believe the things I tell her, and I would show her the number on my arm, and then she would believe. (Levi, 47)

Introduction

The Direct Provision scheme was introduced in Ireland in November 1999 to house asylum seekers in State-designed accommodation centres. There were initially eighty-two centres located across the country, which had grown to more than 120 by 2016; some of the buildings included former convents, army barracks, hotels and holiday homes. Most of these centres were situated on the periphery of towns and cities, this being an institutional decision which reduced integration with the local population significantly, leaving the asylum seekers' community to dwell in a ghettoised environment.

Direct Provision

Within the Direct Provision scheme, the position allocated to asylum seekers objectifies, infantilises and criminalises them. As mentioned above, they live in ghettoes where families with children are often forced to share small rooms: overcrowding, unhygienic conditions and disease are the results. As if they were children or prisoners, the management controls their food, their movements, the supply of bed linen and cleaning materials, exerting their authority, power and control over them with Foucauldian technologies regulating the asylum seekers' movements and the space they inhabit (Foucault, *Discipline and Punish*). In Ronit Lentin's opinion, Direct Provision centres are "holding camps" and "sites of deportability" which "construct their inmates as deportable subjects, ready to be deported any time." These centres rightly match the French anthropologist Marc Augé's concept of the "non-places" characteristic of supermodernity: spaces that cannot be defined as spaces of identity, relational or historical (78–79). Direct Provision centres are the primary focus of my research: this "new" category of institutions that deprive their lodgers of singular identity or relations, where an undefined incarceration is the only existence and where the identity of asylum seekers is unknown by being reduced to having no known identity.

From a slightly different critical perspective, the Free Legal Advice Centre (2009) has referred to these privately owned centres, administered by the Government of Ireland, as a "direct provision industry" which makes a profit on the backs of asylum seekers (Lentin), hence the name "Direct Provision" scheme. To foster the links that there seem to be between Direct Provision, profitability and capitalism, we can also add the photographer and theorist Allan Sekula's description of Bentham's Panopticon as a surveillance system: "[Bentham's] prisons were to function as profit-making establishments, based on the private contracting-out of convict labor. For Foucault, 'Panopticism' provides the central metaphor for modern disciplinary power, based on isolation, individuation, and supervision" ("The Body," 9).

The Direct Provision scheme is a continuation of the history of confinement in Ireland through borstals, industrial schools, Magdalene Laundries, prisons, mother and baby homes and lunatic asylums.[1] When the Irish State initiated the Direct Provision scheme, it deliberately constructed certain spaces where institutional racism could be readily instantiated, explicitly through, for example, the threat of transfer to a different accommodation centre or of deportation. The inmates' constant fear and anxiety transform Direct Provision centres into disciplinary and exclusionary forms of spatial and social enclosure that separate and conceal asylum seekers from mainstream society, ultimately

---

1 For a detailed historical study and analysis of incarcerating institutions in Ireland, see O'Sullivan and O'Donnell.

preventing their long term integration or inclusion. These centres are, as Steve Loyal argues drawing on Erving Goffman's ideas, "total institutions, forcing houses for changing persons, each is a natural experiment on what can be done to the self" (101). Their isolating and exclusionary nature links these centres to contemporary ideas on *communitas* and *immunitas* from the perspective of biopolitics: that is, the need to preserve (some) life and to destroy (other) life. According to Esposito,

> The fact that the growing flux of immigrants is seen – in my view utterly mistaken – as one of the major dangers for our societies shows as well from another side the centrality that the immunitary question has taken on. Wherever new barriers and new checkpoints are set up, new lines of separation appear with respect to something threatening, or at least that appears to threaten, our biological, social, and environmental identity. The contact, the relation, the being in common, immediately appears as crushed by the risk of contamination. (4–5)

One can conclude that asylum seekers are locked/incarcerated in the quarantines/direct provision centres in order to prevent the potential contamination of the Irish State. The immunitary protocol is therefore performed upon the asylum seeker's arrival in a Direct Provision centre; the vaccine of corrective and disciplinary measures.

Figure 9.1: The Old Convent Direct Provision Centre, Ballyhaunis, 2008.

While discussing Nazi concentration camps, Agamben established a link between these spaces and many other similar contemporary enclosures:

> [P]recisely because they were lacking almost all the rights and expectations that we customarily attribute to human existence, and yet were still biologically alive, they came to be situated in a limit zone between life and death, inside and outside, in which they were no longer anything but bare life. If this is true, if the essence of the camp consists in the materialization of the state of exception and in the subsequent creation of a space in which bare life and the juridical rule enter into a threshold of indistinction, then we must admit that we find ourselves virtually in the presence of a camp every time such a structure is created, independent of the kinds of crimes that are committed there and whatever its denomination and specific topography. (159)

In this sense, Direct Provision centres represent "the absence of everything ... the place where the bottom has dropped out of everything, an atmospheric density, a plenitude of the void, or the murmur of silence" (Levinas, 46).

Asylum Archive

Asylum Archive – a repository of asylum experiences and artefacts – originally started as a coping mechanism while I was in the process of seeking asylum in Ireland. During that period, "I kept myself intact by capturing and communicating with the environment through photographs and videos. This creative process helped me to overcome power, authority, detention, and supervision" (Nedeljkovic, "Direct Provision"). Asylum Archive is a project directly concerned with the realities and traumatic lives of asylum seekers: its main objective is to collaborate with asylum seekers, artists, academics and civil society activists with a view to creating an interactive documentary cross-platform online resource which brings forward representations of exile, displacement, trauma, and memory from various critical perspectives.

Asylum Archive is not a singular art project that stands outside of society, distractedly engaged in an internal conversation: rather, it is a platform open for dialogue and discussion inclusive of individuals that have experienced a sense of sociological/geographical displacement, memory loss, trauma, and violence. It has an essential visual, informative, and educational perspective and, as an online archive, it is accessible to any future researchers and scholars who may wish to undertake a study about the conditions of asylum seekers in Ireland.

Although frequently seen as a vehicle for the transmission of "official information and memory," the archive can also reveal its potential for political resistance if interpreted from a different position. In Sekula's words: "The archive has to be read from below, from a position of solidarity with those displaced, deformed, silenced or made invisible by the machineries of profit and progress" ("Reading an Archive," 444). In this spirit, Asylum Archive provides a way of rehearsing and repeating an everyday performance of political resistance whereby Direct Provision centres cannot be exclusively perceived as sites of incarceration, social exclusion, or extreme poverty. Rather, they can be seen to constitute oppositional formations of collectivity and recalcitrance in which different nationalities and ethnic groups exist and persist despite the very conditions of confinement created by the state. In the same vein, Diana Taylor explores how the "archive and the repertoire work together to make political claims, transmit traumatic memory, and forge a new sense of cultural identity," arguing that "trauma expresses itself viscerally, through bodily symptoms, re-enactments and repeats," in which "individual and collective memory and trauma are linked" (51).

Direct Provision Diary[2]

There are many people of different nationalities that speak their native languages. Men, women and children wait impatiently to be assessed. I was brought to a small room where two forensic officials took my fingerprints; my photograph was taken and I was issued an identity card that clearly stated at the back: This is not an Identity Card. I was called to a window where I officially lodged my application for refugee status.

We were brought into a mini bus to one of the Reception Centres. The journey seemed long; we could see from the window the streets and people of Dublin. The long motorway took us to one of the suburbs on the South side of the city. We didn't talk on the bus; we looked at each other with agitation and worry.

Kilmacud House, in Stillorgan, is located on the top of a steep hill, beside the Carmelite Lodge and the bus stop. In front of the old building we can see a large grass area with facilities for children to play. In front of the main building there is a massive pine tree and several palm trees beside the entrance. The manager of Kilmacud House admits that he is from Albania. I admit where I am from. We didn't speak; he was visibly unfriendly, unhelpful and unpleasant. We were brought into our rooms. One room holds around 14 people. There are 7 bunk beds. The beds are metal and painted in black. The room has a high ceiling and there is an oval wall at the back of my bed. I leave my belongings beside the bed. That night, a man beside me talks over the phone with his solicitor. It seems that he is facing deportation. He appears calm and stable. We spoke for a few minutes. That night I had a dream of detention Centres, where Africans are waiting in a long queue for their food. There is an atmosphere of tension and antagonism. In the middle a big elevator is transferring people. People make noises. I observe. They can't see me.

The next morning, a Chinese man serves us our breakfast. Porridge, cereal,

---

2 Editors' note: Following the author's instructions, the diary is reproduced as it was originally written while Nedeljkovic was seeking asylum in Ireland (Nedeljkovic, Unpublished Diary).

poached eggs, toast and juice. The food in Kilmacud House is wonderful. There is a variety of different meals: meat, salads, fruits and deserts. We eat at the canteen, on a large wooden table. The table clothes are coated with plastic with white and red-checkered designs. The plates and cups are made out of aluminium. Residents from the same or neighbouring countries are getting to know each other. They talk and discuss. There is no one from my country. Where is my country located? Where is my country? It used to be called Yugoslavia, before the wars. Now, it is called Serbia. I find it very difficult to explain. We were not aware that we would create, upon our arrival, a diasporic public sphere that succeeded the confinement of the State.

In front of the House, an African man in a wheelchair is laughing. He is from South Africa. His children are playing hide and seek.

That midnight, a young man from Africa is having difficulties with breathing. His elderly mother, dressed in colourful clothes, looks agitated. Her son is having an epileptic seizure; he is in severe pain with his knees on the floor. He faints. The security man calls an ambulance. People are looking at the young man. Some of them would like to help, but they don't know how. Others are just watching. An ambulance comes.

Few days later, I see a young man from Africa, waiting to see a social welfare officer. We are in the same queue. I ask him how is he feeling? He doesn't respond. Perhaps he doesn't speak English. He looks tired and pale.

We collect our weekly payments of 19.10 euros. That is our weekly allowance. We are prohibited from work or study. The medical screening, for transmittable diseases, took place on the top floor of the House in a room that looked on to the garden. We were tested for HIV and Hepatitis amongst other. The bus took us next morning to a local hospital for the examination of our lungs.

"Heimweh" the Germans call this pain; it is a beautiful word, it means longing for one's home, a longing for the home of our childhood, before we were even aware of the consequences of war and displacement (Levi, 61).

The next morning a woman, followed by two security officers, arrives in Kilmacud House. She goes through her papers and calls out some reference numbers; each of us has a reference number that starts with number 69. People start to congregate near the reception forming certain groups. We hear that we will be transferred. Most of us haven't even met our legal representatives. There is no explanation. We take our belongings and enter the bus. It is a hot summer day. We leave our friends behind, without even saying goodbye.

We are told to go on the bus. The bus leaves in 20 minutes. Does the bus driver know who we are? We don't know where we are going. We look through the window. It's a long journey. We see the rivers, the grass fields and the blue sky of the Irish landscape. We arrive in New Ross. It is a Centre for single men, positioned on the hill between the residential houses. The bus driver opens the main gate; we can see a road that leads to The Old Rectory Centre, sheltered from sight and wind by trees, tall plants and hedges.

I see the main building of the Centre. The CCTV camera is attached to the

9. DIRECT PROVISION AND ASYLYM ARCHIVE: POWER & SURVEILLANCE

Figure 9.2: The Old Convent Direct Provision Centre, Ballyhaunis, 2008.

main building; it looks towards the gate. The porch is attached to the main building; it has a glass roof. Further down are the houses that also belong to the Centre. At the back of the houses in a small building, you can see a gym. Some of the residents are trying to keep fit. The pavement outside the main building of the Centre is covered with moss.

There is a Christmas tree in the Centre. The Christmas tree is in the recreational room. At the back of the tree is a wall; at the side of the tree is a small window with a curtain. The Christmas tree is bare. It doesn't have any life in it. The Christmas tree has few Christmas lights that are flickering. It makes me sad to look at the Christmas tree. There are no presents below the Christmas tree. Just the bare tree. I wrote on a piece of paper: 'Another lonely Christmas'! I stick the note on the wall of my room.

My window is divided in half. There are yellow marks at the both sides of the window. The mark on the left side of the window is bigger and wider than the mark on the right side of the window. I can't see anything through the window in my room in the Centre. The yellow marks are covering my view. The yellow marks are on the outside of the window. I can't clean the yellow marks. I don't look through my window. You can only see two big yellow marks if you look through the window in my room.

In the canteen there is an oval wall at the back. On the wall you can see the five windows. The windows are painted in white; there is no natural light in the canteen. On the floor you can see the snack and drink dispenser. Beside is a big red fridge with a Coca-Cola sign on it. I don't know who can purchase drinks and snacks in the Centre.

At the reception in the Centre, I notice a monitor. Every day we have to sign at the reception. The monitor shows the 16 CCTV cameras. One of the cameras is broken. There are at least 15 working CCTV cameras in the Centre.

173

There may be another monitor in the manager's office. I don't know. We rarely go to the manager's office. Only when we decide to complain about our living conditions. We rarely complain.
I walk around the Centre at night. In front of one of the houses I notice a dead chicken head lying on the floor. There is blood everywhere. The blood is on the grass. The blood is on the pavement. The blood is in the Centre. The blood is everywhere. What does the head of the chicken do in the Centre? I feel sorry for the chicken. Where is the body of the chicken? What has happened to the chicken? I can see the head of the chicken and the blood around it.
Outside the main building of the Centre is a wooden bench. The ground, outside the main building of the Centre, is covered with square cement blocks. The wooden bench is wide; several people can sit on it. There are almost no outdoor or indoor activities in the Centre. The residents place two wooden panels on the top of the bench. This will become a table tennis. The wooden panels are not the same size. The left wooden panel is shorter than the right wooden panel. I see residents playing table tennis. There is no net on the tennis table. One of the tennis racquets has a black head and a green handle; the other tennis racquet has a red head and a blue handle. The table tennis ball is not good quality.
I look through my stained window. There are fields in a distance. They seem too far away. I can't see the greenness of the fields. It rains almost every day. The fields are becoming greener every minute. I want to see the fields with my tired, sleepless eyes. I am afraid to leave room 24. I can't smell the fields. I am not able to smell the wildlife. It is just around the corner. There are walls and barriers on the way. I can leave the Centre to see the fields and smell the wildlife; but I am afraid that if I leave the Centre, I won't be able to come into my room again. I could be stopped outside the Centre and asked by a stranger: 'How are things'? or, 'Where are you going'? I could be asked the same question by a local. I wouldn't know what to answer. I want to say: 'I am going for a walk to see the fields and smell the wildlife.' But I am afraid. I say nothing. I make a few steps towards the green fields. They are too far anyway. I will try tomorrow again. I go back to my room. I gently open the window; the smell of the canteen enters my habitat.
We can leave the Centre but we always have to come back to get our daily meals. We have to come back to sign in a daily register. Sometimes I sign using the Cyrillic alphabet; other times I sign using the Latin alphabet. I am not sure who I am anymore. I have lost my identity on the top of the hill freshly paved with new asphalt. We have lost our Identities. A gentle, young man from Afghanistan rushes down the stairs. He cries. He hears that he lost his brother back home. He is severely distressed as the tears are rolling down his cheeks. The gentle, young man is hurt. I don't see him in the canteen that evening. I wonder: is he hungry? How is he? It is beyond terrible that we lose our family members while living in the Centres. It is beyond unacceptable that we can't attend the funerals of our family members; that we are so isolated and lonely. If we leave the Centre, if we leave the State; we will not be allowed to enter the State and / or the Centre again.
It is warm in my room. The floor squeaks under my shoes. I look at the ceiling; there is a fire alarm. It is noon. The dinner will be served soon. I am expecting chicken nuggets and chips. I have gained weight since I am in the Centre. The food is not good quality. Most of the time we are given processed

9. DIRECT PROVISION AND ASYLUM ARCHIVE: POWER & SURVEILLANCE

Figure 9.3: The Old Convent Direct Provision Centre, Ballyhaunis, 2008.

food that doesn't have almost any nutritious value. Our bodies are changing every day. Our minds are changing every single minute. We don't know what to expect. We don't know what is ahead of us. We lose weight or we gain weight. We smile or we cry. Silently. We are in continuous agony. The sound of the cutlery in the canteen reminds me of the first 'calls' to join the Military back home.

I go to the canteen to make instant coffee. You can't drink too many coffees per day. Coffee is expensive. You didn't earn this coffee, someone says. We thought that we got rid of you, someone else says. No, you didn't. I am still here. This is your last coffee. Ok. It is nearly dinner time. What is for dinner? I ask. Nobody replies. What is for dinner, I ask myself? Just wait and see.

In the night, I wake up. I gently open the door of my room. I close the door. The key is in my pocket. I go down the stairs. Nobody is awake. The Centre is asleep. I open the door of the recreation room. On the top of the shelf, just above the fridge, is the yellow container. In the yellow containers there is white sliced bread wrapped in a cellophane. Beside the bread, in the same container, are the butter and jam. The same butter and jam that you can get in some B&B's or even hotels. The CCTV camera is just above the yellow container. I hope nobody is watching. I am afraid to ask the security: 'Can I please get some butter and jam and bread'? I slowly and secretly take white sliced bread, wrapped in cellophane, butter and jam. As I am leaving the recreation room, I can see a fly on the wall. Silent. Almost dead. But still alive.

I open the door of my room. I am not sure what time it is. I don't have to wake up for breakfast. I unwrap the bread. I open the butter and jam. I have no knife. I have to use my fingers to spread butter and jam on the white slice of bread. My hands are not clean. I have to wash them first. I don't have soap

Figure 9.4: Object found in railway centre grounds, Kiltimagh, 2011.

in my room. I have to go to the bathroom that is at the end of the second floor. I have to leave my room again. Which is the best way to get to the bathroom? I take off my shoes. I make my way to the bathroom to wash my hands. I can hear the residents snoring. I open the bathroom door gently. I switch on the lights. There is no soap or washing up liquid in the bathroom at the end of the second floor of the Centre. I wash my hands with water only. In my room; I use my finger to spread the butter on the white bread. Then in the same room I use the same finger to spread the jam on the butter that is already on the white slice of bread. I enjoy it. I was hungry. I can hear the birds chirping. It is almost dawn. In the Centre.

I hear of a man who had an accident while driving. He is in the hospital. We decide to leave the Centre and visit him. It is always difficult to leave the Centre. He is lying in bed. He cannot move. His head is injured. He can't see out of one eye. The glass from the smashed window of his car went into his eye. He can't see out of his left eye. The doctor tells us that he needs to go to surgery. He may be able to see with his left eye only partially. I don't know. I am upset. We leave the hospital. I never see that man again. I don't know what happened. I am afraid to ask the other residents that are living with me in the same Centre.

Another man jumps out of his window in the Centre. He is admitted to psychiatric care in the neighbouring town. We decide to visit him. He is wearing a green pyjama. He has a single room in the hospital. That is good news. The nurses are bringing him food. The nurses are checking his blood pressure. That man doesn't speak good English. He moves the beads on his prayer necklace nervously. I remember him doing the same in the Centre. The necklace has big beads. The necklace is made out of wood. It is a prayer

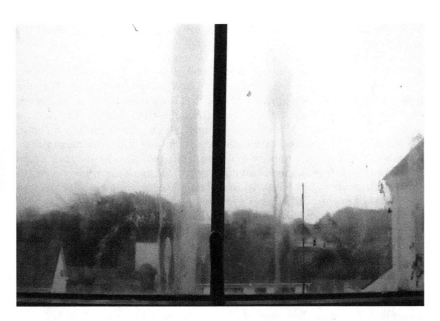

Figure 9.5: The Old Convent Direct Provision Centre, Ballyhaunis, 2008.

necklace. It may bring some relief to this man. I used to know his name.

Nobody was asking for me today. I get no post. That is good news. I can relax now. I am safe for today; unless they come at night. Sometimes they do.

Date: 28-1-00 Time: A.M.

REFUGEE MEDICAL CENTRE

AREA MEDICAL OFFICER'S
VACCINE ***REQUEST FORM***

VACCINE	NO. OF DOSES REQUESTED	BATCH NO.	EXPIRY DATE
DT Single dose	—		
ENERGIX Single dose	20		
MANTOUX TU	3 boxes		
NTOUX U	2 boxes		
	—		

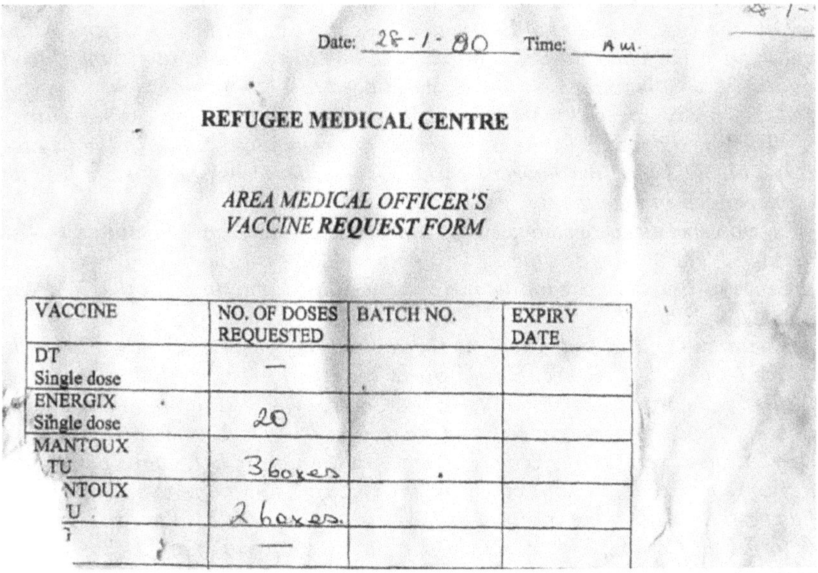

Figure 9.6: Vaccine sheets found in Kilmacud centre, 2013.

I have a sore throat. The right side of my throat is inflamed. I decide not to go and see the doctor. There is always a big queue in the surgery. I decide to wait to feel better. I wait and wait in the Centre hoping to feel better. I look at my table. It is an old table. There are lots of scratches on the table. The scratches look like lines. The lines join and intersect each other. They are forming different shapes, different drawings. I can see the shape of the African Continent; a smiley face with one eye missing; a curly hair; a bone and an arrow; a violin; ryegrass; stars on the brown Sky; a woman holding a fish in her mouth; a giraffe; a long thin seahorse; a baby girl. There is an ashtray on my table. Sometimes I smoke in my room while puffing a smoke outside the window. The ashtray has a rectangular shape; it is made out of plastic. At the front of the ashtray is a beautiful Irish landscape; green grass, blue sea and the mountains behind. The ashes from the smoked cigarettes are covering the ashtray; the ashes are covering the beautiful Irish landscape. You can barely see the landscape anymore. I need to wash the ashtray. A ray of Sun comes briefly into my room. It is the end of the evening. We had our dinner in the Centre. A ray of Sun highlights the ashtray. The Irish landscape looks even more contaminated with the ashes from the cigarettes. I will wash the ashtray tomorrow. It will be bedtime soon. Another sleepless night.

I am drunk in my room in the Centre. I feel no pain; no anxiety. Everything seems fine. The cheap beer, from the local off licence, tastes fine tonight.

My nose is bleeding. I let the blood, from my left nostril, drip into the sink. The sink in my room has red spots from my own blood. I run the tap and let the water wash away my blood. I go to the bathroom to get a tissue. My nose stops bleeding.

I play with my fingertips. I roll my fingertips; touching the thumb and the other fingers on my right hand.

Sometimes I can't breathe in the Centre. My nostrils are blocked; I can't inhale through my nostrils. I have to inhale through my mouth. My mouth is getting dry and I have to drink the water in the Centre. The water is not of good quality. After drinking too much water, I need to go to the toilet. Sometimes I feel that my lungs need more oxygen. It is quite claustrophobic in the Centre.

There is a dead fly in the right corner of my window. How did the fly die? It is a big fly. I can't see any spider webs. The spider webs are invisible. The fly is suspended in the air.

I close my tired, swollen eyes. I am asleep. There are no sounds in the distance. The Centre is quiet. The Centre is asleep. How is that possible? I dream the dreams. I dream the pleasant dreams. I imagine that the Centre is quiet. I need to rest.

I am lonely and lost. I look at the table in my room endlessly. I am safe in the Centre. The silence. It is silent in the Centre. The eternal silence that fulfils the hearts of the residents in the Centre. We need to breathe. We need to inhale fresh air in order to live. One day we will leave the Centre. We can't stay in the Centre forever. The experience in the Centre will shape our future lives. We will cope. We will overcome the Centre. The Centre is an entity that has been created by the Irish State. We need to sleep. We need to rest. We need to forget the Centre. We live in the Centre but we have to imagine that we live somewhere else. We live in the most beautiful, safe and secure places. The grass is green. The roses are red. The walls are yellow. There are no walls. We can walk freely from one place to another. The sky is blue with a few white

9. DIRECT PROVISION AND ASYLUM ARCHIVE: POWER & SURVEILLANCE

Figure 9.7: The Old Convent Direct Provision Centre, Ballyhaunis, 2008.

clouds. The clouds have the shapes of our freedom. The trees are tall and healthy; without berries. We need to imagine that the trees have berries. We imagine to climb on the trees in the Centre that have no fruit. We imagine that the trees are not bare. The trees have the shapes of our phobias. We imagine to climb on a cherry tree. There are no cherry trees in the Centre. There are some cherry trees in Ireland but those trees have no berries. How to get the berries and the fruit in the orchard of nothingness? We go back to our rooms. The silence is part of our lives. The silence is omnipresent. We go to bed. We easily forget about the cherries, berries and other fruit. You can't get them in the Centre anyway. You have to imagine. You have to imagine that you are not in the Centre. But you are. What are you going to do with your knowledge? Can you imagine that you are living in the orchard of nothingness?

I listen to the birds. Can you hear the early morning song of the birds? The birds are singing outside the Centre. You can hear their song in each room of the Centre. You need to listen. You need to be quiet. You need to be still. You need to hear the music of the birds. The birds are singing their song early in the morning. Most of the residents are still asleep. Nobody in the Centre can hear the music of the birds.

Conclusion

It has been more than 100 years since the proclamation of the Irish Free State. Can we talk of evolution in Irish society when, in Direct Provision centres, asylum seekers continue writing their diaries, trying to express their daily experiences of segregation, institutionalism and ghettoisation? Revolution in twenty-first-century Ireland may not be only characterised by the celebrations of the Easter Rising centenary or the successes of the Irish State. Twenty-first-century Ireland is also about the failure of the State; it is about Direct Provision centres and the appalling treatment of asylum seekers.

If we look at relatively recent reports, Direct Provision centres are being categorised as sites of social exclusion, poverty, institutionalism; sites of significantly increased mental health issues that include posttraumatic stress disorder, psychosis, neurosis, insomnia and suicidal tendencies. I may remind you that at least sixty-two asylum seekers have died, since 1990, while in State care. Some of the reasons for these deaths include malnutrition, suicide and heart failure.

There has been some debate in the Irish public sphere as for whether we, as a society, should reform the Direct Provision scheme or completely abolish it by returning to pre-1990 times, when asylum seekers were entitled to social welfare and rent allowance. It seems that we have chosen not to abandon Direct Provision, thus significantly increasing deportations and forced removals from Ireland. If we were more progressive and revolutionary we would have chosen pre-Direct Provision legislation; the times when asylum seekers were treated with more dignity and respect.

Works Cited

Agamben, Giorgio. *Homo Sacer: Sovereign Power and Bare Life*. Stanford University Press, 1995.
Appadurai, Arjun. "Archive and Aspiration." *Information is Alive*, edited by Joke Brouwer and Arjen Mulder, V2_/NAi Publishers, 2003, pp. 14–25.
Augé, Marc. *Non-Places: Introduction to an Anthropology of Supermodernity*. Translated by John Howe. Verso, 1995.
Esposito, Roberto. *Bios: Biopolitics and Philosophy*. Minnesota University Press, 2008
Foucault, Michel. *Discipline and Punish: The Birth of the Prison*. Translated by Alan Sheridan. Penguin, 1991.
Lentin, Ronit. "Anti Deportation Ireland: End Deportations Now." *Free Radikal*, 4 October 2012, www.ronitlentin.net/2012/10/. Accessed 17 Dec. 2019.
Levi, Primo. *If This Is a Man*. Translated by Stuart Wolf, The Orion Press, 1959.
Levinas, Emmanuel. *Time and the Other*. Translated by Richard A. Cohen. Duquesne University Press, 1987.
Loyal, Steven. *Understanding Immigration in Ireland: State, Capital and Labour in a*

Global Age. Manchester University Press, 2011.
Nedeljkovic, Vukasin. Unpublished Direct Provision Diary, 2006–2009.
———. "Direct Provision Diary." *Create News*, vol. 24, June 2018, www.create-ireland.ie/wp-content/uploads/2018/06/Create-News-24.pdf. Accessed 17 Dec. 2019.
O'Sullivan, Eoin and Ian O'Donnell. *Coercive Confinement in Ireland: Patients, Prisoners and Penitents.* Manchester University Press, 2012.
Sekula, Allan. "The Body and the Archive." *October*, vol. 39, 1986, pp. 3–64.
———. "Reading an Archive: Photography between Labour and Capital." *The Photography Reader*, edited by Liz Wells, Routledge, 2002, pp. 443–52.
Taylor, Diana. *The Archive and the Repertoire: Performing Cultural Memory in the Americas.* Duke University Press, 2003.

10

Northern Irish Revolutionary Cinema: From Thriller to Comedy

Stephanie Schwerter

Introduction

This chapter focuses on the radical changes in Northern Irish cinema that followed the first ceasefire declaration of the IRA in 1994. These changes can be considered as revolutionary since significant modifications become manifest in films treating the question of the Troubles. In the following pages, I shall explore Thaddeus O'Sullivan's *Nothing Personal* (1995) and John Forte's *Mad About Mambo* (2000), two films belonging to different genres characteristic of specific periods of contemporary Northern Irish history.[1] Taking the two above mentioned films as examples, I shall argue that the ceasefire generated innovative, radically different films, which challenge traditional Troubles films by taking a revolutionary new direction.

In order to illustrate the striking changes in Northern Irish cinema, a short introduction to the development of films focussing on the Troubles is necessary. Before the ceasefire was declared in 1994, most cinematographic representations of the conflict could be categorised as belonging to the genre of the thriller. Usually based on novels, these films adopted a realistic, almost documentary format. It does not come as a surprise that a great number of Troubles thrillers were set in Belfast due to the city's complex ethno-religious segregation. Formed by a variety of boundary markers, Belfast's sectarian geography lent itself to action films based on tension and excitement. Until today, the borders between Catholic and Protestant areas are indicated by more than twenty-five peace-lines, approximately three hundred murals, as well as several kilometres

---

1   In my analysis, the notion "revolutionary" will be employed according to the definition of the term provided by the Collins English Dictionary, which is "radically new or different" (Sinclair, 1318).

of kerbstone paintings in the colours of the Union Jack or the Irish Tricolour (Calame and Charelworth, 61–81; Shirlow and Murtagh, 57–100). As a result of these visual signs, a substantial part of the city's population can be categorised along religious lines. In Belfast's working class areas, territorial markers such as murals and kerbstone paintings attribute specific ethno-religious connotations to certain areas. In many cases, a person's denomination can therefore be derived from his or her dwelling place. Hugh Jordan claims that Belfast is unique in that it is "quite possible to guess a person's religion based on nothing more than the side of the street on which they chose to walk" (188). This might be particularly true of segregated working class areas at tense periods of the conflict. The city's sectarian geography, highlighted by the above-mentioned boundary markers, plays a central role in the cinematographic depiction of the Troubles.

Most of the Troubles thrillers produced during the 1970s, 1980s, and even at the beginning of the 1990s, paint a pessimistic picture of Belfast, illustrating the city as a gloomy place from which the characters have to escape in order to survive. A peaceful co-existence of Catholics and Protestants is literally impossible. According to Martin Rubin, the most salient features of the thriller genre are suspense, fright, mystery, exhilaration, excitement, speed and movement (5). These elements are also central to traditional Troubles thrillers, where bomb explosions, shootings and abductions drive the narrative forward. Clashes between the paramilitaries of both political camps, the RUC and the British army, are also part of the plot.[2] Due to security reasons, Troubles thrillers made prior to 1994 were shot in cities such as Dublin, London and Manchester (Hill, *Cinema*, 213). Frequent settings of conventional Troubles thriller are gloomy pubs, dark backstreets and derelict factories or deserted building sites. The different boundary markers guide the audience through Belfast's ethno-religious territoriality and, thanks to various visual indicators, the spectator is able to understand whether the characters move through friendly or hostile territory.

In traditional Troubles thrillers, a specific set of recurrent stereotypes can be found. Gerry Smyth categorises the Troubles thrillers' main characters as "the terrorist godfather," "the conscientious gunman," "the reluctant agent," as well as the "*femme fatale*" (114). Bill Rolston extends Smyth's list by adding a further number of stereotypes. Similarly to Smith, he refers to the godfather as a main agent of terrorism. Rolston describes him as a "well-known cypher of mainstream media accounts of the Troubles" (42). As a violent commander, the godfather merely orders killings without being directly involved in them. This type of character is commonly represented as a misogynist who has repressed his homosexual tendencies. Another male character mentioned by Rolston is the villain, an apolitical individual seeking power as an end to itself. Rolston

---

2   In this context, films such as *Angel* (1982) and *Crying Game* (1982) by Neil Jordan, or *Resurrection Man* (1988) by Marc Evans spring to mind.

describes the villain as "a loner who acts out of personal need or psychological inadequacy" (42). Unable to be a leader himself, he is entirely submitted to the terrorist godfather. In his extreme form, the villain is represented as an unpredictable psychopath. Different from the godfather's repressed sexual tendencies, the villain's sexual urges are violent and hedonistic (42). Among the female stereotypes, Rolston names "mothers," "seducers" and "villains." Whereas the mother's role is to protect her children from violence (44), the seducer incites other characters to commit crime (47). The villain, on the contrary, embraces violence with a greater passion than men. However, female villains are often represented as "second class terrorist[s]" as they are prone to self-doubt and tears (51). A rather one-sided depiction of the Northern Irish conflict is also characteristic of conventional Troubles thrillers. This means that the action is entirely set either within the framework of the Protestant or Catholic community, but does not combine views from both sides.

However, after the ceasefire declaration in 1994, a revolutionary tendency towards an ironic as well as humorous depiction of contemporary Northern Ireland can be observed. Filmmakers start moving away from the thriller genre in order to produce carnivalesque comedies in which Belfast is presented in a comic but at the same time optimistic light. The traditional Troubles thriller heroes become gradually replaced by amusing characters.[3]

This new cinematographic trend became possible due to a more relaxed atmosphere in Northern Ireland, generated by the IRA's ceasefire declaration (McLoone, *Irish Film,* 64). Not only the improvement in the region's political climate, but also the emergence of alternative forms of funding encouraged unconventional filmmaking activities which went beyond established traditions. The newly founded Northern Irish Film Council (NIF) as well as the National Lottery were alternative sources for financial support. Martin McLoone maintains that, with the political situation growing more hopeful and the ceasefires continuing to hold, "culture in general and film in particular" became able to start dealing with the "suppressed horror of the recent past" (84). McLoone rightly argues that commercial cinema and state-funded partnerships managed to "open up a space where the legacy of thirty years of violence in Northern Ireland" could be presented (84). Thanks to the changed political situation, the region's history could be revisited and the future imagined with more optimism. Many films produced after 1994 are considered as "Ceasefire cinema" (Hill, *Divorcing Jack,* 229). The term implies that these works have been rendered possible by the ceasefire, not only thanks to the new financial resources

---

3   Well-known comic protagonists are among others Dan Starkey, the clumsy alcoholic journalist representative of the "anti-thriller-hero" in David Cafferey's *Divorcing Jack* (1998) or, Chucky Lurgan, the grotesque main character in Adrian Shergold's BBC series *Eureka Street* (1998). Colum and George, the two ambitious barbers who try to set up an interdenominational hairpiece business in Barry Levinson's *An Everlasting Piece* (2000) share the same debunking impulses.

mentioned above, but also due to a new, much more emotionally distanced view on the Troubles. Whereas a number of Ceasefire films concentrate on the new situation in Northern Ireland generated by the Peace process, others return to troubled periods of the conflict, illustrating them from a more detached angle. Most of the films share a humorous tone and do not adopt the bleak atmosphere of traditional Troubles thrillers.[4]

In the following, I argue that *Nothing Personal* is indebted to the traditional Troubles thriller genre, whereas *Mad About Mambo* can be seen as a representative example of Ceasefire cinema. The analysis of the different contents and form of the two films shall demonstrate the radical evolution of Northern Irish cinema. In order to comprehend the changing cinematographic depiction of Belfast, I will consider the city in sociological terms: that is, as a binary concept which consists of its physical structure and its population. According to the urban sociologist Henry Lefebvre, a city is composed of two contrasting elements: "the city" and "the urban." In Lefebvre's view, the city refers to the "immediate reality" of an urban complex, to its "practico-material and architectural fact" (103). The urban, on the contrary, denotes the "social reality" of the city: that is, its population (103). Lefebvre underlines the interaction of the two elements composing an urban complex, arguing that the city "always had relations with society as a whole" (103). This perception is particularly relevant to Belfast, where societal division is clearly etched into the urban space. In traditional Belfast thrillers, the city, in the sense of Lefebvre's definition, is not only composed of streets, parks and buildings, as in the case of ordinary cities, but also of unusual visual markers such as peace-lines, kerbstone paintings or murals, representing Belfast's social reality in the form of two warring factions. We could argue that, through the conscious inclusion and exclusion of Belfast-typical elements, the film directors attribute a personal perspective to their cinematographic representation of the Northern Irish capital. Following Lefebvre's distinction, in the following, both the city and the urban shall be considered in order to achieve a balanced analysis of Belfast as depicted in the two films.

Nothing Personal: A Traditional Troubles Thriller

The screenplay of *Nothing Personal* was written by Belfast author Daniel Mornin. He took his own novel *All Our Fault* as a basis for his script. Even if the film was released in 1995, one year after the ceasefire, it follows the scheme of a traditional Troubles thriller, probably because Mornin's novel had been published in 1991. Furthermore, the writing of the screenplay and the

---

4   Even if the majority of films produced after the ceasefire takes on a humorous tone, a small number of them, such as *'71* by Yan Demange (2014) and *A Belfast Story* by Nathan Todd (2013), are still produced according to the conventions of the realist thriller.

production of the thriller had started before the ceasefire declaration, so, the film's action was not inspired by the new optimistic atmosphere reigning in Belfast after 1994. *Nothing Personal* is a co-production of Channel Four Films, British Screen and the Irish Film Board (Mulvenna). In contrast to the majority of Troubles thrillers, *Nothing Personal* does not concentrate on the IRA. The film belongs to the rare cinematographic representations of Northern Ireland focussing on loyalist paramilitaries.[5] It is set in Belfast but was shot in Dublin's Ringsend area (McLoone, 197), a fact that for Ruth Barton "detracts from its claim to realism" (165). Nevertheless, even if some of the city's most famous landmarks, such as peace-lines or the construction cranes of the Harland and Wolff ship yard, do not appear, a very Belfast-specific atmosphere is created through kerbstone paintings, murals and the small alleyways and backstreets typical of the working class areas of the city.

The action takes place in 1975 and echoes the violent deeds of the Shankill Butchers, "one of the worst chapters in Belfast's bloody history" (Jordan, 190). The Shankill Butchers were a splinter group of the UVF which terrorised East Belfast's Shankill area between 1975 and 1985. Its members were convicted of 19 killings as well as of countless attempted murders, kidnappings and bombings. Most of their victims were innocent Catholic civilians, whom they tortured and then brutally killed. When brought to Court, the gang received more than forty-two life and prison sentences, amounting to 2,000 years (Jordan, 192).

The thrillers' protagonists are the Catholic Liam (John Lynch), a single father of two, and Kenney (James Frain), a Loyalist paramilitary boss. Whereas the main roles are played by renowned actors, such as Lynch and Frain, the minor characters are played by local actors without international reputation. The film begins with a bomb explosion orchestrated by the IRA in a Protestant pub. In the opening scene, Liam walks through the remains, helping soldiers to pull injured people and dead bodies from beneath the rubble. The story of the film focuses on the UVF's retaliation for the attack and the internal turmoil this provokes in the organisation. The opening credits reading "Belfast 1975" are intended to give *Nothing Personal* a realistic tone. In this way, already at the beginning of the film, the audience is confronted with the image of Belfast as a violent city. As in most traditional Troubles thrillers, violence is explicitly depicted throughout the film and reflects the brutality of the conflict.

---

5   Cécile Bazin attracts attention to the fact that among twenty-three films shot and released between 1975 and 2005, only two films apart from *Nothing Personal* focus on the Loyalist milieu. These films are *Resurrection Man* by Marc Evans (1998) and *As the Beast Sleeps* (2001) by Harry Bradbeer.

1. Belfast's Streets – a Territorial Maze

Concerning the physical appearance of the city, a substantial number of stereotypical Troubles thriller elements can be found in *Nothing Personal*. The most important urban feature appearing in O'Sullivan's film is Belfast's ethno-religious segregation. The city is divided into a myriad of Catholic and Protestant areas with clearly designated borders. Furthermore, Belfast's different territories are controlled by paramilitaries from both sides. The main action takes place at night in gloomy locations, such as dark streets of working class Belfast, backrooms of loyalist pubs, derelict parking lots, deserted factories and a dilapidated gasometer. The city is marked by cruel actions, such as beatings, riots and abductions. Scenes shot inside pubs feature innocent people being tortured. The central story of the film is set during a night of rioting and fighting, and the oppressing atmosphere generated by the choice of locations is underlined by an omnipresent low-key lighting. Veiled in fog, the cityscape appears lugubrious and uninviting and the few sources of light which illuminate the nocturnal scenery are pub windows, searchlights falling from British army helicopters, or street fires caused by riots.

The city is populated with loyalist paramilitaries lurking outside nationalist pubs in order to surprise their innocent victims, while their republican counterparts wait for the right moment to retaliate. The British army helplessly tries to re-establish order. This thrilling urban scenario creates an atmosphere of danger endowing the film with a threatening tone. O'Sullivan claims that in *Nothing Personal* he intended to depict Belfast as a city shaped by working class ghettoes in which Protestant and Catholic areas touch each other. His aim was to render the claustrophobic atmosphere of enclosed communities whose members do not naturally interact (16). O'Sullivan further argues that the streets had been intentionally left empty in order to make them "perform in a dramatic way": "Everything is cleared off the streets and they're lit and presented in a way that is really more theatrical than naturalistic" (16). In the same vein, McLoone praises *Nothing Personal* as "atmospheric cinematography" (198) due to O'Sullivan's unconventional play with light. Through O'Sullivan's choice of lighting, the city is represented as a mercilessly treacherous place for its inhabitants. In this sense, the depiction of the city's "practico-material reality" (Lefebvre, 103) entirely conforms to the conventions of the Troubles thriller.

In *Nothing Personal*, the concept of mental maps plays an important role. The term was coined by sociologist Kevin Lynch in his ground-breaking study *The Image of the City*. Lynch draws attention to the importance of cognitive geography in the interpretation of a city by its inhabitants. He argues that citizens have personal "mental images" of their city, which are "soaked in memories and meanings" (1–2). A mental map is created in the observer's mind through the subconscious selection of various urban aspects which bear personal implications Lynch underlines the importance of mental maps in the process of "way finding," explaining that the "environmental image" held by an individual is "used to interpret information and to guide action" (4). Liam Kennedy further elucidates the concept of mental maps as follows: "Places are charged with emotional and mythical meanings; localised stories, images and memories associated with place and can provide meaningful cultural and historical bearings for urban individuals and communities" (7). These ideas apply in particular to the inhabitants of Belfast, who interpret their personal urban environment according to the city's boundary markers. In this sense, A.T.Q. Stewart highlights the importance of local knowledge in Northern Ireland, claiming that "the Ulsterman carries the map of his religious geography in his mind almost from birth" (180). The characters represented in *Nothing Personal* are guided through the city's urban maze with the help of their individual cognitive geography.

O'Sullivan's film mostly confines Belfast's city space to a few obscure backstreets which turn into dead-ends due to barricades erected by the warring factions. As soon as the characters do not follow their personal sectarian mental map, they expose themselves to danger. Lost on hostile territory or trapped in dead-ends, they are prone to be picked up by paramilitaries and dragged into pubs to be tortured and killed. The characters walk through Belfast's ethno-religious territoriality on the basis of their personal knowledge, experience or history. However, one of the protagonists, a Catholic, loses the grip on his cognitive geography in the aftermath of a riot. Having gone out to man the barricades on the nationalist side, he accidentally enters a Protestant area, where he gets badly beaten up by a loyalist gang. Although he manages to get back to his feet and tries to find his way home, he is disorientated by the darkness and the pain of his injuries. As he is unable to pattern and recognise his surroundings, he loses his habitual frame of reference and fails to interpret the ethno-religious semiotics of his environment. For the protagonist, the city seems to turn into an impenetrable maze. Acoustically, the danger of the situation becomes underlined through thrilling music as well as the constant sound of British army helicopters. Stumbling through Protestant territory, Liam is taken in by Anne (Maria Doyle-Kennedy), the loyalist paramilitary Kenny's former wife, who cleans his wounds. During their time together, Liam and Anne share their feelings about marriage, children and relationships in a politically troubled environment. Thus, we learn that Liam is wandering through Belfast's streets while his children at home are probably worrying about him. His young daughter Kathleen (Jane Courtney), accompanied by her friend Michael (Gareth O'Hare), start looking for him in the city's pubs. As children, they do not have the same sectarian mental map of their urban environment as their adult counterparts. Therefore, they do not hesitate to cross Protestant and Catholic territories in their search of Liam. It is precisely their being children that protects them from becoming a target of violence for the opposite camp.

2. Paramilitary Control of Belfast

Against the background of nocturnal Belfast, the action in *Nothing Personal* unfolds in a complex set of plots and subplots which demonstrates the impact and the range of political violence across three generations of interrelated characters. As mentioned previously, in its depiction of the city's population the film focuses on the Loyalist paramilitaries. Brian McIlroy points out that this thriller works on the following four different levels of discourse:

a) The interactions of the IRA and the UVF leadership;
b) The internal quarrels of UVF members;
c) The view of non-combatants, who unwillingly become drawn into the conflict;
d) The impact of sectarian violence of children. (147)

Paramilitary infighting and clashes between the opposite camps are the traditional ingredients for the conventional Troubles Thriller. References to the lives of children, however, are rather unusual in films belonging to the thriller genre. Among the stereotypical male heroes featuring in *Nothing Personal*, we can count violent commanders, gunmen and psychopaths who kill for the sake of fun, as well as members of the British Army. Stereotypical female characters occurring in the film are women in the role of mothers or seducers. The character of Anne conforms to the stereotype of the caring mother.

In their article "Images of Women in Northern Ireland," Marie-Thérèse McGivern and Margaret Ward criticise the common conception and representation of Northern Irish women as "passive victims of the Troubles, viragoes of the barricades" and "advocates of messianic peace" (67). This very image frequently occurs in traditional Troubles film such as *Nothing Personal*, where Anne is not only a single mother of two small children, but also works as nurse in the local hospital. In this way, her profession enhances the stereotype of women acting as caretakers and innocent victims of violence.

In the scene taking place in Anne's house, Liam and the young woman are visibly attracted to each other, while being aware that they belong to opposite ethno-religious camps. The encounter of the two characters suggests the beginning of a love story crossing the sectarian divide. The so-called "love-across-the-barricades" theme is a typical feature of Troubles film and fiction. Conventionally, a Catholic and a Protestant character try to overcome ethno-religious boundaries in order to get together. In the end, the relationship usually fails not only due to physical intimidation, but also to the psychological pressure exercised by the two communities.[6]

---

6   The term "love-across-the-barricades story" derives from Joan Lingard's novel *Across the Barricades* (1972), which was written for children and young adults. The book seeks to explain the impact of political violence and sectarianisms on young people's private

In *Nothing Personal*, such a relationship does not even begin to develop. Liam leaves Anne's house to continue his way home. He knows that a love affair with a Protestant woman would be too dangerous for both families, since it would be confronted by the paramilitaries on both sides. The scene implies the impossibility of relationships crossing the ethno-religious divide, and this pessimistic message goes hand in hand with the overall gloomy atmosphere of the film. Anne and Liam's encounter illustrates the influence of political violence on civilians, who are not involved in sectarian fighting and resentfully see their lives invaded by the conflict. The film suggests that, whereas in a peaceful environment a love story between the two characters would have been possible, in battle-scarred Belfast a relationship crossing ethno-religious boundaries is unimaginable.

One of the key scenes of the film depicts a meeting of the IRA and the UVF in a derelict factory. Leonard, the leader of the UVF unit (Michael Gambar), meets the IRA boss Cecil (Gerard McSorley) in order to negotiate a ceasefire. Both leaders are followed and supported by members of their respective organisation. According to Smyth's and Rolston's conceptions of stereotypical Troubles thriller characters, both paramilitary bosses can be classified as terrorist godfathers. Kenny, Leonard's follower, could be seen as a combination of a gunman and a commander since he actively participates in violent acts. The other characters in the scene hailing from both sides represent simple gunmen, only carrying out the orders given by their respective godfathers. They are in charge of shootings, killings and bombings, whereas their bosses never get their hands dirty. The hierarchical internal structure of the paramilitary organisations becomes illustrated when several characters are disciplined by their superiors for their actions, considered as not in line with the group's orthodoxy. The character of Ginger (Ian Hart) is the stereotypical psychopath as considered by Rolston (43), since he is a member of the UVF who does not pursue any political aims but kills for the sake of fun, while brutally mutilating his victims. As his random murders shed a bad light on the organisation, Kenny tries to reason with him. Ultimately, due to internal disputes inside the IRA and the UVF, on top of the disagreements between the two paramilitary bosses, a ceasefire fails to be negotiated.

The film ends on a dark note. Liam is violently attacked again after having left Anne's house and, this time, the assailants are Kenny and his men. After having beaten up Liam, Kenny recognises that the latter is a childhood friend with whom he used to play before the beginning of the Troubles and he decides not to kill him but to set him free. This scene happens in front of Liam's family home and is observed by his children and their friend Michael. When young Michael aims with a stolen gun at one of the Loyalists, Liam's daughter Kathleen tries to prevent him from shooting and gets accidently killed. The scene thus

---

lives.

underlines the impact of political violence on children's and teenagers' lives. It terminates with Kenny shooting Ginger for his uncontrollable behaviour and so as to re-establish order among his subalterns. Kenny, on his turn, is shot by the British army, which makes an unexpected and surprising appearance. According to Aaron Kelly, the thriller genre has the function to "investigate and judge" contemporary society (*The Thriller*, 90–91). This applies in particular to *Nothing Personal*, as the ultimate message of the film is that violence generates more violence. Thus, Belfast is represented as a place of death where there is no chance of peace and survival, a depiction of the city that is characteristic of traditional Troubles thrillers.

Mad About Mambo: A Romantic Comedy Belfast-Style

In contrast to *Nothing Personal*, Forte's *Mad About Mambo* takes on an entirely different tone, moving away from the thriller genre. The film captures the changed atmosphere after the ceasefire, while at the same time humorously alluding to the persisting underlying sectarian tensions in Northern Irish society. According to Mikhail Bakhtin, the reversal of received perceptions and value systems gives rise to new world views (*Rabelais*, 16). In this sense, it could be argued that through the comic portrayal of Belfast, the audience is encouraged to see contemporary Northern Irish society in a new light.

Contrary to *Nothing Personal*, physical violence is entirely absent from *Mad About Mambo*. Sectarian tensions are merely alluded to in an ironic way and differences between social classes become more important than ethno-religious animosities. Recurring comic effects aim at the humorous subversion of established social structures. Martin McLoone describes Forte's film as a "romantic comedy" overcoming the "pessimism" of earlier "troubles drama" (218). He explains that there are different reasons for the emergence of the romantic comedy genre in the Northern Irish context. First of all, encouraged by new sources of funding such as the National Lottery, the Northern Irish Film Commission and the Irish Film Board, directors and scriptwriters started aiming at commercial success. By adopting a generic form, they expected their films to appeal to a large audience. Furthermore, this trend towards tragic-comic love stories echoed the revival of romantic comedy, which could be observed in Hollywood in the 1980s and the 1990s. This American tendency was matched in the UK by the success of films such as *Four Weddings and a Funeral* (1994), *Sliding Doors* (1998) and *Notting Hill* (1999) (McLoone, 218). Last but not least, the emergence of the Northern Irish romantic comedy reflects the "new mood of optimism" reigning in Belfast after the ceasefire declaration (Kennedy-Andrews, 189). *Mad About Mambo* is a British-Irish coproduction distributed by USA films. The film was produced and written by John Forte and, similarly to *Nothing Personal*, the action is set in Belfast but shot in Dublin.

1. Mocking Belfast's Society

In *Mad About Mambo* the urban, a notion which, as mentioned above, refers to the city's social reality (Lefebvre, 103), is composed of individuals from both communities as well as characters from outside Northern Ireland, like England and Brazil. Introducing foreign characters into the plot is one of the revolutionary features of Ceasefire cinema.[7] The protagonist of the film is Danny (William Ash), an eighteen-year-old Catholic working-class boy from West-Belfast, who spends most of his time playing football, since his dream is to become a professional football player. One day Danny watches a TV interview with Carlos Rega (Daniel Caltagirone), a Brazilian football star who has just joined the Belfast United team.[8] When Carlos is asked by the journalist how he feels about being the first ever Catholic having been accepted into the team, he answers: "For me, the only religion is football" (00:06:00-05). In a Northern Irish context, this sentence sounds as a subversive hint at the region's sectarian animosities, although a hint which may pass unnoticed to a foreigner. The fact that a Brazilian – and not a Northern Irish player – is the first Catholic to join the club subversively alludes to the remaining discrimination of the Catholic community in post-ceasefire Belfast. The film suggests mockingly that the Protestant team is only willing to tolerate people from a different ethno-religious background as long as they do not come from Northern Ireland.

In order to attribute to his film a humorous tone, the director plays with a number of stereotypes about Brazil. Carlos explains to the journalist that in his country, people learn to dance Samba before they start walking. In a caricature of a Brazilian Portuguese accent, he states: "Well, in Brazil, rhythm is life. We learn to Samba before we learn to walk. When we play football, we don't run with the ball, we dance" (00:06:11-20). This stereotype becomes reinforced through the commentator's statement that Carlos is expected to bring "some much needed Latin flair" (00:05:40-42) to the team.

When Carlos is asked by the journalist what he thinks of Northern Ireland, he confidently answers in broken English: "My family in Brazil they worry, they hear bad things, but me, I love … everyone is so friendly" (00:05:53-56). Danny, who watches the interview in his local chip shop is deeply impressed by the Brazilian football player and decides to take dancing classes in order to

---

7   Other examples of foreigners featuring in Ceasefire films are the American journalist Michael Parker in David Cafferty's *Divorcing Jack* (1998) or the protagonist's French penfriend in Michael Winterbottom's *With or Without You* (1999), who unexpectedly turns up in Belfast.

8   As a fictitious team, Belfast United is clearly inspired by the factually existing Protestant Belfast team Linfield, which, according to Alan Bainer, is supported by the "true Ulster Protestant Working class" (107). Furthermore, the fact that Windsor Park, Linfield's home venue, is located in East-Belfast implies that its supporters hail from the Protestant community (107).

play football as smoothly as Carlos does. The shop owner, Rudy Morelli (Julian Littman), ironically comments on Carlos' optimism when he says: "I give him one week" (00:06:06-07). Thus, he mockingly implies that, perceived from the outside, Northern Ireland might appear as a friendly place, while in reality old animosities still seethe under the surface. Carlos' positive comment about Northern Ireland, made shortly after his arrival in Belfast, receives a comic treatment and the viewer will see him drastically change his attitude as the film goes on. When Danny finally meets his Brazilian idol, Carlos seems to be entirely disillusioned and tells him: "This club is shit. Your money is shit. I hate this job" (01:01:39-46). In this way, the supposed "friendliness" of Northern Irish people is presented in an ironic light.

By focusing in his film on football and dancing, Forte suggests that in post-ceasefire Belfast personal ambitions become more important than sectarian animosities. Contrary to the dark characters featuring in traditional Troubles Thrillers, *Mad About Mambo* abounds with comic heroes so that Belfast's "social reality" is mocked. According to Noël Carroll, the key to comic amusement is a deviation from a supposed norm: that is, the socially acceptable framework that governs the ways "in which we think the world is or should be" (17). For the spectators used to conventional Troubles thrillers, the amusing characters in *Mad About Mambo* come as a surprise. Danny and his friends, all of them West-Belfast Catholic boys, comically stand out against the typical Troubles thriller heroes. They considerably differ from characters such as terrorist godfathers, gunmen or villains (Smyth, 14; Rollstone, 42). Danny's behaviour takes on a grotesque dimension, as the idea of learning to dance in order to improve his football skills seems entirely absurd. Apart from that, the fact that he starts to take dancing lessons does not conform to the typical gender roles found in a male dominated society such as Northern Ireland during the Troubles. In a region whose streets have been dominated by paramilitaries, the RUC and the British army for years, a working class boy interested in dancing goes against the norm. Thus, traditional gender stereotypes become subverted as well. According to Bakhtin's theory of carnivalisation, laughter liberates us from "the sacred," from "prohibition," from "the past" and from "power" (*Rabelais*, 94). In this light, the comic representation of the protagonist's unconventional behaviour could be seen as an ironic subversion of old fashioned values ingrained in Northern Irish society.

Danny's friends Mickey (Stewart McLean) and Gary (Russel Smith) also differ from traditional Troubles thriller characters due to their peculiar job aspirations. Whereas the overweight Mickey dreams of working as a fashion designer in order to date supermodels, Gary's ambition is to become a magician to impress beautiful girls. The only character who assumes a stereotypical male role is Spike (Joe Rea), who loves getting involved in fights and therefore dreams of becoming a well-paid mercenary travelling around the world to kill people. However, Spike's aspirations and stance are exaggerated in such a way that he does not remind the audience of a traditional Troubles thriller hero. A further grotesque character is Mrs Burns (Rosaleen Linehan), the eccentric middle-aged dancing teacher for whom Samba is everything. With overstated gestures, she tries to teach Danny to dance Samba, maternally calling him "darling" (00:10:58-59). Through her comic looks and behaviour, she diverges from the stereotypical female thriller characters, such as the villain, the mother or the seducer (Smyth, 14; Rollstone, 42). According to Vivian Mercier, humour frequently springs from the absurd, which is laughable because it is "untrue or irrational or, at the very least, exaggerated" (1). In this sense, we might say that the above-mentioned characters render a humorous image of Belfast's population, which in *Mad About Mambo* rather seems to be composed of likeable atypical individuals than of malevolent criminals.

By joining a dancing class, Danny enters a neutral space in which denominational differences are irrelevant. However, the protagonist is suddenly confronted with class differences. He encounters Lucy (Keri Russel), whom he initially mistakes for a middle class Protestant due to her posh behaviour and her pretentious English boyfriend Oliver (Theo Fraser). When Oliver learns that Danny takes dancing classes in order to improve his football playing, he proposes a friendly football match between the teams of their respective schools.

Forte uses the football match in order to present a further dimension of Belfast's society in an ironic light. During the match, Danny and Oliver incidentally collide. The latter gets hurt and has to be taken to hospital because of a foot injury. After the accident, Danny gets scolded by Brother Xavier, the headmaster of his all-boys school in West Belfast. Brother Xavier tells him to go to see Oliver to apologise: "Show them that we are not all barbarians in this place" (00:18:25-29). This self-ironic comment hints at the negative reputation of West-Belfast as an IRA stronghold and source of trouble. According to Michael Storey, black humour contains "macabre and grotesque elements," and requires "a sense of distance" (91). Following Storey's ideas, it could be said that the irony created through the priest's comment shows the mental and emotional distance towards the Northern Irish conflict taken on by the director of the film.

Danny is delighted to meet good-looking Lucy again in Oliver's hospital room although he is conscious of the socio-economic distance between the two of them. Contrary to what Danny previously expected, Lucy is not a wealthy Protestant girl, but belongs to the Catholic middle class. Thus, the two characters are not separated by ethno-religious boundaries but by class differences. This configuration subverts the traditional love-across-the-barricades theme, since Lucy and Danny do not correspond to the typical lovers in Troubles film and fiction, who are "destined to overcome the unfortunate legacy of bigotry and militancy which divides them" (Cleary, 240). Thus, in tune with new, brighter prospects, the two characters' relationship does not fail, as, at the end of the film, Lucy leaves her boyfriend for Danny.

2. Subverting Belfast's Sectarian Geography

In *Mad About Mambo*, Belfast's urban space is not marked by dark alleyways, gloomy pubs and derelict building sites. The main locations in which the action takes place are football pitches, dance floors or schools. In the representation of the different parts of Belfast, the focus lies more on the depiction of social class differences than on the portrayal of the city's sectarian geography. Posh middle class areas in East Belfast stand out against modest working class parts of West Belfast. The film opens up with a series of aerial shots from a helicopter of both Catholic and Protestant areas.

A number of scenes are set in West Belfast. Nevertheless, the ill-reputed area is not shown as a gloomy place, as the significance of boundary markers and remaining traces of war are comically subverted. For example, in the streets next to Danny's family home different murals and kerbstone paintings in the colour of the Irish flag can be observed, yet the wall paintings do not feature aggressive paramilitary fighters but slogans in Irish advocating for peace. In the surroundings of Danny's local football pitch, graffiti reading "Brits out" adorn the walls, although the slogans do not actually take on a threatening sectarian tone since nobody seems to notice them. Apart from that, the British soldiers patrolling the streets of the area do not offer a terrifying picture of the British army.

In Oliver's hospital room, Danny gets to know Sid, Lucy's father (Brian Cox). Sid is represented as a grotesque character, whose massive cowboy hat farcically makes him look like a Texan rancher. He takes a liking to Danny since he grew up and lived in working West Belfast himself before becoming a wealthy businessman. Sid is well aware that his economic success made it possible for him to leave West Belfast and that it is thanks to his money that he managed to become a member of the board of the Belfast United Football Club despite being a Catholic. With self-irony, he states: "I'm the worst nightmare, I'm a Catholic with cash" (00:21:53-54). According to Bakhtin, laughter caused by absurd situations amounts to "the world's second truth" (*Rabelais*, 48), and, in this light, Sid's comic comment subversively suggests that in contemporary Belfast, ethno-religious boundaries can be easily overcome with money.

Benefiting from his respected position in society, Sid promises Danny to introduce him to the United Belfast coach, encouraging him to live up to his dreams. When Sid gives Danny a lift home to West-Belfast, he states nostalgically: "I haven't been around here for years," while Lucy disparagingly replies to her father's remark: "Is that any wonder?" (00:30:24-28). The two characters' contrasting attitude towards the west of the city spring from their different cognitive geography of Belfast: whereas on Sid's mental map, West Belfast is associated with his childhood, for Lucy, the area is connected to negative images of the Troubles. The class differences between the characters become particularly evident when Danny's neighbours contemplate, all stupefied, Danny's arrival in Sid's Rolls-Royce. A further example of the characters' dissimilar socio-economic origins takes place in West-Belfast: when Lucy drives Danny home in her father's company car and they are stopped by the British army. Unaccustomed to seeing soldiers in the street, Lucy seems to be worried. Danny, however, merely answers in an untroubled way: "It's only the Brits. They have been here a few years in case you haven't noticed" (00:30:24-28). Even if both characters are from the same ethno-religious community, the fact that they belong to different social classes makes them perceive the city in different ways. Whereas for Danny the British army is part of his everyday scenario in West Belfast, soldiers do not belong to Lucy's mental map of the city at all because they are absent from wealthy middle class areas. When Lucy asks one of the soldiers whether he would know a nice restaurant in the area, the latter wryly answers that there is nothing but trouble in this part of town. The spectators are here confronted with a further view of the city: according to the soldier's cognitive geography, West Belfast is still a war-zone.

The depiction of working class West Belfast is contrasted by a scene taking place in Oliver's family house in a wealthy middle class area. In order to welcome Oliver back home after his hospital stay, his family organises a party. The spacious house is surrounded by a big garden and, apart from antique furniture, it also contains a private swimming pool. This is an environment where Danny and his friends, who attend the party, seem entirely out of place. When Gary tells one of the guests that he is from West-Belfast, the latter asks him: "Have you ever shot anybody?" (00:50:34-36). The conversation between the two characters humorously suggests that for moneyed inhabitants of the city, West Belfast represents a no-go area in which everybody is connected to crime.

Conclusion

As representative cinematographic works of two different periods of the Troubles, O'Sullivan's *Nothing Personal* and Forte's *Mad About Mambo* demonstrate the revolutionary development of Northern Irish film after 1994. Whereas *Nothing Personal* belongs to the traditional Troubles thriller genre, *Mad About Mambo* is a carnivalesque romantic comedy reflecting the optimistic atmosphere reigning in the region after the IRA's ceasefire declaration. In O'Sullivan's thriller, Belfast is depicted as a bleak place in which survival is impossible. *Mad About Mambo*, however, moves towards a representation of the Northern Irish capital as a city of multiple opportunities. The revolutionary dimension of the film is that the remaining animosities between Catholics and Protestants receive a comic subversion, so that Belfast's post-ceasefire society is approached ironically. According to Bakhtin, laughter does not "deny seriousness but purifies and completes it" (*Rabelais,* 122). In this sense, it could be argued that numerous comic scenes in which the absurdities of everyday life in the city are exposed function to sharpen the spectators' view for remaining traces of atavistic value systems.

Mad About Mambo communicates the feeling that in contemporary Belfast everything is achievable: the character of Danny suggests that it is feasible to be accepted in a Protestant football team despite being a Catholic. It is also possible to have a love relationship with a beautiful wealthy girlfriend, even if you are from a modest working class area of town. The comic Sid stands for a Belfast version of the American dream. His financial and social success imply that, notwithstanding an underprivileged background, he can still become a rich businessman. This atmosphere of general optimism insinuates that socio-economic as well as ethno-religious boundaries can be overcome in contemporary Belfast. Furthermore, the introduction of Brazilian culture through the football star Carlos as well as Danny's growing passion for Latin dancing open up the film to a wider range of topics beyond the sectarian tensions depicted in traditional Troubles thrillers. Through a character from Brazil, the director attributes to the film not only an exotic dimension, but also communicates a foreign perspective on contemporary Northern Ireland. The omnipresence of joyous music replaces the gloomy soundtracks of Troubles thrillers, frequently counterpointed by the sound of army helicopters. In *Mad About Mambo,* the focus on youth also contributes to creating a more positive image of Belfast: a new generation is on-screen, occupied with their personal aspirations and refusing to get involved in the remaining and paralysing sectarian animosities. The comic reversion of traditional power structures and established societal hierarchies reflect the director's striving for new forms of artistic expression. The humorous approach followed by Forte indicates a general revolutionary tendency in Northern Irish cinema towards an optimistic depiction of Belfast's post-ceasefire evolution.

Works Cited

Bairner, Alan. "'Up to their Knees?' Football, Sectarianism, Masculinity and Working-class Identity." *Who are "The People"? Unionism, Protestantism and Loyalism in Northern Ireland,* edited by Peter Shirlow and Mark McGovern, Pluto, 1997, pp. 95–113.

Bakhtin, Mikhail. *Rabelais and His World.* Translated by Hélène Iswolsky. Indiana University Press, 1984.

——."Epic in the Novel." *The Dialogic Imagination,* edited and translated by M. Holquist, University of Texas Press, 1988, pp. 259–442.

Barton, Ruth. *Irish National Cinema.* Routledge, 2004.

Bazin, Cécile. "Images of the Protestants in Northern Ireland: A Cinematic Deficit or an Exclusive Image of Psychopaths?" *In Media*, vol. 3, 2013, pp. 2–12.
Calame, Jon and Esther Charlesworth. *Divided Cities. Belfast, Beirut, Jerusalem, Mostar and Nicosia*. University of Pennsylvania Press, 2000.
Carroll, Noël. *Humour*. Oxford University Press, 2014.
Cleary, Joe. "'Fork-Tongued on the Border Bit': Partition and the Politics of Form in Contemporary Narratives of the Northern Irish Conflict." *The South Atlantic Quarterly*, vol. 95, no 1, 1996, pp. 227–76.
Forte, John, director. *Mad About Mambo*. Universal DVD, 2003 (2000).
Hill, John. *Cinema and Northern Ireland. Film, Culture and Politics*. British Film Institute, 2006.
———. McFarlane, Wallflower Press, 2005.
Jordan, Hugh. *Milestones in Murder: Defining Moments in Ulster's Terror War*. Mainstream Publishing, 2002.
Kelly, Aaron. *The Thriller and Northern Ireland since 1969. Utterly Resigned Terror*. Ashgate, 2005.
———. "*Terror*-torial Imperatives: Belfast in Eoin McNamee's *Resurrection Man*." *The Cities of Belfast*, edited by Nicholas Allen and Aaron Kelly, Four Courts Press, 2003, pp. 168–82.
Kennedy-Andrews, Elmer. *(De-)constructing the North: Fiction and the Northern Ireland Troubles Since 1969*. Four Courts Press, 2003.
Kennedy, Liam. *Race and Urban Space in Contemporary American Literature*. Edinburgh University Press, 2000.
Lefebvre, Henri. "The Right to the city." *Writings on Cities: Henri Lefebvre*, edited and translated by Elenore Kofman and Elizabeth Lebas, Blackwell, 1996, pp. 147–59.
Lingard, Joan. *Across the Barricades*. Puffin, 1973.
Lynch, Kevin. *The Image of the City*. MIT Press, 1960.
McGivern, Marie-Thérèse and Margaret Ward. "Images of Women in Northern Ireland." *Crane Bag*, vol. 4, no.1, 1980, pp. 66–72.
McIlroy, Brian. *Shooting to Kill: Filmmaking and the Troubles in Northern Ireland*. Flicks Books, 1998.
McLoone, Martin. *Irish Film. The Emergence of a Contemporary Cinema*. British Film Institute, 2000.
Mercier, Vivian: *The Irish Comic Tradition*. Oxford University Press, 1962.
Mulvenna, Gareth. "In the Shadow of the Butchers. Loyalist Paramilitaries on Film." *Balaclava Street*, 28 August 2015, balaclavastreet.wordpress.com/2015/08/28/in-the-shadow-of-the-butchers-loyalist-paramilitaries-on-film/. Accessed 28 April 2019.
O'Sullivan, Thaddeus, director. *Nothing Personal*. Cinema Club DVD, 2003 (1995).
———. "Fanatic Heart." *Film West*, vol. 7, July 1995, p. 18.
Rolston, Bill. "Escaping from Belfast: Class Ideology and Literature in Northern Ireland." *Race & Class*, vol. 20, no. 1, 1978, pp. 41–61.
———. "Mothers, Whores and Villains: Images of Women in Novels of the Northern Ireland Conflict." *Race & Class*, vol. 1, no. 1, 1989, pp. 41–57.

Rubin, Martin. *Thrillers.* Cambridge University Press, 1999.
Sinclair, J.M. *Collins English Dictionary. 21st Century Edition.* Harper Collins, 2001.
Shirlow, Peter and Brendan Murtagh. *Belfast. Segregation, Violence and the City.* Pluto Press, 2006.
Smyth, Gerry. *The Novel and the Nation.* Pluto Press, 1997.
Stewart, A.T.Q. *The Narrow Ground. Aspects of Ulster 1609–1969.* The Black Staff Press, 1977.
Storey, Michael. *Representing the Troubles in Irish Short Fiction.* Catholic University of America Press, 2004.
Titley, Alan. "Rough Rug-Headed Kerns: The Irish Gunman in the Popular Novel." Éire-Ireland: A Journal of Irish Studies, vol. 15, no. 4, 1980, pp.15–38.

11

Interview with Sarah Clancy: Poetry and Social Activism

Sara Martín-Ruiz

Sarah Clancy is a page and performance poet from Galway, Ireland. She is the author of three collections of poetry, including *Stacey and the Mechanical Bull* (2011), *Thanks for Nothing, Hippies* (2012) and *The Truth and Other Stories* (2014). Along with fellow Galway poet Elaine Feeney, she released a poetry CD called *Cinderella Backwards* in 2013. She has won or been shortlisted for many of Ireland's written and performance poetry competitions. In 2015, she was named The Bogman's Cannon People's Poet and, in 2016, she was the Lingo Festival's Poet Laureate. We had the pleasure of having Sarah Clancy performing as a guest artist in the AEDEI International Conference, 2016, which was held in Zarazoga, Spain.

Sara Martín-Ruiz: *First of all, let me thank you for doing this interview with me. I would like to congratulate you on your latest literary achievement, as you have been named as Lingo's Poet Laureate of 2016, where you have shared stage with Sorcha Fox and with the renowned Palestinian activist and poet Rafeef Ziadah. What has this recognition meant for you?*

Sarah Clancy: Thank you! The Lingo Festival in Ireland is a really excellent spoken word celebration. This was its third year and it is run very professionally by a group of performers and artists who are based in Dublin. I would say it is likely to go from strength to strength in years to come. The people who started the festival and selected me as their Laureate are all my poetry peers. They are fellow performing poets and friends whom I know from various events, gigs and festivals over the years and so I was very honoured that they chose me. I would have to point out though, because it may not be apparent from elsewhere, that the title of Laureate for the festival is very tongue in cheek – and not exactly Bob Dylan's Nobel or anything. So of course I was very moved to receive such a vote of confidence from my peers and of course, like any Irish person, I was mortified with embarrassment at it ... But in terms of "recognition," as it might generally be thought of in poetry terms, this would be on a different register, a more DIY or grass roots type of accolade than the more established prizes and awards.

It was great to perform with Sorcha Fox and Rafeef Ziadah in Liberty Hall – the headquarters of one of Ireland's largest Trade Unions. The combination of performers, the place, and a really receptive and on-side audience, made it an extraordinarily powerful gig. I was in the audience for both Rafeef and Sorcha's performances and people were really, really moved. Sorcha's performance (and the musicians who accompanied her) brought a decade-long conflict over the construction of an onshore gas processing plant and pipe line in a rural coastal community in Ireland to the stage, and back to the forefront of people's minds, in an almost spiritual way. It was an extraordinary piece of theatre.

SMR: *You have often been referred to as a political poet. Even though this fact is undeniable, what do you think has been more influential in your categorisation as a political poet: the content of your poems, or the specific venues in which you have performed them?*

SC: I would say I have written more love poems than political poems. Although I sometimes mix the two up ... But as regards politics I was involved in various forms of campaigning before I ever started writing poetry. In fact, when I began writing with any degree of application in around 2009, I was working in Ireland for Amnesty International, and I began attending a poetry workshop in the evenings in order to stop my life becoming all work and no play. Before that, though, in my life, poetry and literature were always present. My mother was a children's book buyer for various bookshops and so we always had and loved a huge selection of books. On the other hand, I did not develop really any sort of political consciousness until quite late in life, beginning in my mid to late twenties I think. I put this down to not having attended university, where I probably would have engaged earlier with politics (I worked in the rural countryside buying and selling horses for ten years after I finished second level school). I became very interested in, fascinated with, and eventually enraged by politics in my late twenties and early thirties, which coincided with me returning to education, and it was after that point that I began to write poems.

I think that both the content and the venues or events that I have performed at lead to me being called a political poet, and to be honest, it's not really a term used to compliment my work! There is still in Ireland a love of the pastoral and somewhat disengaged poem – the poet immersed in nature, or say celebrating one of life's great events, and, while there are people who are both more political and better poets than me, the capacity of their work to make people uncomfortable often means that they do not get great recognition. In my case, in some ways the opposite has been the case- "recognition" for me has resulted from my having something to say about things.

11. INTERVIEW WITH SARAH CLANCY: POETRY AND SOCIAL ACTIVISM

SMR: *Your visible participation in social activism (going from LGTBQ+ rights, to women's rights, water rights, migrant rights, housing rights, etc.), which is reflected in your poetry, together with your performing of it in activist circles, makes the connection between poetry and social activism very clear. This interview is going to be published in an academic book, which, in its turn, has its origins in an academic conference, where both yourself and Vukasin Nedeljkovic, whose art is also very politically engaged, where invited as guest artists. I know you have also been invited and participated in other international academic events. What is your view on the relationship between academia and wider society and, more specifically, between academia and social activism?*

SC: In the circles I move in in Ireland, at least in social activism, we have for the last number of years had the benefit of having a good number of the best type of community-oriented academics making themselves available to social movements, campaigns, workshops, talks, demonstrations, etc. These may not be the majority of academics, but they are very valuable to activists, and I think we greatly appreciate them.

In terms of the worlds of art or literature, I have very little experience of what the relationship between the production of literature and the analysis of it might be. I have, of course, on occasions come under mild fire from people within academia who think they know what a poem should be, and what subjects it should address in order to be of merit ... But I would say that they are "dinosaurs." If I can refer to something as vague as a "poetry establishment" – by which I mean academics and literary critics, and the general muted babble that surrounds poetry –, clearly in this sphere there are people who think that poetry should be removed to some non-existent universal and unbiased territory and speak from there. But I do not really pay much attention to them; their days are numbered (that is not a threat!).

As an aside, I recently spotted a well-known and very decent white, middle-class, male poetry critic, writing in one of our national papers, who said the following about the poet W.S. Merwin:[1] "At a time when insularity and identity politics seem, daily, to be set upon reducing and simplifying the complexity of the world, his new work shows off the cosmopolitan virtues of this great American poet" (McAuliffe). It is this type of thing that we face in Ireland as political poets, the notion that there is somewhere an unpolitical place to write from – that those of us who have needed identity politics to protect us are somehow reducing culture from where it should be up on a non-identity pedestal of mostly cis[2] male privilege... You know the score. They do not mean any harm.

---

1   W.S. Merwin died on 15 March 2019.
2   Editors' note: here "cis" is an abbreviation for "cisgender," a term that applies to people who identify with the gender of their birth.

SMR: *You describe yourself equally as "a page and stage poet." Taking into account your habit of sharing just-written poems on Facebook, have you thought of including "screen poet" to your self-description? Or do you not consider your sharing of poems on social media at the same level as having them on print or performing them in front of an audience?*

SC: I do not consider my poems much at all. I often write straight to Facebook for convenience and from habit. I have lost dozens of poems, I would say, that I wrote that way: posted and then forgot about. If I write something I like, I retrieve it from Facebook, and if necessary I edit it, and if I like it more then I will learn it and perform it somewhere. I am lazy about submitting poems to magazines and the like and have also all but given up entering competitions, even though I found all of these things really useful when I was starting out a few years ago. Now, I cannot be bothered waiting ages for someone who I do not know to tell me whether they like or choose my poem or not, so I often just post them on social media and let them off into the world that way. Often then someone will ask me if they can publish or use the poem from there. I often record poems for RTÉ – the national radio station in Ireland, and often they are ones that the programme's producer has seen on Facebook and asked me for. At the moment, I have a lot of poems that have been out in the world in various forms but never published in a collection, and this is a bit of a dilemma for me. I have probably lost interest in some of those poems and would rather be working on new poems to publish, but then I wonder if even for my own personal satisfaction, I should not let those poems disappear without putting them in a book.

SMR: *Related to the previous question and your answer to it ... What is the difference, for you personally as a poet, between those different media (page, stage, social media, and radio)? In terms of audience, feedback, experience ...*

SC: The best way for me is on the very rare occasions when I get to perform or read a good poem well to a good audience – where something is added by the exchange between me and them. It happens rarely, but it is a very special feeling. I also really love reading poetry for the radio – it is the almost perfect medium for poetry.

SMR: *You recently acknowledged that, despite having been openly queer and mostly in relationships with women for years, it was not until the 2015 Referendum on same-sex marriage in Ireland that you actually gave some active thought to your sexual identity and ended up owning it ("Poetry's Unintended Consequences," 191). This might seem surprising to your readers, since there are several poems of yours in which you openly talk about non-heteronormative relationships, both in Thanks for Nothing, Hippies (in poems such as "Dear John / Jane" or "Sad Bear's Dance") and in The Truth and Other Stories ("Lobotomised" or "Homecoming Queen").*

SC: I have readers? But yes, there is I think a difference in publicly accepting something like one's own sexuality and taking psychological-level ownership of it or inhabiting that aspect of your life fully. I think very often that the experience of being a queer person is understood to follow a certain sequential path in a person's life. That is, you discover you are queer, and then you come out when you feel ready. However, I think that is a simplification, and I would say that most cis, straight, and queer people become themselves in fits and starts over their lifetimes. I also should point out that it is quite possible for me to write about something that I do not feel, or do not feel in the way I am writing it. I like poetry that rings true, that has truth at its core but that does not have to be true in the sense of factual detail, it can be true in the sense and feeling that I am investigating when I am writing.

SMR: *In the same essay, you also state that "sometimes it is the act of making something unspoken public that makes poetry political" (193). In fact, I would say that this is precisely the thread that connects all of your poetic production: from those poems with a more confessional tone, to those with a more openly political content, you speak out loud about all these uncomfortable truths in your poetry. While your first published collection of poetry seems somewhat isolated from your latter production, there is a very clear connection between* Thanks for Nothing, Hippies *and* The Truth and Other Stories, *besides the thematic leitmotifs that appear in both collections. The former ends with "For the Living and the Dead," a poem in which the word "Truth" is repeated 32 times with different definitions. The title of your last collection,* The Truth and Other Stories, *seems to resume from the last poem of the previous one, and it ends with a break-up poem: "Some Thoughts on the Prospect of Internet Dating during the Future which is Taking Place, Despite Itself, Just a few Short Years after Our Break Up." Following this trend, should we expect your next printed collection to be connected to this last poem?*

SC: No (laughs). Had I realised that I would call my collection *The Truth and Other Stories,* I would have kept "For the Living and the Dead" for it. There is no great poetic project that I am embarking on, no planning. I just have a habit that I like and enjoy of responding in words to the quicksilver continuous present, and sometimes I catch some sentiment or emotion or feeling in words that can be passed between me and a reader in a way that only a poem can do, and that is what I write for.

SMR*: If we take into account your production as a "social media poet" on Facebook, it would seem that your latest writing is less concerned with romantic relationships and more with issues of social justice. I'm thinking of "Combating the Pull Factor (Direct Provision – This is How We Do It Here)" (posted 28 August 2016), "Poem for a migrant poet waiting to make her crossing" (posted 4 September 2016), and "Things I learned from Black writers" (posted 15 October 2016). It would seem that certain topics that were already latent in your poetry have finally taken centre stage. Are you aware of* *this trend? Has it been a conscious decision?*

SC: I would not say there is such a trend. I have written a good few very whimsical or wistful poems as well as the ones you mention above. Over the last year I have, by my own standards, written very little, as I have had a hectic full time job which I needed badly to get me out of debt. Because of this I have been very much kept to the humdrum grindstone, and the humdrum grindstone I work at is community work – running a participatory democracy project – and so that has become the prevailing topic that concerns me. I have also been lucky enough to have had a large number of poetry gigs to perform at over the year and, in fact, grateful as I am for this, it is all becoming a bit much. I have been doing less than justice to the organisers of some events recently so something has to give – as I am not writing much and beginning not to enjoy the readings. I am, however, enjoying being able to pay my bills and, for the first time in years, to have a bit of stability and a lovely relationship in my life. I will fix the work art balance one way or another soon ...

SMR: *One of your last poems published on Facebook, "Things I learned from Black Writers," seems a continuation of your poem "Bull," from your latest printed collection. While in "Bull" you recognise the impact that South American writers and poets such as Roberto Bolaño, Nicanor Parra, Roque Dalton, or Pablo Neruda have had on you, in "Things I learned from Black Writers" you pay tribute to bell hooks, Chinua Achebe, Frantz Fanon, Alice Walker, Frederick Douglass or Warsan Shire, among others. In some of your previous poems, you also mention some Irish writers, such as Yeats (in "The Centre Never Held Anything Anyway") or Heaney (in "In Cill Rialaig Trying Not to Write 'Digging'"). In fact, in "In Cill Rialaig Trying Not to Write 'Digging'" you question the need of Irish writers to mimic their forefathers, and you admit to be "a prisoner of theory and culture." Which other writers, theories, and cultures have shaped you and your poetry?*

SC: I think very often that I am probably unaware of the writers who shaped my poetry and me ... Maybe it is actually Enid Blyton and Patricia Cornwell who shaped me! However, books that taught me both how I might think and how I might write include: everything by Eduardo Galeano; almost everything by Adrienne Rich, except maybe some of her early poems; Walt Whitman; Roberto Bolaño, over and over again, for the possibilities he opens up; *The Fire Next Time* by James Baldwin; *The Price of Our Souls* by Bernadette Devlin; every book I swallowed up by the great Irish travel writer Dervla Murphy; Paulo Freire; and the dastardly union organiser Saul Alinksy's *Rules for Radicals*. Recently I fell in love with the light deft work of American poet Kay Ryan, though I could never emulate it. Then, of course, the chapbook *'Teaching my mother how to give birth'* from Warsan Shire, which has become essential reading; Emer McBride's novel *A Girl is a Half Formed Thing* opened a few writing doors for me that

I had not previously spotted; and Claudia Rankine's experimental lessons in race relations and racism are unforgettable. Close by the inimitable Rita Ann Higgins was and is a great lesson in how you can do whatever you want and say whatever you want in a poem if you have a quick enough wit and a sharp enough pen. That's probably enough to be going on with ...

SMR: *Finally, I would like to ask you about the ambiguous relationship that you seem to have with Ireland in your poetry, which I think is best exemplified in two consecutive poems which appear in Thanks for Nothing, Hippies: "Don't Think I Won't" and "She Takes Me Back." The former depicts Irish culture as "suffocating" and Irish people as "self-deprecating" and unable to make a change, and ends up with your resolution to walk away from your "arranged marriage / with this unforgiving country." In the latter poem, which is dedicated to "this Atlantic rock we live on," it seems that Ireland haunts you and you are doomed to go back to her again and again. Where do you stand now?*

SC: I have an ambiguous relationship with Ireland and I probably always will. At the same time, I am at my most at ease and at home when I am somewhere near the Atlantic, and I miss the warmth and humour and mischievousness of the people whenever I live or travel abroad. When I travel to countries like New Zealand or the United States I always feel a sense of admiration for the wide family structures that many of us have the benefit of in Ireland. It is these same families I think, rather than political ideologies or actions, that have kept Ireland as a reasonably stable and relatively prosperous country since the end of the Civil War. This is double edged too, of course, with those very families often having being horrendous places for children and horrendous weights around adults who sought to be free.

Most women who are in any way awake would have similar reservations about the Republic because of the ways in which the religious/state apparatus has treated women since the foundation of the state. That other places are worse does not really diminish this feeling. In many ways, we in Ireland as a people are less than the sum of our parts – this is evidenced in the way things like Direct Provision, Magdalene Laundries and Industrial Schools have managed to persist right up to the present. No generation has yet existed in the Free State which has not had a system of quasi-legal incarceration of people who the state did not approve of flourishing alongside it. And the thing about these systems, like the current one of Direct Provision, is that it is almost impossible to find anyone outside of government who is in favour of it. So it persists because in some ways as a people we refuse to refuse it, and this happened too with all the other forms of separation or incarceration we have practiced to date. We refuse to refuse what we find unacceptable, and we go on with the unacceptable persisting in some sort of Beckettian way. We cannot go on like this, but somehow we always do.

Works Cited

Clancy, Sarah. *Stacey and the Mechanical Bull*. Lapwing Press, 2011.
———. *Thanks for Nothing, Hippies*. Salmon Poetry, 2012.
———. *The Truth and Other Stories*. Salmon Poetry, 2014.
———. "Poetry's Unintended Consequences …" *Beyond the Centre. Writers in their Own Words*, edited by Declan Meade, New Island Books, 2016, pp. 184–94.
McAuliffe, John. "Poetry: Edged with Nightmares and Inspired by Troubadours." *The Irish Times*, 10 December 2016, www.irishtimes.com/culture/books/poetry-edged-with-nightmares-and-inspired-by-troubadours-1.2885596. Accessed 29 May 2019.

New Poems

Sarah Clancy

Things I was Thinking when she Said she Wanted to Feed me
For Anne Mulhall

I want to feed her the sting of wind burned cheeks of streaming eyes
I want to make her use that land's end too-much distance squint
I want to feel the sea-salt thickening of her hair and with her listen
to smooth stones moving against each other as the sea draws back.
I want us to shelter somewhere tin-roofed and breathe in time with
the steady beat of rain, I want her to hear the low moans
an orphan wind makes at dusk when it is forced to beg for welcome
from every manmade thing, I want to offer her the discomfort flush
of wet thigh jeans or the cold-hands, warm-torso feel of Abbey Hill
or Capawalla on some blue and bracing day, I want her to welcome
the nothing feeling that comes from fossils in limestone
from the persistence of ring forts or from watching the Scots Pines
that someone planted sometime scraping at a washed out winter sky.

I want to offer her the faded votive ribbons on the naked Blackthorn
that marks the holy well, I want to feast with her on the wishes
of the unseen pilgrims who came and still come at it petitioning
I want us to walk the pathways feral goats take at night time
and know the tangled closeness they sleep in when no one is around
I want her to see how red-warm cattle huddle together for comfort
in their own sort of *meithal* giving and receiving all at once
and I want to parcel these parallel worlds for her,
so that while we age in squares of love, of artificial light
and comfort, while we go about our business, we know
that outside and elsewhere things are happening without us
and I want to offer her this even if it isn't mine to give, and she,
she wants to take me in and feed me and I'm okay with this.

Cherishing for Beginners

Cherish the meek
cherish the ranchers
cherish the guards
cherish the bankers
cherish the virgins
then ride them and cherish their sisters,
cherish tax exiles and entrepreneurs
cherish the rewards of intergenerational privilege
or if that's too hard for beginners
sure cherish the Rose of Tralee for starters,
cherish the goal and the point and the foul
cherish the priest's dirty sheets
but not the woman who washes them,
don't mention her
or what she might need,
go on and cherish the IFSC
and its type of laundries –
those ones are fine, they are grand sure.
Cherish Them.

Cherish the men
because they couldn't help it
if the women and girls went and fell pregnant,
cherish the foetus, the heartbeat,
but not the person it's in
then cherish the small graves
in their undisclosed wastelands
cherish the shovels
and boot soles that dug them –
let there be no doubt about it:
Yes We Can!
cherish the children
if they're from the right class
aren't travelling people
and are not for god's sake
seeking asylum,
don't forget too that we must
cherish the mute
and cherish the sheepish
but hate those in need,

worship Fr Peter McVerry himself,
go ahead make him an icon
but don't hear what he's saying
about anything.

Cherish the poor
for how you can use them
to frighten those who are just one rung above
cherish the people
who learned early and often
what happens to those
with big mouths,
cherish your local TDs,
and the crowd in Listowel
who didn't care that he raped her
sure wasn't he one of their own?
Yea cherish the rapist,
why don't you.

Cherish the golf course
and its sprinklers
sure Irish Water will save us
cherish piece work and internships,
and zero hour contracts
aren't you lucky you have a job at all,
do you not remember the coffin ships
and are you not grateful?
Yea cherish your own exploitation
cherish the school board,
for our lack of gay teachers,
cherish women's place in the home
then cut their allowances,
sure they don't deserve them
having all of those children
repeat after me – Cherish Privatisation;
and if you don't then you better learn
to cherish the knock on your door
in the morning – consider this a warning.

Cherish Dev and Pearse
and blood sacrifice
but don't mention James Connolly

who said until Ireland's women are free
none of us will be, most of all though
cherish outsourcing and remember
your call is important,
you too will be cherished equally
if you can afford it
as soon as an operator
becomes available
which may well take
another hundred years.

Notes on Editors and Contributors

Editors

Constanza del Río-Álvaro is Senior Lecturer in British and Irish Literature at the University of Zaragoza. Her research centres on contemporary Irish fiction, narrative and critical theory and popular narrative genres. She has published on these subjects and on writers Flann O'Brien, Seamus Deane, Eoin McNamee, William Trevor, Jennifer Johnston, Dorothy Nelson, Kate O'Riordan, Patrick McCabe and Sebastian Barry, among others. She is co-editor of *Memory, Imagination and Desire in Contemporary Anglo-American Literature and Film* (Universitätsverlag Winter, 2004) and of *Traumatic Memory and the Ethical, Political and Transhistorical Functions of Literature* (Palgrave, Macmillan, 2017).

José Carregal-Romero is Assistant Lecturer at the University of Huelva. His PhD dissertation, which he completed in 2016 at the University of Vigo, received the Inés Praga Terente Award by the Spanish Association of Irish Studies (AEDEI). His research focuses on the intersections between gender, sexuality and culture in contemporary Irish literature. His publications have appeared in several Irish Studies journals, including *New Hibernia Review*, *Irish University Review* and *Estudios Irlandeses*.

Contributors

María Amor Barros-del Río is Assistant Professor at the University of Burgos, Spain, where she teaches English language, culture and literatures. Her research focuses mainly on gender studies and contemporary fiction in English with a special interest in Irish fiction. She is the Secretary of the Spanish Association for Irish Studies (AEDEI) and in 2017 she was awarded an ESSE Bursary to conduct research on Irish female migration. She is the author of *A Practical Guide to Address Gender Bias in Academia and Research* (2016), *El trabajo de las mujeres pobres* (2010) and *Metáforas de su tierra: Breve historia de las mujeres*

Irlandesas (2004). She has published extensively in peer-reviewed journals and collective works. Other fields of interest are critical pedagogy and second language teaching for which she was funded the Erasmus+ Research Project VIR_TEACH (2018–2021), virteachproject.eu.

Thomas Earls FitzGerald completed his PhD on violence in revolutionary Ireland in June 2018 at Trinity College Dublin under the supervision of Professor Eunan O'Halpin. His dissertation was supported by a Government of Ireland postgraduate fellowship from the Irish Research Council. He has since held postdoctoral fellowships at the Trinity Centre for Contemporary Irish History and from the Ireland–Canada University Foundation at the Department of Irish Studies at Concordia University Montreal. Dr Earls FitzGerald is a historian of modern Ireland with particular interests in the role of political violence and its impact on wider society throughout the twentieth and twenty-first centuries, together with social and cultural attempts at nation building in the early twentieth century. His first publication was a contribution to the volume edited by David Fitzpatrick *Terror in Ireland 1916–1923* (2012) and he has since published in a number of journals and edited collections. He is also a frequent contributor to the Dublin Review of Books.

Cécile Gordon is Senior Archivist at Military Archives of Ireland and works as Project Manager of the Military Service (1916–1923) Pensions Project. She has been involved in this project from the very first day back in May 2008. Prior to this, Cécile was the County Archivist for Kildare, Meath and Wicklow County Councils. She holds a BA in American and English History and Literature from Lyon II University, France and later obtained a Higher Diploma and Masters in Archives and Records Management from University College Dublin. Cécile has been working as a qualified archivist for 13 years and her current research interests include the role of the archivist during the centenaries and the link between archives, identity, commemorations and collective memory.

Robert McEvoy is an archivist employed on the Military Service (1916–1923) Pensions Collection with the Military Archives, Rathmines, Dublin 6. He has been working on the project since 2012. His duties include processing material for release to the public and undertaking promotional activities. Robert qualified with a Masters in Archives and Records Management and has over ten years' experience as a professional archivist. He has worked in a range of institutions in both the private and public sector including the National Library of Ireland, National Archives of Ireland, University College Dublin, Arts Council of Ireland and a number of local authorities. Prior to qualification, Robert studied history to postgraduate level with a specific interest in twentieth-century Irish history and Northern Ireland.

Sara Martín-Ruiz is a PhD Candidate at the University of the Balearic Islands. Her research focuses on contemporary Irish literature written by female immigrants, with a special interest in the intersection of gender, class, and race.

Vukasin Nedeljkovic holds a Masters in Visual Arts Practice at Dunlaoghaire Institute of Arts, Design and Technology. He has exhibited both nationally and internationally. His recent contributions include *Reiterating Asylum Archive: Documenting Direct Provision in Ireland* (2018) and *Asylum Archive: an Archive of Asylum and Direct Provision in Ireland* (2016) He was awarded recently an Arts and Activism bursary from the Arts Council and has recently published the book *Asylum Archive* (2018). He initiated the multidisciplinary project Asylum Archive.

Maurice O'Keeffe is a native of Tralee, Co. Kerry. He was educated by the Christian Brothers in Tralee, and later by the Carmelite fathers in Terenure Boarding School, Dublin. He holds a qualification from University College Cork in local and regional studies. Maurice's previous occupations were in auctioneering, specialising in antique furniture, antiquarian books, charts and maps. Irish Life and Lore was founded by Maurice and Jane O'Keeffe in 1990. Maurice is joint principal, with his wife Jane, of Irish Life and Lore, an educational and commercial organisation based in Tralee, Co. Kerry and dedicated to recording, cataloguing and archiving oral history in Ireland. Since its inception, over 4,000 hours of recordings have been compiled and archived. The work is commissioned principally by Local Authorities, colleges, public and private bodies and government departments. Fieldwork is carried out all over Ireland, and individual oral history collections are compiled from the resultant recordings. Utilising information gathered from these oral history recordings, a number of books have been written by Jane O'Keeffe and their daughter, Dr. Helene O'Keeffe. A full overview of the work of Irish Life and Lore in recording and writing may be seen at www.irishlifeandlore.com.

Paul O'Mahony is an Irish academic from Cork, Ireland. He has a BA degree in English and New Media from the University of Limerick and a master degree from the University of Granada, Spain. He has worked as a teacher all over the world in countries such as Spain, Ireland, England, Australia, Argentina, New Zealand and the Czech Republic. He presented his master thesis at the Irish Studies conference in La Rioja, Spain in 2017. He has recently returned from the UAE where he was working as an English teacher and he is hoping to continue his studies by doing a PhD in the near future.

Stephanie Schwerter is professor of Anglophone literature at the Université Polytechnique Hauts-de-France. Previously, she spent six years in Northern Ireland, working at the University of Ulster and at Queen's University Belfast. Her research interest lies in Northern Irish Film and Fiction as well as in the intertextual links between Irish, French, German and Russian poetry

Melania Terrazas is on the Executive Board of AEDEI (The Spanish Association for Irish Studies), head of the Centre of Irish Studies BANNA/ BOND (EFACIS-European Federation of Associations and Centres of Irish Studies), Senior Lecturer in English Studies and involved in the International Mobility Programs Coordinator at the University of La Rioja (Spain). She is the author of *Relational Structures in Wyndham Lewis's Fiction: Complexity and Value* (Lincom Europa, 2005), the editor of *Journal of English Studies*, vol. 8. (2010), guest editor of *Gender Issues in Contemporary Irish Literature* (*Estudios Irlandeses*, vol. 13.2, 2018) and the editor of *Trauma and Identity in Contemporary Irish Culture* (Peter Lang *Reimagining Ireland* Series, 2019). She helped set up the Wyndham Lewis Project websites through grants from the AHRC and the Spanish Ministry of Science and Competitiveness. She has published extensively on a number of British and Irish modernist and contemporary authors and film directors, and on applied linguistics. Her work has been recognized by positive reviews in international journals, grants and awards received to date.

Mariana Vignoli Figueroa is an independent researcher from Argentina. She holds a master's degree in English Literature and Linguistics from the University of Granada, Spain, and a bachelor's degree in English Teaching from the National University of San Juan (UNSJ), Argentina. Her research interests are in the area of Discourse Analysis, Applied Linguistics and Irish History.

José M. Yebra is a Lecturer in English at the University of Zaragoza, Spain. He has recently published articles on literatures in English such as "Re-framing Vulnerability and Wound Ethics: Colm Tóibín's *The Testament of Mary*" in *The Journal of Language, Literature and Culture*, "Transmodern Motion or the Rhizomatic Updated in *In a Strange Room*, 'Take me to Church' and *Babel*" in *Anglia* and "Acheronta Movebo: Violence and Dystopia in Naomi Alderman's *The Power*" in *Orbis Litterarum*. He has co-edited the volume *Transmodern Perspectives on Contemporary Literatures in English* (Routledge, 2019) with Jessica Aliaga-Lavrijsen. His current research interests include literatures in English, transmodernism, and gender studies.

Index

Abortion 9, 11, 120, 122, 124, 126; Eighth Amendment 11, 122, 136.
Anglo-Irish Treaty 11, 45.
Arendt, Hannah ix, 4.
Army Pensions Act 23–24, 26, 32, 35.
Benjamin, Walter 108.
Black and Tans 57, 62, 68–71, 73–75.
British Army 11, 23, 38, 45, 63, 98, 109, 192, 194, 196–197.
Bureau of Military History (1913–1921) 3, 22–23, 44, 46, 69.
Catholic Church 7–8, 10, 119, 126, 150, 153; Catholicism 7, 10, 119, 126, 150, 153; Catholics in Northern Ireland 11, 184, 193; sexual abuse 10, 150, 152–55;
Celtic Tiger 9, 12, 164.
Civil War 25, 27, 31, 33–34, 36–37, 39, 45–46, 54–58, 62, 83, 119, 207.
Clancy, Sarah; *Thanks for Nothing, Hippies* 201, 204–05, 207; *The Truth and Other Stories* 204–05; "Dear John/Jane" 204; "Sad Bear's Dance" 204; "Lobotomised" 204; "Homecoming Queen" 204; "For the Living and the Dead" 205; "Some Thoughts on the Prospect of Internet Dating during the Future which is Taking Place, Despite Itself, Just a few Short Years after Our Break Up" 205; "Combating the Pull Factor (Direct Provision – This is How We Do It Here)" 205; "Poem for a migrant poet waiting to make her crossing" 205; "Things I learned from Black writers" 205–06; "Bull" 206; "The Centre Never Held Anyway" 206; "In Cill Rialaig Trying Not to Write 'Digging'" 206; "Things I was Thinking when she Said she Wanted to Feed me" 209; "Cherishing for Beginners" 210–12.
1937 Constitution 8–10, 119–20, 122, 126, 136.
Conlon, Evelyn; Irishwomen United 135–136, 145–146; *Not the Same Sky* 141; "What Happens at Night" 136–46.
Connaught Rangers 27–28.
Connolly, James 6, 35, 44, 53, 112, 211.
Connolly, Linda 10, 136, 140.
Crown forces 13, 34, 62–65, 68–76.
Cumman na mBan 23, 26, 29, 32, 33, 44, 61, 69, 73, 75, 84, 90, 62.
De Valera, Éamon 9, 43, 45, 119, 157.
Deane, Seamus 2, 99–100, 103.
Devotional Revolution 132, 134–35, 142–143.
Diaspora 9, 14, 104, 122–23, 125, 135, 142–44, 147.
Direct Provision 12, 16, 167–80, 205, 207.
Easter Rising i, 1–6, 12–14, 16, 21–22, 27, 30, 32, 34–35, 38, 43–45, 50–53, 57–58, 61, 79–80, 83–85, 86–92, 98–99, 101–104, 106–12, 180.
Familism 7, 134–35, 143.
Fanon, Frantz 5, 99, 110–11, 206.
Feminism, first-wave 9, 132, 135, 140,

217

143; second-wave 10, 15, 121, 142–43, 145, 149.
Ferriter, Diarmaid 3, 8, 9, 11, 21, 37, 39, 83.
Fianna Fáil 7–8, 12, 23, 44.
Fisk, Robert 104, 106–108.
Forte, John; *Mad About Mambo* 186, 192–197.
Foster, Roy 4, 98, 101, 106.
Frawley, Oona 141–146.
Gallimore, Andrew; *Easter 1916: The Enemy Files* 98, 104–08.
Gay rights 136, 150–52, 156, 164, 211; same-sex marriage 11, 136, 204.
Great Famine 1, 7–8, 15, 97, 132, 134–35, 137, 139, 143, 152.
Hayes, Edwin 132, 136, 138–40.
Higgins, Michael D. 13, 39, 44, 131.
HIV/AIDS 150–51, 155–57.
Home Rule 11, 33, 45, 98.
IRA 5, 11, 13, 16, 23, 26–27, 29, 31–34, 36–37, 44, 57, 62–65, 68–73, 75–76, 83, 124, 183, 190–91, 195.
Irish Citizen Army (ICA) 4, 12, 23, 44, 50, 84, 98.
Irish Free State 2, 43, 45, 64, 101, 103, 119, 134, 139, 180.
Irish independence 83, 85, 92, 139.
Irish Life and Lore 44, 49–58.
Joyce, James 113, 118, 120.
Keenan, Marie; "Perfect Celibate Clerical Masculinity" 153, 158–60.
Kiberd, Declan 8, 84, 99, 104, 106.
Lloyd, David 99–100.
Lynch, Kevin; "mental map" 188–189, 197.
Magan, Ruán and Pat Collins; *1916: The Irish Rebellion* 104–05, 109–12.
Markievicz, Constance 6, 84.
Military Service Pensions 3, 12, 21–26, 83.
Nationalism 6, 8–9, 84, 88, 91, 99, 103, 105, 124, 144.
Nedeljkovic, Vukasin; Asylum Archive 170–71; Direct Provision Diary 171–79.

O'Brien, Edna; *The Country Girls* 119–20; *August is a Wicked Month* 120; *Night* 120; *Mother Ireland* 121; *Wild Decembers* 122; *The Light of Evening* 123; *House of Splendid Isolation* 123; *Down by the River* 124; *Little Red Chairs* 124–25; *Girl* 125.
O'Sullivan, Thaddeus; *Nothing Personal* 186–192.
Postcolonialism 2, 99–104, 112, 119.
Purser, Sarah 133, 135–36, 138–40.
Revisionism 99, 102–103.
Revolution ix, 2–5, 183.
Said, Edward 99, 105–06, 109–10.
Sinn Féin 4–5, 7–8, 84.
Tóibín, Colm; *The Blackwater Lightship* 151, 155–58; "A Priest in the Family" 158–59; "The Pearl Fishers" 160–63.
Townshend, Charles 3, 21, 73, 75.
Troubles, the 11, 16, 58, 102, 107, 124, 126, 183–87, 190–92, 194, 197–98; Troubles thrillers 183–87, 192, 194, 198.
Virgin Mary 120–21, 160.
War of Independence 4–5, 12, 22, 25, 27, 31, 33–35, 36–38, 43, 45, 57–58, 62, 68–75.
Women; women in the Easter Rising 29–31, 83–92; discrimination under Pensions Acts 32, 51; women in the War of Independence and Civil War 33–34, 39–40; violence against women in revolutionary Ireland 62–70, 74–76; women's rights and struggles 119–22, 124, 135–36, 140–41, 149, 203, 207.
World War I 10, 38, 72, 98, 112.

CPSIA information can be obtained
at www.ICGtesting.com
Printed in the USA
BVHW010536141020
590951BV00002B/6